高 等 院 校 英 语 系 列 教 材

英国文学经典名篇选读

顾铁军 ◎ 编

Selected Readings from British Literary Classics

CUCP 中国传媒大学出版社
·北京·

Contents

Part A

Text and Reading Tasks

A

Unit 1

The Canterbury Tales

I. Introduction

1. The author

Geoffrey Chaucer, born in 1340, London, and died on October 25, 1400, London, is considered the outstanding English poet before Shakespeare. His *The Canterbury Tales* ranks as one of the greatest poetic works in English. He also contributed importantly in the second half of the 14th century to the management of public affairs as courtier, diplomat, and civil servant. In that career he was trusted and aided by three successive kings—Edward III, Richard II, and Henry IV. But it is his avocation—the writing of poetry—for which he is remembered. Perhaps the chief characteristics of Chaucer's works are their variety in subject matter, genre, tone, style, and in the complexities presented concerning man's pursuit of a sensible existence. Yet his writings also consistently reflect an all-pervasive humour, combined with serious and tolerant consideration of important philosophical questions. From his writings Chaucer emerges as poet of love, both earthly and divine, whose presentations range from lustful cuckoldry to spiritual union with God. Thereby, they regularly lead the reader to speculation about man's relation both to his fellows and to God, while simultaneously providing delightfully entertaining views of the frailties and follies, as well as the nobility, of mankind.

2. *The Canterbury Tales*

Geoffrey Chaucer wrote *The Canterbury Tales*, a collection of stories in a frame story, between 1387 and 1400. It is the story of a group of thirty people who travel as pilgrims to Canterbury (England). The pilgrims, who come from all layers of society, tell stories to each other to kill time while they travel to Canterbury. He never finished his enormous project and even the completed tales were not finally revised. Scholars are uncertain about the order of the tales. As the printing press had yet to be invented when Chaucer wrote his works, *The Canterbury Tales* has been passed down in several handwritten manuscripts.

3. "General Prologue"

"General Prologue" is the key to *The Canterbury Tales* that narrates about the gathering of a group of people in an inn that intend to go on a pilgrimage to Canterbury (England) next morning. In "General Prologue", the narrator of *The Canterbury Tales*, who is one of the intended pilgrims, provides more or less accurate depictions of the members of the group and describes why and how *The Canterbury Tales* is told. If we trust the General Prologue, Chaucer determined that each pilgrim should tell two tales on the way to Canterbury and two tales on the way back. The host of the inn offers to be and is appointed as judge of the tales as they are told and is supposed to determine the best hence winning tale. Unfortunately, *The Canterbury Tales* was never finished.

II. Text

General Prologue

(with the interlinear translation)

Here bygynneth the Book of the Tales of Caunterbury.

Here begins the Book of the Tales of Canterbury.

Whan that Aprill with his* shoures soote* — its/sweet
When April with its sweet-smelling showers
The droghte of March hath perced to the roote,
Has pierced the drought of March to the root,
And bathed every veyne[1] in swich* licour* — such/liquid
And bathed every vein (of the plants) in such liquid
Of which vertu[2] engendred is the flour;
By the power of which the flower is created;
Whan Zephirus[3] eek* with his sweete breeth — also
When the West Wind also with its sweet breath,
Inspired hath in every holt* and heath* — grove/field
In every wood and field has breathed life into
The tendre croppes, and the yonge sonne*[4] — shoots
The tender new leaves, and the young sun
Hath in the Ram his half cours yronne,
Has run half its course in Aries,
And smale foweles maken melodye,
And small fowls make melody,
That slepen al the nyght with open ye* — eye
Those that sleep all the night with open eyes

1. I.e., in plants.
2. by the power of which.
3. The west wind.
4. The sun is young because it has run only halfway through its course in Aries, the Ram—the first sign of the zodiac in the solar year.

(So priketh hem* Nature in hir corages[1]), them
(So Nature incites them in their hearts),
Thanne longen folk to goon* on pilgrimages, go
Then folk long to go on pilgrimages,
And palmeres[2] for to seken straunge strondes,
And professional pilgrims (long) to seek foreign shores,
To ferne halwes, kowthe* in sondry londes; know
To (go to) distant shrines, known in various lands;
And specially from every shires ende
And specially from every shire's end
Of Engelond to Caunterbury they wende,
Of England to Canterbury they travel,
The hooly blisful martir[3] for to seke,
To seek the holy blessed martyr,
That hem hath holpen* whan that they were seeke*. Helped/sick
Who helped them when they were sick.
Bifil that in that seson on a day,
It happened that in that season on a day,
In Southwerk[4] at the Tabard as I lay
In Southwark at the Tabard Inn as I lay
Redy to wenden on my pilgrymage
Ready to go on my pilgrimage
To Caunterbury with ful* devout corage, very
To Canterbury with a very devout spirit,
At nyght was come into that hostelrye
At night had come into that hostelry
Wel nyne and twenty in a compaignye
Well nine and twenty in a company
Of sondry folk, by aventure* yfalle chance

1. their hearts.
2. palmers, wide-ranging pilgrims,especially those who sought out the"staunge strondes"(foreign shores) of the Holy Land."Ferne halwes": fat-off shrines.
3. St. Thomas à Becket, murdered in Canterbury Cathedral in 1170.
4. Southwark, site of the Tabard Inn, was then a suburb of London, south of the Tames River.

Of various sorts of people, by chance fallen
26 In felaweshipe, and pilgrimes were they alle,
In fellowship, and they were all pilgrims,
27 That toward Caunterbury wolden* ryde. — would
Who intended to ride toward Canterbury.
28 The chambres and the stables weren wyde,
The bedrooms and the stables were spacious,
29 And wel we weren esed* atte beste[1]. — accommodated
And we were well accommodated in the best way.
30 And shortly, whan the sonne was to reste[2],
And in brief, when the sun was (gone) to rest,
31 So hadde I spoken with hem everichon* — every one
I had so spoken with everyone of them
32 That I was of hir felaweshipe anon*, — at once
That I was of their fellowship straightway,
33 And made forward[3] erly for to ryse,
And made agreement to rise early,
34 To take oure wey ther as”[4] I yow devyse*. — describe
To take our way where I (will) tell you.
35 But nathelees*, whil I have tyme and space[5], — nevertheless
But nonetheless, while I have time and opportunity,
36 Er* that I ferther in this tale pace*, — before/pass
Before I proceed further in this tale,
37 Me thynketh it acordaunt to resoun[6]
It seems to me in accord with reason
38 To telle yow al the condicioun
To tell you all the circumstances
39 Of ech of hem, so as it semed me,

1. In the best possible way.
2. Had set.
3. I.e., (we) made an agreement.
4. “Ther as”: where.
5. I.e., opportunity.
6. It seems to me according to reason.

Of each of them, as it seemed to me,
40 And whiche they weren, and of what degree,
And who they were, and of what social rank,
41 And eek in what array that they were inne;
And also what clothing that they were in;
42 And at a knyght than* wol I first bigynne. knyght / then
And at a knight then will I first begin.
…
270 A MARCHANT was ther with a forked berd,
There was a MERCHANT with a forked beard,
271 In mottelee[1], and hye on horse he sat;
Wearing parti-colored cloth, and in a high saddle he sat on his horse;
272 Upon his heed a Flaundryssh* bever hat, Flemish
Upon his head (he wore a) Flemish beaver hat,
273 His bootes clasped faire and fetisly*. elegantly
His boots were buckled handsomely and elegantly.
274 His resons* he spak ful solempnely, opinions
His opinions he spoke very solemnly,
275 Sownynge* alwey th' encrees of his wynnyng. sounding
Concerning always the increase of his profits.
276 He wolde the see were kept for any thyng[2]
He wanted the sea to be guarded at all costs
277 Bitwixe Middelburgh and Orewelle.
Between Middelburgh (Holland) and Orwell (England).
278 Wel koude he in eschaunge sheeldes[3] selle.
He well knew how to deal in foreign currencies.
279 This worthy man ful wel his wit bisette*: employed
This worthy man employed his wit very well:
280 Ther wiste* no wight that he was in dette, knew

1. It was not suitable because of his position.
2. I.e., he wished the sea to be guarded at all costs. The sea route between Middelburgh (in the Netherlands) and Orwell (in Suffolk) was vital to the Merchant's export and import of wool-the basis of England's chief trade at the time.
3. Shields, *ecus* (French coins): he made a profit trading on international credit and exchange rates.

There was no one who knew that he was in debt,

281 So estatly* was he of his governaunce[1]   dignified

He was so dignified in managing his affairs

282 With his bargaynes[2] and with his chevyssaunce.

With his buying and selling and with his financial deals.

283 For sothe he was a worthy man with alle,

Truly, he was a worthy man indeed,

284 But, sooth to seyn, I noot* how men hym calle.   don't know

But, to say the truth, I do not know what men call him.

...

285 A CLERK[3] ther was of Oxenford also,

There was also a CLERK (scholar) from Oxford,

286 That unto logyk hadde longe ygo[4].

Who long before had begun the study of logic.

287 As leene was his hors as is a rake,

His horse was as lean as is a rake,

288 And he nas nat right fat, I undertake,

And he was not very fat, I affirm,

289 But looked holwe*, and therto sobrely.   hollow

But looked emaciated, and moreover abstemious.

290 Ful thredbare was his overeste courtepy,[5]

His short overcoat was very threadbare,

291 For he hadde geten hym yet no benefice,

For he had not yet obtained an ecclesiastical living,

292 Ne was so worldly for to have office*.   secular employment

Nor was he worldly enough to take secular employment.

293 For hym was levere[6] have at his beddes heed

---

1. The management of his affairs.
2. Bargainings."Chevissaunce": borrowing.
3. The Clerk is a student at Oxford; in order to become a student, he would have had to signify his intention of becoming a cleric, but he was not bound to proceed to a position of responsibility in the church.
4. Who had long since matriculated in philosophy?
5. Outer cloak."Benefice": ecclesiastical living, such as the income a parish priest receives.
6. He would rather.

For he would rather have at the head of his bed
294 Twenty bookes, clad in blak or reed,
Twenty books, bound in black or red,
295 Of Aristotle and his philosophie
Of Aristotle and his philosophy
296 Than robes riche, or fithele, or gay sautrie*.[1] fiddle
Than rich robes, or a fiddle, or an elegant psaltery.
297 But al be that he was a philosophre[2],
But even though he was a philosopher,
298 Yet hadde he but litel gold in cofre*; offer
Nevertheless he had but little gold in his strongbox;
299 But al that he myghte of his freendes hente*, take
But all that he could get from his friends,
300 On bookes and on lernynge he it spente,
He spent on books and on learning,
301 And bisily gan for the soules preye
And diligently did pray for the souls
302 Of hem that yaf hym wherwith to scoleye*. study
Of those who gave him the wherewithal to attend the schools.
303 Of studie took he moost cure* and moost heede. care
He took most care and most heed of study.
304 Noght o* word spak he moore than was neede, one
He spoke not one word more than was needed,
305 And that was seyd in forme[3] and reverence,
And that was said with due formality and respect,
306 And short and quyk* and ful of hy sentence;[4] lively
And (was) short and lively and full of elevated content;
307 Sownynge* in moral vertu was his speche, sounding
His speech was consonant with (his) moral virtue,

1. Psaktery (a kind of harp).
2. The word may also mean“alchemist”.
3. With decorum.
4. Elevated thought.

308 And gladly wolde he lerne and gladly teche.
And gladly would he learn and gladly teach.

III. Reading Tasks

1. Read the interlinear translation and the original text, and note the difference between Middle English and Modern English.

2. Rewrite the text in prose without omission in meanings.

3. Fill in the following chart of comparison:

	appearance	speech	ideas	properties	character
the businessman					
the scholar					

4. What functions does "General Prologue" perform for the whole work of *The Canterbury Tales*?

5. How is "General Prologue" begun? Why does the poet make a description of the spring here?

Unit 2

Poems by Shakespeare

I. Introduction

1. The author

William Shakespeare (1564-1616) occupies a position unique in world literature. Other poets, such as Homer and Dante, and novelists, such as Leo Tolstoy and Charles Dickens, have transcended national barriers; but no writer's living reputation can compare with that of Shakespeare, whose plays, written in the late 16th and early 17th centuries for a small repertory theatre, are now performed and read more often and in more countries than ever before. The prophecy of his great contemporary, the poet and dramatist Ben Jonson, that Shakespeare "was not of an age, but for all time," has been fulfilled. It may be audacious

even to attempt a definition of his greatness, but it is not so difficult to describe the gifts that enabled him to create imaginative visions of pathos and mirth that, whether read or witnessed in the theatre, fill the mind and linger there. He is a writer of great intellectual rapidity, perceptiveness, and poetic power. Other writers have had these qualities, but with Shakespeare the keenness of mind was applied not to abstruse or remote subjects but to human beings and their complete range of emotions and conflicts. Other writers have applied their keenness of mind in this way, but

Shakespeare is astonishingly clever with words and images, so that his mental energy, when applied to intelligible human situations, finds full and memorable expression, convincing and imaginatively stimulating. As if this were not enough, the art form into which his creative energies went was not remote and bookish but involved the vivid stage impersonation of human beings, commanding sympathy and inviting vicarious participation. Thus Shakespeare's merits can survive translation into other languages and into cultures remote from that of Elizabethan England.

2. *Hamlet, Prince of Denmark*

Tragedy in five acts by William Shakespeare, performed in 1600-1601 and published in a quarto edition in 1603 from a reported text, with reference to an earlier play. The play opens with Hamlet's mourning for his father, who has been killed, and lamenting the behaviour of his mother, Gertrude, who married his uncle Claudius within a month of his father's death. The ghost of his father appears to Hamlet, informs him that he was poisoned by Claudius, and asks Hamlet to avenge his death. Hamlet hesitates, desiring further evidence of foul play. His uncertainty and inability to act make him increasingly melancholy, and to everyone around him Hamlet seems to be going mad. Driven by a guilty conscience, Claudius attempts to ascertain the cause of Hamlet's odd behaviour by hiring Hamlet's friends Rosencrantz and Guildenstern to spy on him. Hamlet quickly sees through the scheme and begins to act the part of a madman in front of them. To the pompous old courtier Polonius, it appears that Hamlet is lovesick over Polonius' daughter Ophelia. Despite Ophelia's loyalty to him, Hamlet thinks that she, like everyone else, is turning against him; he feigns madness with her also and treats her cruelly as if she were representative, like his own mother, of her treacherous sex. Hamlet contrives a plan to test the ghost's accusation. With a group of visiting actors, Hamlet arranges the performance of a story representing circumstances similar to those described by the ghost, under which Claudius poisoned Hamlet's father. When the play is presented as planned, the performance clearly unnerves Claudius. Despite Claudius' evident guilt, Hamlet still is unable to act, to avenge his father's wrongful murder. He nevertheless confronts his mother and kills the eavesdropping Polonius. Justly fearing for his own life, Claudius sends Hamlet to England with Rosencrantz and Guildenstern, who carry secret orders to have Hamlet killed. When Hamlet discovers the orders, he alters them to make his two friends the victims instead. Upon his return to Denmark, Hamlet hears that Ophelia has killed herself and that her brother Laertes seeks to avenge Polonius' murder. Claudius is only too eager to arrange the duel. Carnage ensues. Both Hamlet and Laertes are struck by the sword that Claudius has had dipped in poison. Gertrude, also present at the duel, drinks from the cup of poison that Claudius has had placed near Hamlet to ensure his death. Before Hamlet himself dies, he manages to stab Claudius and to entrust the clearing of his honour to his friend Horatio.

Judged by its reception, Hamlet must be regarded as Shakespeare's most successful play. It has unceasing theatrical vitality, and the character of Hamlet himself has become a figure of literary mythology. For a time during the 20th century, many critics argued that in Hamlet Shakespeare did not make a psychologically consistent play out of a plot that retained much of the crudity of an earlier kind of "revenge" drama—that he was trying to transform a barbaric "revenge" hero into a subtle Renaissance prince but did not succeed. Even if this opinion has become unacceptable, it nevertheless taught critics to search out elements such as Shakespeare's artistic balance in presenting the play's moral problems. It is likely that an artist will make his work more interesting if he leaves a dilemma morally ambiguous rather than explicit. The revenge situation in Hamlet, moreover, is one charged with emotional excitement as well as moral interest. Simply put, the good man (Hamlet) is weak, and the bad man (Claudius) is strong. The good man has suffered a deep injury from the bad man, and he cannot obtain justice because justice is in the hand of the strong bad man. Therefore, the weak good man must go around and around in order to achieve a kind of natural justice; and the audience watches in suspense while the weak good man by subtlety attacks and gets his own back upon the strong bad man and the strong bad man spends his time evading the weak good man. Hamlet is given a formidable opponent: Claudius is a hypocrite, but he is a successful one. He achieves his desired effect on everybody. His hypocrisy is that of a skilled politician. He is not dramatically shown as being in any way unworthy of his station—he upholds his part with dignity. He is a "smiling villain" and is not exposed until the final catastrophe. The jealous Hamlet heaps abuse upon him, but Shakespeare makes Claudius the murderer self-controlled. Thus, theatrically, the situation is much more exciting.

3. Sonnet

The term derives from the Italian *sonetto* a "little sound" or "song". The ordinary sonnet consists of fourteen lines, usually in iambic pentameters with considerable variations in rhyme scheme. The three basic sonnet forms are: (1) the Petrarchan, or Italian, which comprises an octave rhyming abbaabba and a sestet rhyming cdecde or cdcdcd, or in any combination except a rhyming couplet; (2) the Spenserian of three quatrains and a couplet, rhyming abab,bcbc, cdcd,ee; (3) the Shakespearean, again with three quatrains and a couplet, rhyming abab, cdcd, efef, gg. The Italian form is the commonest. The octave develops one thought; there is then a"turn" or *volta*, and the sestet grows out of the octave, varies it and completes it. In the other two forms a different idea is expressed in each quatrain; each grows out of the one preceding it; and the argument, theme and dialectic are concluded,"tied up" in the binding end-couplet.

II. Text

1. Hamlet's Soliloquy[1]

To be, or not to be[2] , that is the question:
Whether 'tis nobler in the mind to suffer
The slings and arrows[3] of outrageous[4] fortune
Or to take arms against[5] a sea of troubles,
And by opposing end them[6]. To die—to sleep—
No more; and by a sleep to say we end
The heartache, and the thousand natural shocks

---

1. The whole soliloquy is written in blank verse.
2. To be, or not to be — to live on n this world or die (or, to take action or do nothing).
3. The slings and arrows — injuries.
4. outrageous — cruel, furious.
5. take arms against — fight against.
6. end them— put an end to the troubles by fighting against them.

That flesh* is heir to[1]. 'Tis a consummation[2]	human body
Devoutly to be wish'd. To die—to sleep.	
To sleep—perchance* to dream: ay*, there's the rub[3]!	possibly, maybe / yes
For in that sleep of death what dreams may come	
When we have shuffled off this mortal coil*[4],	turmoil
Must give us pause[5]. There's the respect*	consideration, thought
That makes calamity of so long life[6].	
For who would bear the whips and scorns of time[7],	
Th' oppressor's wrong, the proud man's contumely*,	insolence, contempt
The pangs of despis'd love[8], the law's delay[9],	
The insolence of office[10], and the spurns*	insults
That patient merit of th' unworthy takes[11],	
When he himself might his quietus make[12]	
With a bare bodkin[13]? Who would these fardels* bear,	burdens
To grunt* and sweat under a weary life,	groan
But that the dread of something after death—	
The undiscover'd country[14], from whose bourn*	boundary
No traveller returns—puzzles* the will,	confuse, perplexes
And makes us rather bear those ills we have	
Than fly to others[15] that we know not of?	
Thus conscience[16] does make cowards of us all,	

1. flesh* is heir to — the many kinds of sufferings that naturally come to a human being.
2. consummation — conclusion, final settlement of all accounts.
3. there's the rub — there lies the obstacle (that is the point at which doubt or difficulty arises, there's difficulty, or hitch).
4. shuffled off this mortal coil — ended this life. "Mortal coil" refers to human life.
5. give us pause — make us hesitate.
6. makes calamity of so long life — makes a long life seem to be a great misfortune.
7. whips and scorns of time — the unpleasant things and miseries we suffer in our epoch."Time" means the age we live in.
8. despised love— rejected love, love held in contempt.
9. the law's delay — the long-drawn-out lawsuits.
10. The insolence of office — the haughty and contemptuous behaviour shown by holders of high governmental posts.
11. That patient merit of th' unworthy takes — that people of worth and fortitude endure at the hands of the unworthy.
12. might his quietus make — might end his life. "Quietus" means the final settlement of account.
13. a bare bodkin — a mere dagger.
14. The undiscover'd country — the place unknown to us (where we go after death).
15. fly to others — go to others, i.e., other ills or evils.
16. conscience — serious thought, reflection, consciousness, contemplation.

And thus the native* hue* of resolution — natural / colour
Is sicklied* o'er* with the pale cast of thought[1], — covered / over
And enterprises of great pith* and moment*[2] — height / importance
With this regard[3] their currents turn awry[4]
And lose the name of action[5].

2. Sonnet 18

Shall I compare thee to a summer's day?
Thou art more lovely and more temperate:
Rough winds do shake the darling buds of May,
And summer's lease hath all too short a date[6]:
Sometime[7] too hot the eye of heaven[8] shines,
And often is his gold complexion dimmed;
And every fair[9] from fair[10] sometime declines,
By chance, or nature's changing course [11] untrimmed[12];
But thy eternal summer shall not fade,
Nor lose possession of that fair thou ow'st*[13]; — ownest, own
Nor shall death brag thou wand'rest in his shade[14],
When in eternal lines to time thou grow'st.
So long as men can breathe or eyes can see,
So long lives this, and this gives life to thee.

---

1. Is sicklied* o'er* with the pale cast of thought— a natural decision becomes weakened by melancholy thought."The pale cast of thought" means the pale look of melancholy.
2. enterprises of great pith* and moment — actions of great importance.
3. With this regard — in this consideration of this, on this account.
4. their currents turn awry — turn awry their currents, i.e., turn their course aside; deviate from their original purpose.
5. lose the name of action — fail to be put into action.
6. a date — a limited period of time.
7. sometime — sometimes, now and then, from time to time.
8. the eye of heaven — refers to the Sun.
9. every fair — every beautiful object, every beautiful person or thing.
10. fair — beauty.
11. By chance, or by nature's course — either by fortune or by the normal course of change in the natural world.
12. untrimm'd — sripped of beauty.
13. Though ow'st — thou ownest, you own, you possess.
14. Nor shall Death brag thou wand'rest in his shade — Nor shall Death boast that you roam about in his darkness, i.e., you shall not fall under the threat of Death. Here"Death" is personified;"thou wand'rest" = thou wanderest.

3. Sonnet 29

When, in disgrace with fortune and men's eyes,
I all alone beweep[1] my outcast state[2],
And trouble deaf heaven with my bootless[3] cries,
And look upon myself and curse my fate,
Whishing me like to one[4] more rich in hope,
Feature'd like him[5], like him with friends possess'd,
Desiring this man's art[6], and that man's scope[7],
With what I most enjoy contented least;[8]
Yet in these thoughts myself almost despising,
Haply[9] I think on thee; and then my state
Like to the lark at break of day arising
From sullen earth, sings hymns at heaven's gate:
For thy sweet love remember'd such wealth brings,
That then I scorn to change my state with kings.

III. Reading Tasks

1. Hamlet's Soliloquy

(1) Read aloud the poem.

(2) Write on the lines the relationships of these main characters in the play.

---

1. beweep (obsolete) — deplore, weep over.
2. my outcast state — my state of being ignored by the society.
3. bootless — unavailing, useless.
4. Wishing me like to one — whishing me to resemble someone.
5. Featur'd like him — with personal appearance (or features) similar to his (implying a handsome appearance).
6. art — learning, literary or other accomplishment.
7. scope — range of genius.
8. With what I most enjoy contented least — least contented with what I possess in abundance.
9. haply — fortunately, luckily (ordinarily"haply" means"by chance").

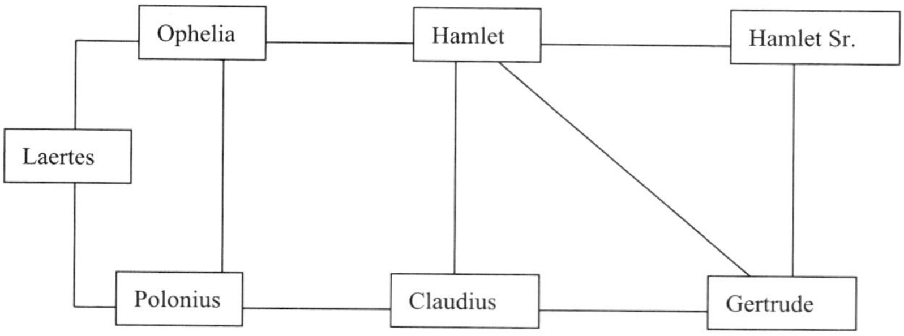

(3) Explain Hamlet's reasoning process in this soliloquy.

(4) Questions for discussion

① What is a soliloquy? In a soliloquy, who is the speaker and who is the listener?

② What idea is Hamlet dwelling on in this soliloquy? Why does not he talk the idea over with a friend, such as Ophelia, Laetes, etc.

③ What kind of life attitude is revealed in this soliloquy? optimistic or pessimistic? Quote some of Hamlet's dissatisfactions of life mentioned in this soliloquy.

④ Why, according to the soliloquy, does man hesitate to end his life? What results come from this hesitation?

2. Sonnet 18

(1) Recite Sonnet 18.

(2) Name and explain the figures of speech contained in this poem.

(3) Mark the rhyme scheme and comment upon the verse form employed.

(4) Give a rendering of the content of the poem in your own words to show that you have fully understood its meaning.

(5) Questions for discussion:

① In what ways does the poet praise his lover's beauty.

② The word"fair" is used twice in line 7. How do you understand the meanings of the word respectively?

3. Sonnet 29

(1) Recite Sonnet 29.

(2) Explain the contrast and comparison employed to stress the value of love.

(3) Give a paraphrase of the poem in simple language.

(4) Questions

① What mood is suggested in the first 9 lines? What happenings lead to the formation of the mood?

② Does the poem fall in a happy ending or a sad ending?

③ What is the theme of the poem?

Unit 3

Of Studies

I. Introduction

1. The author

Francis Bacon (1561-1626) was a statesman, philosopher, and essayist: as a thinker, one of the most formative minds in European thought during the last 500 years; as a prose writer, an important influence on the development of English rational (as distinct from poetic and imaginative) expression; as a statesman, he reached the highest political and judicial office (the Lord Chancellorship) from which, however, he was dismissed for accepting bribes in 1621. The combination of greatness of thought with mediocrity of conduct provoked the poet Pepe's description of him, a century later, as "the wisest, brightest, meanest of mankind."

2. Essay

Essay is a literary composition of moderate length, dealing in an easy, cursory way with a single subject, usually representing the writer's personal experience and outlook. The form was invented in the late 16th century by the French writer Michel de Montaigne, who chose the name essai to emphasize that his compositions were attempts or endeavours, feeling their way toward the expression of his personal thoughts and experiences. The reflective Montaigne wrote about himself with startling frankness, capturing his fancies about the intimate things of life with superb skill and setting them down in a vivid and arresting way. His Essais, published in their final form in 1588, are still considered among the finest of their kind. Francis Bacon was the first great English essayist, although his Essayes (1597; enlarged editions in 1612 and 1625) are utterly different from those of Montaigne. The topics were grave and weighty—"Of Ambition","Of Truth","Of Great Place", and the like—and the style is lofty and often austere. Abraham Cowley (1618-1667) was the first English writer of distinction to follow Montaigne's example, echoing the Frenchman's personal touch in such essays as"Of Myself." In the 18th century the English essay enjoyed a great vogue, taking shape in the hands of such masters as Addison and Steele, Samuel Johnson, and Oliver Goldsmith. Among the greatest of the English essayists was Charles Lamb (1775-1834), whose"Essays of Elia," which began to appear in 1820, are universally recognized as landmarks of the genre. Lamb's essays combine humour, fantasy, and sentiment with a gift for perceptive observation of life, all expressed in a highly personal style. Another outstanding essay writer was Thomas De Quincey (1785-1859), whose works include such highly polished and imaginative pieces as"On Murder as One of the Fine Arts" and"On the English Mail Coach." In the latter half of the 19th century, the essays of Robert Louis Stevenson are of the same class as those of Montaigne and Lamb, and he approached far more closely than his contemporaries to their level of excellence. In the United States the essay had been written with genius by Thoreau in *Walden*; and Emerson's Essays, though not in the tradition of Montaigne and Lamb, were rich in lofty thought and utterance. Although invented by a great French writer, the essay was very late in making itself at home in France. During the 20th century the essay has been reborn as a playful kind of literature, and such humorists as James Thurber and Dorothy Parker excelled in the art.

Of Bacon's 58 essays, "Of Studies" is one of the shortest, but also one of the better known and the more widely read. In the essay Bacon attempts to discuss rather analytically the use and abuse of studies, the proper and improper ways to pursue one's studies, and also the effect of the different kinds of studies upon human character. Though the essay was written nearly four centuries ago and parts of it are therefore outdated and of little interest to us, a number of the remarks in it were based on the author's own wide experience as a scholar and as a practical man of affairs and consequently they still deserve our attention today. Conciseness of expression and simplicity of diction are the two chief distinguishing features of the prose style of Bacon who was among the earliest of English essayists.

II. Text

Of Studies

Studies serve for delight, for ornament, and for ability. Their chief use for delight is in privateness and retiring;[1] for ornament, is in discourse[2]; and for ability, is in the judgment and disposition of business[3]. For expert men[4] can execute, and perhaps judge of particulars, one by one[5]; but the general counsels[6], and the plots and marshalling of affairs[7] come best from those that are learned[8]. To spend too much time in studies is sloth; to use them too much for ornament is affectation; to make judgment wholly by their rules is the humour of a scholar[9]. They perfect nature, and are perfected by experience[10]; for natural abilities are like natural plants, that need proyning[11] by study; and studies themselves do give forth directions too much at large[12], except they be bounded in by experience[13]. Crafty men[14] contemn studies, simple men admire them, and wise men use them, for they teach not their own use; but that is a wisdom without them, and above them, won by observation[15].

---

1. in privateness and retiring — when one is alone and away from company.
2. in discourse — when one is engaged in conversation.
3. in the judgement and disposition of business — when one forms a judgment and makes definite arrangements about the affairs of the world.
4. expert men — men with much experience.
5. judge of particulars, one by one — form opinions of specific matters separately.
6. the general counsels — the giving of advice on general topics.
7. the plots and marshalling of affairs — the planning and the directing of affairs.
8. those that are learned — learned men, scholars.
9. the humour of a scholar — the mental peculiarity of a scholar.
10. They perfect nature, and are perfected by experience — they (studies) improve a person's natural abilities and are themselves made more complete by experience.
11. proyning — old spelling for"pruning", meaning: trimming, or cutting off the superfluous and burdensome parts.
12. too much at large — too general or impractical.
13. be bounded in by experience — restricted by experience.
14. crafty men — men who have some special skill("crafty"= skilful, ingenious, having some special kill).
15. but that is a wisdom without them and above them, won by observation — but that (to make good use of studies) is a wisdom that lies beyond and above the realm of studies, attainable only through a keen observation of things.

Read not to contradict and confute, nor to believe and take for granted, nor to find talk and discourse, but to weigh and consider. Some books are to be tasted, others to be swallowed, and some few to be chewed and digested; that is, some books are to be read only in parts; others to be read, but not curiously[1]; and some few to be read wholly, and with diligence and attention. Some books also may be read by deputy[2], and extracts[3] made of them by others, but that would be only in the less important arguments, and the meaner sort of books[4]; else distilled books[5] are like common distilled waters, flashy things[6]. Reading maketh a full man[7], conference[8] a ready man[9], and writing an exact man[10]. And therefore, if a man write little, he had need have a great memory[11]; if he confer[12] little, he had need have a present wit: and if he read little, he had need have much cunning, to seem to know, that he doth not. Histories make men wise; poets, witty; the mathematics, subtile; natural philosophy, deep; moral, grave; logic and rhetoric, able to contend[13]. *Abeunt studia in mores*[14]. Nay, there is no stond[15] or impediment in the wit but may be wrought out by fit studies; like as[16] diseases of the body may have appropriate exercises. Bowling[17] is good for the stone and reins[18], shooting for the lungs and breast, gentle walking for the stomach, riding for the head, and the like. So if a man's wit

---

1. curiously — with thoroughness and care.
2. read by deputy — read with the assistance of others.
3. extracts — passages taken from books.
4. but that would be only in the less important argument, and the meaner sort of books — but to read by deputy and to have extracts made of books by other persons should be done only in the case of books with less important subject-matter and of little value ("argument" =the content or subject matter of books.).
5. distilled books — books from which the better parts have been extracted.
6. flashy things — flat and tasteless things.
7. a full man — a man with a wide knowledge of things.
8. conference — consultation, conversation.
9. a ready man — a man who can answer things readily and freely.
10. an exact man — a man who speaks and writes with accuracy.
    Abeunt studia in mores (Latin) — Studies go into forming one's character.
11. if a man write little, he had need have a great memory —"write"= take notes;"had need have" = would need to have.
12. confer — converse, speak.
13. Histories make men wise; poets witty; the mathematics subtile; natural philosophy deep; moral grave; logic and rhetoric able to contend — The study of history books makes men wise; the study of poetry makes men brilliant in conversation; the study of mathematics makes men subtile (able to see fine differences between things,"subtile" = old spelling for subtle"); the study of natural philosophy (physics) enables men to see into the depth of things; the study of moral philosophy makes men serious and dignified; the study of logic and rhetoric enables men to argue well about things.
14. Abeunt studia in mores (Latin) — Studies go into forming one's character.
15. stond — hindrance, drawback.
16. like as (archaic) = as.
17. bowling — playing at bowls ("bowls": tools in shape of ball used in the game).
18. stone and reins — the bladder and kidneys.

be wandering[1], let him study the mathematics; for in demonstrations[2], if his wit be called away never so little[3], he must begin again. If his wit be not apt to distinguish or find differences, let him study the Schoolmen[4], for they are *cymini sectores*[5]. If he be not apt to beat over matters[6] and to call up one thing to prove and illustrate another, let him study the lawyer's cases. So every defect of the mind, may have a special receipt[7].

III. Reading Tasks

1. Put the passage into several sections and give the main idea of each of them.

2. Name as many essays on the same subject by other writers as possible and try to compare the ideas and the writing styles.

3. What ideas provided in this essay are still of great value today? Which ideas, in your opinion, are out of date? Why?

4. What are the differences and similarities between an essay and an academic researcher paper?

---

1. if a man's wit be wandering — if a man's mind cannot concentrate on anything to make analyses of things.
2. demonstrations — ways of finding proofs in solving a problem in mathematics.
3. if his wit be called away never so little — if his mind should be diverted to other things even lightly (her"never" actually ="ever").
4. the schoolman — the philosophers or theologians of the schools of the Middle Ages, who were skilled in a making fine distinctions in the matters under discussion in theology and philosophy.
5. cymini sectores (Latin) — dividers of cumin-seed, i.e., hair-splitters (persons who spend much time and energy in making fine distinctions about very abstract things).
6. to beat over matters — to make thorough examinations of things, to go over the ground and search carefully (like beaters who in hunting search the ground carefully to rouse the game).
7. receipt — a recipe, a remedy given in a prescription.

Unit 4

Robinson Crusoe

I. Introduction

1. The author

Daniel Defoe (1660-1731) was a man of many talents and author of an extraordinary range and number of works. Defoe remains in many ways an enigmatic figure. A man who made many enemies, he has been accused of double-dealing, of dishonest or equivocal conduct, of venality. Certainly in politics he served in turn both Tory and Whig; he acted as a secret agent for the Tories and later served the Whigs by "infiltrating" extremist Tory journals and toning them down. But Defoe always claimed that the end justified the means, and a more sympathetic view may see him as what he always professed to be, an unswerving champion of moderation. At the age of 59 Defoe embarked on what was virtually a new career, producing in Robinson Crusoe the first of a remarkable series of novels and other fictional writings that resulted in his being called the father of the English novel. Defoe's last years were clouded by legal controversies over allegedly unpaid bonds dating back a generation, and it is thought that he died in hiding from his creditors. His character Moll Flanders, born in Newgate Prison, speaks of poverty as "a frightful spectre,"

and it is a theme of many of his books.

2. The story

Robinson Crusoe is a sailor. In one of his voyages he is shipwrecked. All the other men are drowned. He alone finds himself cast away on the shore of an uninhabited island. He lives there alone for many years. With the few things he gets from the wrecked ship, he builds a dwelling place. He grows barley and rice, domesticates the goats, fights against the savages, and saves one savaged named Friday from death and makes him his servant. Finally he is brought back to England by an English ship.

II. Text

Extract 2.1 Crusoe Visits the Wreck

A little after Noon I found the Sea very calm, and the Tyde ebb'd[1] so far out, that I could come within a Quarter of a Mile of the Ship; and here I found a fresh renewing of my Grief, for I saw evidently, that if we had kept on board, we had been all safe, that is to say, we had all got safe on Shore, and I had not been so miserable as to be left entirely destitute of all Comfort and Company, as I now was; this forc'd Tears from my Eyes again, but as there was little Relief in that, I resolv'd, if possible, to get to the Ship, so I pull'd off my Clothes, for the Weather was hot to Extremity, and took the Water, but when I came to the Ship, my Difficulty was still greater to know how to get on board, for as she lay a ground[2], and high out of the Water, there was nothing within my Reach to lay hold of; I swam round her twice, and the second Time I spy'd a small Piece of a Rope, which I wonder'd I did not see at first, hang down by the Fore-Chains[3] so low, as that with great Difficulty I got hold of it, and by the help of that Rope, got up into the Forecastle of the Ship; here I found that the Ship was bulg'd[4], and had a great deal of Water in her Hold, but that she lay so on the Side of a Bank of hard Sand, or rather Earth, that her Stern lay lifted up upon the Bank, and her Head low almost to the Water; by this Means all her Quarter was free, and all that was in that Part was dry; for

1. the Tyde ebb'd = the tide ebbed. In this novel, the first letter of key words in a sentence is often capitalized. The suffix "-ed" is written as "-'d".
2. lay a ground = lay aground, meaning"be stuck onto or on a shore or the bottom of the body of water".
3. Fore-Chain — chains which brace the ships mast.
4. bulg'd — staved or broken in her bilge.

you may be sure my first Work was to search and to see what was spoil'd and what was free; and first I found that all the Ship's Provisions were dry and untouch'd by the Water, and being very well dispos'd to eat, I went to the Bread-room and fill'd my Pockets with Bisket[1], and eat it as I went about other things, for I had no time to lose; I also found some Rum in the great Cabbin, of which I took a large Dram, and which I had indeed need enough of to spirit me for what was before me: Now I wanted nothing but a Boat to furnish my self with many things which I forsaw would be very necessary to me.

It was in vain to sit still and wish for what was not to be had, and this Extremity rouz'd my Application; we had several spare Yards[2], and two or three large sparrs of Wood, and a spare Top-mast or two in the Ship; I resolv'd to fall to work with these, and I flung as many of them over board as I could manage for their Weight, tying every one with a Rope that they might not drive away; when this was done I went down the Ship's Side, and pulling them to me, I ty'd four of them fast together at both Ends as well as I could, in the Form of a Raft, and laying two or three short Pieces of Plank upon them cross-ways, I found I could walk upon it very well, but that it was not able to bear any great Weight, the Pieces being too light; so I went to work, and with the Carpenter's Saw I cut a spare Top-mast into three Lengths, and added them to my Raft, with a great deal of Labour and Pains, but hope of furnishing myself with Necessaries, encourag'd me to go beyond what I should have been able to have done upon another Occasion.

My Raft was now strong enough to bear any reasonable Weight; my next Care was what to load it with, and how to preserve what I laid upon it from the Surf of the Sea; But I was not long considering this, I first laid all the Plank or Boards upon it that I could get, and having consider'd well what I most wanted, I first got three of the Seamens Chests, which I had broken open and empty'd, and lower'd them down upon my Raft; the first of these I fill'd with Provision, viz[3]. Bread, Rice, three Dutch Cheeses, five Pieces of dry'd Goat's Flesh, which we liv'd much u'pon, and a little Remainder of European Corn which had been laid by for some Fowls which we brought to Sea with us, but the Fowls were kill'd; there had been some Barly and Wheat together, but, to my great Disappointment, I found afterwards that the Rats had eaten or spoil'd it all; as for Liquors, I found several Cases of Bottles belonging to our Skipper, in which some Cordial Waters, and in all about five or six Gallons of Rack, these I stow'd by themselves, there

1. bisket = biscuit.
2. spare Yards — extra poles.
3. viz = videlicet (Latin), namely.

being no need to put them into the Chest, nor no room for them. While I was doing this, I found the Tyde began to flow, tho' very calm, and I had the Mortification to see my Coat, Shirt, and Wast-coat which I had left on Shore upon the Sand, swim away; as for my Breeches which were only Linnen and open knee'd, I swam on board in them and my Stockings: However this put me upon rummaging for Clothes, of which I found enough, but took no more than I wanted for present use, for I had other things which my Eye was more upon, as first Tools to work with on Shore, and it was after long searching that I found out the Carpenter's Chest, which was indeed a very useful Prize to me, and much more valuable than a Ship Loading of Gold would have been at that time; I got it down to my Raft, even whole as it was, without losing time to look into it, for I knew in general what it contain'd.

My next Care was for some Ammunition and Arms; there were two very good Fowling-pieces in the great Cabbin, and two Pistols, these I secur'd first, with some Powder-horns, and a small Bag of Shot, and two old rusty Swords; I knew there were three Barrels of Powder in the Ship, but knew not where our Gunner had stow'd them, but with much search I found them, two of them dry and good, the third had taken Water, those two I got to my Raft, with the Arms, and now I thought my self pretty well freighted, and began to think how I should get to Shore with them, having neither Sail, Oar, or Rudder, and the least Cap full of Wind would have overset all my Navigation[1].

I had three Encouragements, 1. A smooth calm Sea, 2. The Tide rising and setting in to the Shore, 3. What little Wind there was blew me towards the Land; and thus, having found two or three broken Oars belonging to the Boat, and besides the Tools which were in the Chest, I found two Saws, an Axe, and a Hammer, and with this Cargo I put to Sea; For a Mile, or thereabouts, my Raft went very well, only that I found it drive a little distant from the Place where I had landed before, by which I perceiv'd that there was some Indraft of the Water, and consequently I hop'd to find some Creek or River there, which I might make use of as a Port to get to Land with my Cargo.

Extract 2.2 The Footprint

It happen'd one Day about Noon going towards my Boat, I was exceedingly surpriz'd with the Print of a Man's naked Foot on the Shore, which was very plain to be seen in the Sand: I stood like one Thunder-struck, or as if I had seen an Apparition; I listen'd, I look'd

---

1. and the least cap full of Wind would have overset all my Navigation — and a slight blow of wind would overturn my boat along with its cargo.

round me, I could hear nothing, nor see any Thing, I went up to a rising Ground to look farther, I went up the Shore and down the Shore, but it was all one, I could see no other Impression but that one, I went to it again to see if there were any more, and to observe if it might not be my Fancy; but there was no Room for that, for there was exactly the very Print of a Foot, Toes, Heel, and every Part of a Foot; how it came thither, I knew not, nor could in the least imagine. But after innumerable fluttering Thoughts, like a Man perfectly confus'd and out of my self, I came Home to my Fortification, not feeling, as we say, the Ground I went on, but terrify'd to the last Degree, looking behind me at every two or three Steps, mistaking every Bush and Tree, and fancying every Stump at a Distance to be a Man; nor is it possible to describe how many various Shapes affrighted Imagination represented Things to me in, how many wild Ideas were found every Moment in my Fancy, and what strange unaccountable Whimsies came into my Thoughts by the Way.

When I came to my Castle, for so I think I call'd it ever after this, I fled into it like one pursued; whether I went over by the Ladder as first contriv'd, or went in at the Hole in the Rock, which I call'd a Door, I cannot remember; no, nor could I remember the next Morning, for never frighted Hare fled to Cover, or Fox to Earth, with more Terror of Mind than I to this Retreat.

Extract 2.3 Crusoe Saves Friday from the Cannibals

While I was thus looking on them, I perceived by my Perspective, two miserable Wretches dragg'd from the Boats, where it seems they were laid by, and were now brought out for the Slaughter. I perceived one of them immediately fell, being knock'd down, I suppose with a Club or Wooden Sword, for that was their way, and two or three others were at work immediately cutting him open for their Cookery, while the other Victim was left standing by himself, till they should be ready for him. In that very Moment this poor Wretch seeing himself a little at Liberty, Nature inspir'd him with Hopes of Life, and he started away from them, and ran with incredible Swiftness along the Sands directly towards me, I mean towards that part of the Coast, where my Habitation was.

I was dreadfully frighted, (that I must acknowledge) when I perceived him to run my

Way; and especially, when as I thought I saw him pursued by the whole Body, and now I expected that part of my Dream was coming to pass, and that he would certainly take shelter in my Grove; but I could not depend by any means upon my Dream for the rest of it, (viz.) that the other Savages would not pursue him thither, and find him there. However I kept my Station, and my Spirits began to recover, when I found that there was not above three Men that follow'd him, and still more was I encourag'd, when I found that he outstrip'd them exceedingly in running, and gain'd Ground of them[1], so that if he could but hold it for half an Hour, I saw easily he would fairly get away from them all.

There was between them and my Castle, the Creek which I mention'd often at the first part of my Story, when I landed my Cargoes out of the Ship; and this I saw plainly, he must necessarily swim over, or the poor Wretch would be taken there: But when the Savage escaping came thither, he made nothing of it, tho' the Tide was then up, but plunging in, swam thro' in about Thirty Strokes or thereabouts, landed and ran on with exceeding Strength and Swiftness; when the Three Persons came to the Creek, I found that Two of them could Swim, but the Third cou'd not, and that standing on the other Side, he look'd at the other, but went no further; and soon after went softly back again, which as it happen'd, was very well for him in the main.

I observ'd, that the two who swam, were yet more than twice as long swimming over the Creek, as the Fellow was, that fled from them: It came now very warmly upon my Thoughts, and indeed irresistibly, that now was my Time to get me a Servant, and perhaps a Companion, or Assistant; and that I was call'd plainly by Providence to save this poor Creature's Life; I immediately run down the Ladders with all possible Expedition, fetches my two Guns, for they were both but at the Foot of the Ladders, as I observ'd above; and getting up again, with the same haste, to the Top of the Hill, I cross'd toward the Sea; and having a very short Cut, and all down Hill, clapp'd my self in the way, between the Pursuers, and the Pursu'd; hallowing aloud to him that fled, who looking back, was at first perhaps as much frighted at me, as at them; but I beckon'd with my Hand to him, to come back; and in the mean time, I slowly advanc'd towards the two that follow'd; then rushing at once upon the foremost, I knock'd him down with the Stock of my Piece I was loath to fire, because I would not have the rest hear; though at that distance, it would not have been easily heard, and being out of Sight of the Smoke too, they wou'd not have easily known what to make of it: Having

1. and gain'd Ground of them — and kept a distance from them.

knock'd this Fellow down, the other who pursu'd with him stopp'd, as if he had been frighted; and I advanc'd a-pace towards him; but as I came nearer, I perceiv'd presently, he had a Bow and Arrow, and was fitting it to shoot at me; so I was then necessitated to shoot at him first, which I did, and kill'd him at the first Shoot; the poor Savage who fled, but had stopp'd; though he saw both his Enemies fallen, and kill'd, as he thought; yet was so frighted with the Fire, and Noise of my Piece, that he stood Stock still, and neither came forward or went backward, tho' he seem'd rather enclin'd to fly still, than to come on; I hollow'd again to him, and made Signs to come forward, which he easily understood, and came a little way, then stopp'd again, and then a little further, and stopp'd again, and I cou'd then perceive that he stood trembling, as if he had been taken Prisoner, and had just been to be kill'd, as his two Enemies were; I beckon'd him again to come to me, and gave him all the Signs of Encouragement that I could think of, and he came nearer and nearer, kneeling down every Ten or Twelve steps in token of acknowledgement for my saving his Life: I smil'd at him, and look'd pleasantly, and beckon'd to him to come still nearer; at length he came close to me, and then he kneel'd down again, kiss'd the Ground, and laid his Head upon the Ground, and taking me by the Foot, set my Foot upon his Head; this it seems was in token of swearing to be my Slave for ever; I took him up, and made much of him, and encourag'd him all I could. But there was more work to do yet, for I perceived the Savage who I knock'd down, was not kill'd, but stunn'd with the blow, and began to come to himself; so I pointed to him, and showing him the Savage, that he was not dead; upon this he spoke some Words to me, and though I could not understand them, yet I thought they were pleasant to hear, for they were the first sound of a Man's Voice, that I had heard, my own excepted, for above Twenty Five Years. But there was no time for such Reflections now, the Savage who was knock'd down recover'd himself so far, as to sit up upon the Ground, and I perceived that my Savage began to be afraid; but when I saw that, I presented my other Piece at the Man, as if I would shoot him, upon this my Savage, for so I call him now, made a Motion to me to lend him my Sword, which hung naked in a Belt by my side; so I did: he no sooner had it, but he runs to his Enemy, and at one blow cut off his Head as cleaverly, no Executioner in Germany, could have done it sooner or better; which I thought very strange, for one who I had Reason to believe never saw a Sword in his Life before, except their own Wooden Swords; however it seems, as I learn'd afterwards, they make their Wooden Swords so sharp, so heavy, and the Wood is so hard, that they will cut off Heads even with them, ay and Arms, and that at one blow too; when he had done this, he comes laughing to me in Sign of Triumph, and brought me the Sword again, and with abundance of Gestures which I did not understand, laid it down with the Head of the Savage, that he had kill'd just before me.

But that which astonish'd him most, was to know how I had kill'd the other Indian so far off, so pointing to him, he made Signs to me to let him go to him, so I bad him go, as well as I could, when he came to him, he stood like one amaz'd, looking at him, turn'd him first on one side, then on t'other, look'd at the Wound the Bullet had made, which it seems was just in his Breast, where it had made a Hole, and no great Quantity of Blood had follow'd, but he had bled inwardly, for he was quite dead; He took up his Bow, and Arrows, and came back, so I turn'd to go away, and beckon'd to him to follow me, making Signs to him, that more might come after them.

Upon this he sign'd to me, that he should bury them with Sand, that they might not be seen by the rest if they follow'd; and so I made Signs again to him to do so; he fell to Work, and in an instant he had scrap'd a Hole in the Sand, with his Hands, big enough to bury the first in, and then dragg'd him into it, and cover'd him, and did so also by the other; I believe he had bury'd them both in a Quarter of an Hour; then calling him away, I carry'd him not to my Castle, but quite away to my Cave, on the farther Part of the Island; so I did not let my Dream come to pass in that Part[1], viz. That he came into my Grove for shelter.

Here I gave him Bread, and a Bunch of Raisins to eat, and a Draught of Water, which I found he was indeed in great Distress for, by his Running; and having refresh'd him, I made Signs for him to go lie down and sleep; pointing to a Place where I had laid a great Parcel of Rice Straw, and a Blanket upon it, which I used to sleep upon my self some times; so the poor Creature laid down, and went to sleep.

He was a comely handsome Fellow, perfectly well made; with straight strong Limbs, not too large; tall and well shap'd, and as I reckon, about twenty six Years of Age. He had a very good Countenance, not a fierce and surly Aspect; but seem'd to have something very manly in his Face, and yet he had all the Sweetness and Softness of an European in his Countenance too, especially when he smil'd. His Hair was long and black, not curl'd like Wool; his

1. so I did not let my Dream come to pass in that Part — so I did not allow what I had dreamed to come true.

Forehead very high, and large, and a great Vivacity and sparkling Sharpness in his Eyes. The Colour of his Skin was not quite black, but very tawny; and yet not of an ugly yellow nauseous tawny, as the Brasilians, and Virginians, and other Natives of America are; but of a bright kind of a dun olive Colour, that had in it something very agreeable; tho' not very easy to describe. His Face was round, and plump; his Nose small, not flat like the Negroes, a very good Mouth, thin Lips, and his line Teeth well set, and white as Ivory. After he had slumber'd, rather than slept, about half an Hour, he wak'd again, and comes out of the Cave to me; for I had been milking my Goats, which I had in the Enclosure just by: When he espy'd me, he came running to me, laying himself down again upon the Ground, with all the possible Signs of an humble thankful Disposition, making a many antick Gestures show it: At last he lays his Head flat upon the Ground, close to my Foot, and sets my other Foot upon his Head, as he had done before; and after this, made all the Signs to me of Subjection, Servitude, and Submission imaginable, to let me know, how he would serve me as long as he liv'd; I understood him in many Things, and let him know, I was very well pleas'd with him; in a little Time I began to speak to him, and teach him to speak to me; and first, I made him know his Name should be *Friday,* which was the Day I sav'd his Life; I call'd him so for the Memory of the Time; I likewise taught him to say *Master,* and then let him know, that was to be my Name; I likewise taught him to say, YES, and No, and to know the Meaning of them; I gave him some Milk, in an earthen Pot, and let him see me Drink it before him, and sop my Bread in it; and I gave him a Cake of Bread, to do the like, which he quickly comply'd with, and made Signs that it was very good for him.

III. Reading Tasks

1. How did Crusoe manage to get onto the ship?

2. Name all the items in groups of foods, drinks, cloths, ammunitions and arms, tools, etc. that Crusoe obtained from the ship.

3. What preparations did Crusoe make for his coming life on the island?

4. Make a comment on Crusoe's character.

5. Questions for discussion:

(1) From whose point of view is the story narrated? Does this point of view bring any special effectiveness?

(2) What role did Crusoe play in the fight between the escaper and the pursuers?

(3) What are the main factors that contribute to Crusoe's successful survival on the island almost single-handed?

(4) How did Crusoe consider his relationship with the island, the aborigines there, and Friday in particular?

Unit 5

Tom Jones

I. Introduction

1. The author

Henry Fielding (1707-1754), a novelist and playwright, who, with Samuel Richardson, is considered a founder of the English novel. Sir Walter Scott called Henry Fielding the "father of the English novel," and the phrase still indicates Fielding's place in the history of literature. Though not actually the first English novelist, he was the first to approach the genre with a fully worked-out theory of the novel; and in *Joseph Andrews*, *Tom Jones*, and *Amelia*, which a modern critic has called comic epic, epic comedy, and domestic epic, respectively, he had established the tradition of a realism presented in panoramic surveys of contemporary society that dominated English fiction until the end of the 19th century.

2. The story

Tom Jones (the full title being *The History of Tom Jones, a Foundling*), generally considered Fielding's most important novel, consists of eighteen "books". The story begins with the discovery of Tom Jones, a foundling, in the bed of a wealthy squire, Mr. Allworthy, who gives him a home and an education. Allworthy's nephew, young Blifil, who is a thorough-going hypocrite, hates Tom and speaks ill of him before Allworthy until the latter drives Tom out of his house. Sophia Western, the beautiful daughter of a neighbouring landlord, Squire Western, loves Tom and flees from her home when her father forces her to marry Blifil. Lengthy accounts are given of the various adventures of Tom and then of Sophia as both travel to London. Then, after further complications involving the hero and the heroine in the English capital, Tom is eventually discovered to be Allworthy's nephew and young Blifil's half-brother and is happily united to Sophia while Blifil's hypocrisy and villainy are finally exposed to view.

II. Text

Chapter 13, Book 4

A DREADFUL ACCIDENT WHICH BEFEL SOPHIA. THE GALLANT BEHAVIOUR OF JONES, AND THE MORE DREADFUL CONSEQUENCE OF THAT BEHAVIOUR TO THE YOUNG LADY; WITH A SHORT DIGRESSION IN FAVOUR OF THE FEMALE SEX

Mr. Western grew every day fonder and fonder of Sophia, insomuch that his beloved dogs themselves almost gave place to her in his affections; but as he could not prevail on himself to abandon these, he contrived very cunningly to enjoy their company, together with that of his daughter, by insisting on her riding a hunting with him.

Sophia, to whom her father's word was a law, readily complied with his desires, though she had not the least delight in a sport, which was of too rough and masculine a nature to suit with her disposition. She had however another motive, beside her obedience, to accompany the old gentleman in the chase; for by her presence she hoped in some measure to restrain his impetuosity, and to prevent him from so frequently exposing his neck to the utmost hazard.

The strongest objection was that which would have formerly been an inducement to her, namely, the frequent meeting with young Jones, whom she had determined to avoid; but as the end of the hunting season now approached, she hoped, by a short absence with her aunt, to reason herself entirely out of her unfortunate passion; and had not any doubt of being able to meet him in the field the subsequent season without the least danger.

On the second day of her hunting, as she was returning from the chase, and was arrived within a little distance from Mr. Western's house, her horse, whose mettlesome spirit required a better rider, fell suddenly to prancing and capering in such a manner that she was in the most imminent peril of falling. Tom Jones, who was at a little distance behind, saw this, and immediately galloped up to her assistance. As soon as he came up, he leapt from his own horse, and caught hold of hers by the bridle. The unruly beast presently reared himself on end on his hind legs, and threw his lovely burthen from his back, and Jones caught her in his arms.

She was so affected with the fright, that she was not immediately able to satisfy Jones, who was very solicitous to know whether she had received any hurt. She soon after, however, recovered her spirits, assured him she was safe, and thanked him for the care he had taken of her. Jones answered,"If I have preserved you, madam, I am sufficiently repaid; for I promise you, I would have secured you from the least harm at the expense of a much greater misfortune to myself than I have suffered on this occasion."

"What misfortune?" replied Sophia eagerly, "I hope you have come to no mischief?"

"Be not concerned, madam," answered Jones."Heaven be praised you have escaped so well, considering the danger you was in. If I have broken my arm, I consider it as a trifle, in comparison of what I feared upon your account."

Sophia then screamed out,"Broke your arm! Heaven forbid."

"I am afraid I have, madam," says Jones:"but I beg you will suffer me first to take care of you. I have a right hand yet at your service, to help you into the next field, whence we have but a very little walk to your father's house."

Sophia seeing his left arm dangling by his side, while he was using the other to lead her, no longer doubted of the truth. She now grew much paler than her fears for herself had made her before. All her limbs were seized with a trembling, insomuch that Jones could scarce support her; and as her thoughts were in no less agitation, she could not refrain from giving Jones a look so full of tenderness, that it almost argued a stronger sensation in her mind, than even gratitude and pity united can raise in the gentlest female bosom, without the assistance of a third more powerful passion.

Mr. Western, who was advanced at some distance when this accident happened, was now returned, as were the rest of the horsemen. Sophia immediately acquainted them with what had befallen Jones, and begged them to take care of him. Upon which Western, who had been much alarmed by meeting his daughter's horse without its rider, and was now overjoyed to find her unhurt, cried out,"I am glad it is no worse. If Tom hath broken his arm, we will get a joiner to mend it again."

The squire alighted from his horse, and proceeded to his house on foot, with his daughter and Jones. An impartial spectator, who had met them on the way, would, on viewing their several countenances, have concluded Sophia alone to have been the object of compassion: for as to Jones, he exulted in having probably saved the life of the young lady, at the price only of a broken bone; and Mr. Western, though he was not unconcerned at the accident which had befallen Jones, was, however, delighted in a much higher degree with the fortunate escape of his daughter.

The generosity of Sophia's temper construed this behaviour of Jones into great bravery; and it made a deep impression on her heart: for certain it is, that there is no one quality which so generally recommends men to women as this; proceeding, if we believe the common opinion, from that natural timidity of the sex, which is, says Mr. Osborne,"so great, that a woman is the most cowardly of all the creatures God ever made;"—a sentiment more remarkable for its bluntness than for its truth. Aristotle, in his Politics, doth them, I believe, more justice, when he says,"The modesty and fortitude of men differ from those virtues in women; for the fortitude which becomes a woman, would be cowardice in a man; and the modesty which becomes a man, would be pertness in a woman." Nor is there, perhaps, more of truth in the opinion of those who derive the partiality which women are inclined to show to the brave, from this excess of their fear. Mr. Bayle (I think, in his article of Helen) imputes this, and with greater probability, to their violent love of glory; for the truth of which, we have the authority of him who of all others saw farthest into human nature, and who introduces the heroine of his Odyssey, the great pattern of matrimonial love and constancy, assigning the glory of her husband as the only source of her affection towards him.

However this be, certain it is that the accident operated very strongly on Sophia; and, indeed, after much enquiry into the matter, I am inclined to believe, that, at this very time, the charming Sophia made no less impression on the heart of Jones; to say truth, he had for some time become sensible of the irresistible power of her charms.

Chapter 14, Book 12

WHAT HAPPENED TO MR. JONES IN HIS JOURNEY FROM ST. ALBANS

They were got about two miles beyond Barnet, and it was now the dusk of the evening, when a genteel-looking man, but upon a very shabby horse, rode up to Jones, and asked him whether he was going to London; to which Jones answered in the affirmative. The gentleman replied,"I should be obliged to you, sir, if you will accept of my company; for it is very late, and I am a stranger to the road." Jones readily complied with the request; and on they travelled together, holding that sort of discourse which is usual on such occasions.

Of this, indeed, robbery was the principal topic: upon which subject the stranger expressed great apprehensions; but Jones declared he had very little to lose, and consequently as little to fear. Here Partridge could not forbear putting in his word."Your honour," said he,"may think it a little, but I am sure, if I had a hundred-pound bank-note in my pocket, as you have, I should be very sorry to lose it; but, for my part, I never was less afraid in my life; for we are four of us, and if we all stand by one another, the best man in England can't rob us. Suppose he should have a pistol, he can kill but one of us, and a man can die but once.—That's my comfort, a man can die but once."

Besides the reliance on superior numbers, a kind of valour which hath raised a certain nation among the moderns to a high pitch of glory, there was another reason for the extraordinary courage which Partridge now discovered; for he had at present as much of that quality as was in the power of liquor to bestow.

Our company were now arrived within a mile of Highgate, when the stranger turned short upon Jones, and pulling out a pistol, demanded that little bank-note which Partridge had mentioned.

Jones was at first somewhat shocked at this unexpected demand; however, he presently recollected himself, and told the highwayman, all the money he had in his pocket was entirely at his service; and so saying, he pulled out upwards of three guineas, and offered to deliver it; but the other answered with an oath, That would not do. Jones answered coolly, he was very sorry for it, and returned the money into his pocket.

The highwayman then threatened, if he did not deliver the bank-note that moment, he must shoot him; holding his pistol at the same time very near to his breast. Jones instantly caught hold of the fellow's hand, which trembled so that he could scarce hold the pistol in it, and turned the muzzle from him. A struggle then ensued, in which the former wrested the pistol from the hand of his antagonist, and both came from their horses on the ground together, the highwayman upon his back, and the victorious Jones upon him.

The poor fellow now began to implore mercy of the conqueror: for, to say the truth, he was in strength by no means a match for Jones."Indeed, sir," says he,"I could have had no intention to shoot you; for you will find the pistol was not loaded. This is the first robbery I ever attempted, and I have been driven by distress to this."

At this instant, at about a hundred and fifty yards' distance, lay another person on the ground, roaring for mercy in a much louder voice than the highwayman. This was no other than Partridge himself, who, endeavouring to make his escape from the engagement, had been thrown from his horse, and lay flat on his face, not daring to look up, and expecting every minute to be shot.

In this posture he lay, till the guide, who was no otherwise concerned than for his horses, having secured the stumbling beast, came up to him, and told him his master had got the better of the highwayman.

Partridge leapt up at this news, and ran back to the place where Jones stood with his sword drawn in his hand to guard the poor fellow; which Partridge no sooner saw, than he cried out,"Kill the villain, sir, run him through the body, kill him this instant!"

Luckily, however, for the poor wretch, he had fallen into more merciful hands; for Jones having examined the pistol, and found it to be really unloaded, began to believe all the man had told him, before Partridge came up: namely, that he was a novice in the trade, and that he had been driven to it by the distress he mentioned, the greatest indeed imaginable, that of five hungry children, and a wife lying in of the sixth, in the utmost want and misery. The truth of all which the highwayman most vehemently asserted, and offered to convince Mr. Jones of it, if he would take the trouble to go to his house, which was not above two miles off; saying,"That he desired no favour, but upon condition of proving all he had alledged."

Jones at first pretended that he would take the fellow at his word and go with him, declaring that his fate should depend entirely on the truth of his story. Upon this the poor fellow immediately expressed so much alacrity, that Jones was perfectly satisfied with his veracity, and began now to entertain sentiments of compassion for him. He returned the fellow his empty pistol, advised him to think of honester means of relieving his distress, and gave him a couple of guineas for the immediate support of his wife and his family; adding,"he wished he had more for his sake, for the hundred pound that had been mentioned was not his own."

Our readers will probably be divided in their opinions concerning this action; some may applaud it perhaps as an act of extraordinary humanity, while those of a more saturnine temper will consider it as a want of regard to that justice which every man owes his country. Partridge certainly saw it in that light; for he testified much dissatisfaction on the occasion, quoted an old proverb, and said, he should not wonder if the rogue attacked them again before they reached London.

The highwayman was full of expressions of thankfulness and gratitude. He actually dropt tears, or pretended so to do. He vowed he would immediately return home, and would never afterwards commit such a transgression: whether he kept his word or no, perhaps may appear hereafter.

Our travellers having remounted their horses, arrived in town without encountering any new mishap. On the road much pleasant discourse passed between Jones and Partridge, on the subject of their last adventure: in which Jones exprest a great compassion for those highwaymen who are, by unavoidable distress, driven, as it were, to such illegal courses as generally bring them to a shameful death:"I mean," said he,"those only whose highest guilt extends no farther than to robbery, and who are never guilty of cruelty nor insult to any person, which is a circumstance that, I must say, to the honour of our country, distinguishes the robbers of England from those of all other nations; for murder is, amongst those, almost inseparably incident to robbery."

"No doubt," answered Partridge,"it is better to take away one's money than one's life; and yet it is very hard upon honest men, that they can't travel about their business without being in danger of these villains. And to be sure it would be better that all rogues were hanged out of the way, than that one honest man should suffer. For my own part, indeed, I should not care to have the blood of any of them on my hands; but it is very proper for the law to hang them all. What right hath any man to take sixpence from me, unless I give it him? Is there any honesty in such a man?"

"No, surely," cries Jones,"no more than there is in him who takes the horses out of another man's stable, or who applies to his own use the money which he finds, when he knows the right owner."

These hints stopt the mouth of Partridge; nor did he open it again till Jones, having thrown some sarcastical jokes on his cowardice, he offered to excuse himself on the inequality of firearms, saying,"A thousand naked men are nothing to one pistol; for though it is true it will kill but one at a single discharge, yet who can tell but that one may be himself?"

III. Reading Tasks

1 Give some examples of Mr. Western's concern for his daughter.

2 Why did Sophia avoid Tom at fist? How did Tom win Sophia's love finally?

3 What kind of narrative tone is assumed by the author in this novel, comic or serious?

4 Was Tom Jones a rebel at his time? What are the similarities and differences

between Tom and Jia Baoyu, the protagonist in the Chinese novel *The Dreams in the Red Mansion*?

Mr. Thwackum the Divine, and Mr. Square the Philosopher

Unit 6

Pomes by 18th Century poets

I. Introduction

1. Romanticism

In English literature, the poetic movement led by Wordsworth, Coleridge, Keats, Shelley, and Byron between 1795 and about 1830. The Romantic poets were concerned mainly with (a)The need to fabricate a new mythology to explain the universe and the individual's place in it; (b) emotion over reason (in this they had much in common with the German STURM-UND-DRANG movement of the 1770s); (c) spontaneity over "art," although the Romantic poets' letters, journals, and revisions of poems now being re-examined reveal that they did not entirely resist technique and form; and (d) a realistic rather than an idealistic view of nature, even if this approach led such poets as Wordsworth and Shelley into certain tenets of idealism (for example, the idea of progress and ultimate perfectibility).

By 1798, when Wordsworth published his Preface to the *Lyrical Ballads*, a kind of manifesto for the Romantic movement, the concept of the GREAT CHAIN OF BEING seemed no longer adequate to explain the makeup of the universe; the eighteenth-century poetry based on that idea no longer seemed relevant to the turn-of-the-century mood. Eighteenth-century poetry had not assumed progress or ultimate perfectibility; it had been more concerned with the place of abstract "Man" in the "Chain" and with how to live the good life. In contrast to this attitude, the Romantic poet was concerned with self-discovery; looking within and asking, "Who am I?"

Moreover, the Romantic poets, intent on expressing themselves in what Wordsworth called"language really used by men" were less concerned about making contact with their audience than with the need for self-expression; the poet must express the spirit within, audience or not. In turning away from NEO-CLASSICAL notions about "ideal Nature", the Romantics preferred to seek their reality through spontaneous and personal acts of the IMAGINATION. As Keats said in a letter, "I am certain of nothing but the holiness of the heart's affection and the truth of the Imagination." He could not perceive how anything could be known except through "personal identity." They also sought their reality through the RENDERING of personal experience, especially through IMAGERY, the concrete particular ("a violet by a mossy stone," "the lone and level sands," "those caves of ice!").

Among other characteristics of the Romantics: They preferred the countryside (the Lake Windemere country, for instance) to the materialistic city("Getting and spending, we lay waste our powers"); preferred longing or mysterious aspiration (as reflected in Keats's "Ode on a Grecian Urn") rather than fulfilled desire. They attempted to connect, indeed to fuse, certain worlds—Truth and Beauty for Keats; the Platonic paradise and the realm of concrete phenomena for Shelley. Wordsworth sought to incorporate the object—the external world of nature—into himself, the subject.

What almost every poet of the Romantic movement shared was a desire to bring nature, God and man, the finite and the infinite, the familiar and the mysterious, into unity through the shaping power of the individual's imagination.

II. Text

1. The Chimney Sweeper

by William Blake (1757-1827)

A little black thing in the snow,
Crying "'weep! weep!" in notes of woe!
"Where are they father and mother? Say?"
"They are both gone up to the church to pray.

"Because I was happy upon the heath,

And smiled among the winter's snow;
They clothed me in the clothes of death,
And taught me to sing the notes of woe.

"And because I am happy and dance and sing,
They think they have done me no injury,
And are gone to praise God and his priest and king,
Who make up a heaven of our misery."

2. A Red, Red Rose[1]

by Robert Burns (1759-1796)

O my Luve's like a red, red rose,
That's newly sprung in June:
O my Luve's like the melodie,
That's sweetly play'd in tune.

As fair art thou, my bonnie lass,
So deep in luve am I;
And I will luve thee still, my dear,
Till a' the seas gang dry.

Till a' the seas gang dry, my dear,
And the rocks melt wi' the sun;
And I will luve thee still, my dear,
While the sands o' life shall run.

And fare-thee-weel, my only Luve!
And fare-thee-weel, a while!

1. Like many of Burns's lyrics, this one incorporates elements from several current folk songs.

And I will come again, my Luve,
Though it were ten thousand mile!

3. I Traveled among Unknown Men

by William Wordsworth (1770-1850)

I traveled among unknown men.
In lands beyond the sea;
Nor, England! did I know till then
What love I bore to thee.

This past, that melancholy dream!
Nor will I quit thy shore
A second time; for still I seem
To love thee more and more.

Among thy mountains did I feel
The joy of my desire;
And she I cherished turned her wheel
Beside an English fire.

Thy mornings showed, thy nights concealed,
The bowers where Lucy played;
And thine too is the last green field
That Lucy's eyes surveyed.

4. Upon the Westminster Bridge

by William Wordsworth

Earth has not anything to show more fair:
Dull would he be of soul who could pass by
A sight so touching in its majesty:
This City now doth, like a garment, wear
The beauty of the morning; silent, bare,
Ships, towers, domes, theatres, and temples lie
Open unto the fields, and to the sky;
All bright and glittering in the smokeless air.
Never did sun more beautifully steep
In his first splendour, valley, rock, or hill;
Ne'er saw I never felt, a calm so deep!
The river glideth at his own sweet will:
Dear God! the very houses seem asleep;
And all that mighty heart is lying still!

5. When We Parted

by George Gordon Byron (1788-1824)

When we two parted
In silence and tears,
Half broken-hearted
To sever for years,
Pale grew thy cheek and cold,
Colder thy kiss;
Truly that hour foretold
Sorrow to this.

The dew of the morning

Sunk chill on my brow—
It felt like the warning
Of what I feel now.
Thy vows are all broken,
And light is thy fame;
I hear thy name spoken,
And share I its shame.

They name thee before me,
A knell to mine ear;
A shudder comes o'er me—
Why wert thou so dear?
They know not I knew thee,
Who knew thee too well—
Long, long shall I rue thee,
Too deeply to tell.

In secret we met —
In silence I grieve,
That thy heart could forget,
Thy spirit deceive.
If I should meet thee
After long years,
How should I greet thee?—
With silence and tears.

6. Ozymandias[1]

by Percy Bysshe shelley (1792-1822)

I met a traveler from an antique land,
Who said—Two vast and trunkless legs of stone
Stand in the desert … Near them, on the sand,
Half sunk a shattered visage lies, whose frown,
And wrinkled lip, and sneer of cold command,
Tell that is sculptor well those passions read
Which yet survive, stamped on these lifeless things,
The hand that mocked them, and the heat that fed[2];
And on the pedestal, these words appear:
My name is Ozymandias, King of Kings,
Look on my works, ye Mighty, and despair!
Nothing beside remains, Round the decay
Of that colossal wreck, boundless and bare
The lone and level sands stretch far away.

7. Ode to a Nightingale[3]

by John Keats (1795-1821)

1

My heart aches, and a drowsy numbness pains

1. According to Diodorus Siculus, Greek historian of the 1st century B.C., the largest statue in Egypt had the inscription:"I am Ozymandias, king of kings; if anyone wishes to know what I am and where I lie, let him surpass me in some of my exploits." Ozymandias was the Greek name for Ramses II of Egypt, 13th century B.C.
2. "The hand" is the sculptor's, who had"mocked" (both imitated and derided) the sculptured passions;"the heart" is the king's, which has"fed" his passions.
3. Charles Brown, with whom Keats was then living in Hampstead, wrote:"In the spring of 1819 a nightingale had built her nest near my house. Keats felt a tranquil and continual joy in her song; and one morning he took his chair from the breakfast table to the grass plot under a plum tree, where he sat for two or three hours. When he came into the house, I perceived he had some scraps of paper in his hand, and these he was quietly thrusting behind the books. On inquiry, I found those scraps, four or five in number, contained his poetic feeling on the song of our nightingale."

My sense, as though of hemlock[1] I had drunk,
Or emptied some dull opiate to the drains
One minute past, and Lethe-wards[2] had sunk:
This not through envy of thy happy lot,
But being too happy in thine happiness, —
That thou, light-winged Dryad of the trees,
In some melodious plot
Of beechen green, and shadows numberless,
Singest of summer in full-throated ease.

2

O, for a draught of vintage! that hath been
Cool'd a long age in the deep-delved earth,
Tasting of Flora[3] and the country green,
Dance, and Provencal song[4], and sunburnt mirth!
O for a beaker full of the warm South,
Full of the true, the blushful Hippocrene[5],
With beaded bubbles winking at the brim,
And purple-stained mouth;
That I might drink, and leave the world unseen,
And with thee fade away into the forest dim.

3

Fade far away, dissolve, and quite forget
What thou among the leaves hast never known,
The weariness, the fever, and the fret
Here, where men sit and hear each other groan;
Where palsy shakes a few, sad, last gray hairs,

1. A poisonous herb, not the North American evergreen tree.
2. Toward Lethe, the river in Hades whose waters cause forgetfulness.
3. Roman goddess of flowers, or the flowers themselves.
4. Provence, in southern France, was in the late Middle Ages renowned for its troubadours, the writers and singers of love songs.
5. Fountain of the Muses on Mt. Helicon; hence, the waters of inspiration, here applied metaphorically to a beaker of wine.

Where youth grows pale, and spectre-thin, and dies[1];
Where but to think is to be full of sorrow
And leaden-eyed despairs,
Where Beauty cannot keep her lustrous eyes,
Or new Love pine at them beyond to-morrow.

4

Away! away! for I will fly to thee,
Not charioted by Bacchus and his pards,
But on the viewless wings of Poesy[2],
Though the dull brain perplexes and retards:
Already with thee! tender is the night,
And haply the Queen-Moon is on her throne,
Cluster'd around by all her starry Fays[3];
But here there is no light,
Save what from heaven is with the breezes blown
Through verdurous[4] glooms and winding mossy ways.

5

I cannot see what flowers are at my feet,
Nor what soft incense hangs upon the boughs,
But, in embalmed[5] darkness, guess each sweet
Wherewith the seasonable month endows
The grass, the thicket, and the fruit-tree wild;
White hawthorn, and the pastoral eglantine[6];
Fast fading violets cover'd up in leaves;
And mid-May's eldest child,

---

1. Keats's brother, Tom, wasted by tuberculosis, had died the preceding winter.
2. I.e., not by getting drunk on wine (the"vintage" of stanza2), but on the invisible ("viewless") wings of the poetic imagination. (Bacchus, god of wine, was sometimes represented in a chariot drawn by"pards" —leopards.)
3. Fairies.
4. Green-foliaged.
5. Perfumed.
6. Sweetbrier, or honeysuckle.

The coming musk-rose, full of dewy wine,
The murmurous haunt of flies on summer eves.

6

Darkling[1] I listen; and, for many a time
I have been half in love with easeful Death,
Call'd him soft names in many a mused[2] rhyme,
To take into the air my quiet breath;
Now more than ever seems it rich to die,
To cease upon the midnight with no pain,
While thou art pouring forth thy soul abroad
In such an ecstasy!
Still wouldst thou sing, and I have ears in vain —
To thy high requiem become a sod.

7

Thou wast not born for death, immortal Bird!
No hungry generations tread thee down;
The voice I hear this passing night was heard
In ancient days by emperor and clown:
Perhaps the self-same song that found a path
Through the sad heart of Ruth[3], when, sick for home,
She stood in tears amid the alien corn;
The same that oft-times hath
Charm'd magic casements, opening on the foam
Of perilous seas, in faery lands forlorn.

8

Forlorn[4]! the very word is like a bell

---

1. in the dark.
2. Meditated.
3. The young window in the Biblical Book of Ruth."com"(line 67): i.e. wheat.
4. One critic has said that"forlorn"—which means"long past" as well as"sorrowful" —"has its feet in two worlds," the fairyland of imagination and the woe of reality to which the word reawakens the lyric speaker.

To toil me back from thee to my sole self!
Adieu! the fancy[1] cannot cheat so well
As she is fam'd to do, deceiving elf.
Adieu! adieu! thy plaintive anthem[2] fades
Past the near meadows, over the still stream,
Up the hill-side; and now 'tis buried deep
In the next valley-glades:
Was it a vision, or a waking dream?
Fled is that music: Do I wake or sleep?

8. Ode on a Grecian Urn[3]

by John Keats

1

Thou still unravish'd bride of quietness,
Thou foster-child of silence and slow time,
Sylvan[4] historian, who canst thus express
A flowery tale more sweetly than our rhyme:
What leaf-fring'd legend haunts about thy shape
Of deities or mortals, or of both,

1. I.e., imagination,"The viewless wings of Poesy" of line 33.
2. Hymn.
3. This urn, with its sculptured reliefs of Dionysian ecstasies, panting young lovers in flight and pursuit, a pastoral piper under spring foliage, and the quiet celebration of communal pieties, resembles parts of various vases, sculptures, and paintings; but it existed in all its particulars only in Keats's imagination. In the urn—which captures moments of intense experience in attitudes of grace and immobilizes them in marble—Keats found the perfect correlative for his concern with the long for permanence in a world of change, The interpretation of the details with which he develops this concept, however, is hotly disputed, all the way from the opening phrase—is"still" an adverb ("as yet") or an adjective ("motionless")? —to the two concluding lines, which have already accumulated as much critical discussion as the"two-handed engine" in Milton's *Lycidas* or the cruxes in Shakespeare's plays. These disputes testify to the enigmatic richness of meaning in the five stanzas, and show that the ode has become a central point of reference in the criticism of the English lyric.
4. Rustic, representing a woodland scene.

In Tempe or the dales of Arcady[1]?
What men or gods are these? What maidens loth?
What mad pursuit? What struggle to escape?
What pipes and timbrels? What wild ecstasy?

2

Heard melodies are sweet, but those unheard
Are sweeter; therefore, ye soft pipes, play on;
Not to the sensual ear[2], but, more endear'd,
Pipe to the spirit ditties of no tone:
Fair youth, beneath the trees, thou canst not leave
Thy song, nor ever can those trees be bare;
Bold Lover, never, never canst thou kiss,
Though winning near the goal - yet, do not grieve;
She cannot fade, though thou hast not thy bliss,
For ever wilt thou love, and she be fair!

3

Ah, happy, happy boughs! that cannot shed
Your leaves, nor ever bid the Spring adieu;
And, happy melodist, unwearied,
For ever piping songs for ever new;
More happy love! more happy, happy love!
For ever warm and still to be enjoy'd,
For ever panting, and for ever young;
All breathing human passion far above,
That leaves a heart high-sorrowful and cloy'd,
A burning forehead, and a parching tongue.

4

Who are these coming to the sacrifice?

1. Tempe is a beautiful valley in Greece which has come to represent supreme rural beauty. The"dales of Arcady" are the valleys of Arcadia, a state in ancient Greece often used as a symbol of the pastoral ideal.
2. The ear of sense (as opposed to that of the"spirit" , or imagination).

To what green altar, O mysterious priest,
Lead'st thou that heifer lowing at the skies,
And all her silken flanks with garlands drest?
What little town by river or sea shore,
Or mountain-built with peaceful citadel,
Is emptied of this folk, this pious morn?
And, little town, thy streets for evermore
Will silent be; and not a soul to tell
Why thou art desolate, can e'er return.

5

O Attic[1] shape! Fair attitude! with brede
Of marble men and maidens overwrought[2],
With forest branches and the trodden weed;
Thou, silent form, dost tease us out of thought
As doth eternity: Cold Pastoral!
When old age shall this generation waste,
Thou shalt remain, in midst of other woe
Than ours, a friend to man, to whom thou say'st,
"Beauty is truth, truth beauty[3],"— that is all
Ye know on earth, and all ye need to know.

III. Reading Tasks

1. Try to give the content of the poems in your own words.
2. Name and explain the figures of speech contained the poems.

---

1. Greek. Attica was the region of Greece in which Athens was located.
2. Ornamented all over ("overwrought") with an interwoven pattern ("brede").
3. The quotation marks around this phrase are found in the volume of poems Keats published in 1820; but there are no quotation marks in the version printed in *Annals of the Fine Arts* that same year, or in the four transcripts of the poem made by Keats's friends. This discrepancy has multiplied the diversity of critical interpretations of the last two lines. Leading critics disagree whether the whole of these lines is said by the urn, or"Beauty is truth, truth beauty" by the urn and the rest by the lyric speaker; whether the"ye" in the last line is addressed to the lyric speaker, to the readers, to the urn, or to the figures on the urn; whether"all ye know" is that beauty is truth, or this plus the statement in lines 46-48; and whether"beauty is truth" is a profound metaphysical proposition, or an overstatement uttered in the course of a dramatic dialogue, or simply nonsensical.

3. Mark the thyme scheme and comment upon the verse form employed.

4. Enumerate the images employed in the poems and try to explain their significance and effectiveness.

5. Analyse the tone and the theme of the poems.

Unit 7

Pride and Prejudice

I. Introduction

1. The author

Jane Austen (1775-1817), English writer who first gave the novel its distinctly modern character through her treatment of ordinary people in everyday life. Austen created the comedy of manners of middle-class life in the England of her time in such novels as *Sense and Sensibility* (1811), *Pride and Prejudice* (1813), *Mansfield Park* (1814), *Emma* (1815), and *Northanger Abbey* and *Persuasion* (published posthumously, 1817).

2. The story

Mr and Mrs Bennet belong to the minor gentry, and live at Longbourne near London. Mr Bennet is witty and intelligent, and bored with his foolish wife. They have five daughters, whose marriage prospects are Mrs Bennet's chief interest in life, since the estate is "entailed"—i.e. by the law of the period it will go on Mr Bennet's death to his nearest male relation, an absurd clergyman called Mr Collins. The main part of the story is concerned with the relationship between the witty and attractive Elizabeth Bennet and the haughty and fastidious

Fitzwilliam Darcy, who at first considers her beneath his notice, and later, on coming to the point of asking her to marry him, finds that she is resolutely prejudiced against him. His friend Charles Bingley is in love with the eldest daughter, Jane, but they are kept apart by the jealous snobbishness of his sisters and (at first) the fastidious disapproval of Darcy. Meanwhile, Elizabeth is subjected to an insolent offer of marriage by Mr Collins and the arrogant condescension of his patroness, Lady Catherine de Bourgh, Darcy's aunt. Those who regard the Bennet family as foolish and vulgar have their opinion justified when Lydia Bennet elopes with an irresponsible young officer, George Wickham; by this time, however, Darcy has been chastened by finding in Elizabeth a fastidiousness and pride that exceed his own, and, despite the family scandal, they are united.

II. Text

Chapter 1

It is a truth universally acknowledged, that a single man in possession of a good fortune must be in want of a wife.

However little known the feelings or views of such a man may be on his first entering a neighbourhood, this truth is so well fixed in the minds of the surrounding families, that he is considered as the rightful property of some one or other of their daughters.

"My dear Mr. Bennet," said his lady to him one day,"have you heard that Netherfield Park is let at last?"

Mr. Bennet replied that he had not.

"But it is," returned she, "for Mrs. Long has just been here, and she told me all about it."

Mr. Bennet made no answer.

"Do not you want to know who has taken it?" cried his wife impatiently.

"You want to tell me, and I have no objection to hearing it."

This was invitation enough.

"Why, my dear, you must know, Mrs. Long says that Netherfield is taken by a young man of large fortune from the north of England; that he came down on Monday in a chaise and four to see the place, and was so much delighted with it that he agreed with Mr. Morris immediately; that he is to take possession before Michaelmas, and some of his servants are to be in the house by the end of next week."

"What is his name?"

"Bingley."

"Is he married or single?"

"Oh! single, my dear, to be sure! A single man of large fortune; four or five thousand a year. What a fine thing for our girls!"

"How so? How can it affect them?"

"My dear Mr. Bennet," replied his wife,"how can you be so tiresome! You must know that I am thinking of his marrying one of them."

"Is that his design in settling here?"

"Design! nonsense, how can you talk so! But it is very likely that he may fall in love with one of them, and therefore you must visit him as soon as he comes."

"I see no occasion for that. You and the girls may go, or you may send them by themselves, which perhaps will be still better; for, as you are as handsome as any of them, Mr. Bingley might like you the best of the party."

"My dear, you flatter me. I certainly have had my share of beauty, but I do not pretend to be any thing extraordinary now. When a woman has five grown up daughters, she ought to give over thinking of her own beauty."

"In such cases, a woman has not often much beauty to think of."

"But, my dear, you must indeed go and see Mr. Bingley when he comes into the neighbourhood."

"It is more than I engage for, I assure you."

"But consider your daughters. Only think what an establishment it would be for one of them. Sir William and Lady Lucas are determined to go, merely on that account, for in general, you know they visit no new comers. Indeed you must go, for it will be impossible for us to visit him, if you do not."

"You are over-scrupulous, surely. I dare say Mr. Bingley will be very glad to see you; and I will send a few lines by you to assure him of my hearty consent to his marrying which ever he chuses of the girls; though I must throw in a good word for my little Lizzy."

"I desire you will do no such thing. Lizzy is not a bit better than the others; and I am sure she is not half so handsome as Jane, nor half so good humoured as Lydia. But you are always giving *her* the preference."

"They have none of them much to recommend them," replied he, "they are all silly and ignorant like other girls; but Lizzy has something more of quickness than her sisters."

"Mr. Bennet, how can you abuse your own children in such way? You take delight in vexing me. You have no compassion on my poor nerves."

"You mistake me, my dear. I have a high respect for your nerves. They are my old friends. I have heard you mention them with consideration these twenty years at least."

"Ah! you do not know what I suffer."

"But I hope you will get over it, and live to see many young men of four thousand a year come into the neighbourhood."

"It will be no use to us if twenty such should come, since you will not visit them."

"Depend upon it, my dear, that when there are twenty I will visit them all."

Mr. Bennet was so odd a mixture of quick parts, sarcastic humour, reserve, and caprice, that the experience of three and twenty years had been insufficient to make his wife understand his character. Her mind was less difficult to develope. She was a woman of mean understanding, little information, and uncertain temper. When she was discontented, she fancied herself nervous. The business of her life was to get her daughters married; its solace was visiting and news.

Chapter 2

Mr. Bennet was among the earliest of those who waited on Mr. Bingley. He had always intended to visit him, though to the last always assuring his wife that he should not go; and till the evening after the visit was paid, she had no knowledge of it. It was then disclosed in the following manner. Observing his second daughter employed in trimming a hat, he suddenly addressed her with,

"I hope Mr. Bingley will like it, Lizzy."

"We are not in a way to know *what* Mr. Bingley likes," said her mother resentfully,"since we are not to visit."

"But you forget, mama," said Elizabeth,"that we shall meet him at the assemblies, and that Mrs. Long has promised to introduce him."

"I do not believe Mrs. Long will do any such thing. She has two nieces of her own. She is a selfish, hypocritical woman, and I have no opinion of her."

"No more have I," said Mr. Bennet, "and I am glad

to find that you do not depend on her serving you."

Mrs. Bennet deigned not to make any reply, but unable to contain herself, began scolding one of her daughters.

"Don't keep coughing so, Kitty, for heaven's sake! Have a little compassion on my nerves. You tear them to pieces."

"Kitty has no discretion in her coughs," said her father, "she times them ill."

"I do not cough for my own amusement," replied Kitty fretfully.

"When is your next ball to be, Lizzy?"

"To-morrow fortnight."

"Aye, so it is," cried her mother,"and Mrs. Long does not come back till the day before; so it will be impossible for her to introduce him, for she will not know him herself."

"Then, my dear, you may have the advantage of your friend, and introduce Mr. Bingley to *her*."

"Impossible, Mr. Bennet, impossible, when I am not acquainted with him myself, how can you be so teazing?"

"I honour your circumspection. A fortnight's acquaintance is certainly very little. One cannot know what a man really is by the end of a fortnight. But if we do not venture, somebody else will; and after all, Mrs. Long and her nieces must stand their chance; and therefore, as she will think it an act of kindness, if you decline the office, I will take it on myself."

The girls stared at their father. Mrs. Bennet said only,"Nonsense, nonsense!"

"What can be the meaning of that emphatic exclamation?" cried he."Do you consider the forms of introduction, and the stress that is laid on them, as nonsense? I cannot quite agree with you *there*. What say you, Mary? for you are a young lady of deep reflection I know, and read great books, and make extracts."

Mary wished to say something very sensible, but knew not how.

"While Mary is adjusting her ideas," he continued,"let us return to Mr. Bingley."

"I am sick of Mr. Bingley," cried his wife.

"I am sorry to hear *that*; but why did not you tell me so before? If I had known as much this morning, I certainly would not have called on him. It is very unlucky, but as I have actually paid the visit, we cannot escape the acquaintance now."

The astonishment of the ladies was just what he wished; that of Mrs. Bennet perhaps surpassing the rest; though when the first tumult of joy was over, she began to declare that it was what she had expected all the while.

"How good it was in you, my dear Mr. Bennet! But I knew I should persuade you at last. I was sure you loved our girls too well to neglect such an acquaintance. Well, how pleased I am! and it is such a good joke, too, that you should have gone this morning, and never said a word about it till now."

"Now, Kitty, you may cough as much as you chuse," said Mr. Bennet; and, as he spoke, he left the room, fatigued with the raptures of his wife.

"What an excellent father you have, girls," said she, when the door was shut."I do not know how you will ever make him amends for his kindness; or me either, for that matter. At our time of life, it is not so pleasant I can tell you, to be making new acquaintance every day; but for your sakes, we would do anything. Lydia, my love, though you *are* the youngest, I dare say Mr. Bingley will dance with you at the next ball."

"Oh!" said Lydia stoutly,"I am not afraid; for though I *am* the youngest, I'm the tallest."

The rest of the evening was spent in conjecturing how soon he would return Mr. Bennet's visit, and determining when they should ask him to dinner.

III. Reading Tasks

1. These two chapters are mainly composed by the characters' conversations, in what ways is it different from the descriptive narration in terms of the function and effectiveness?

2. Jane Austin is noted for her delicate depictions of man's manner and mind in everyday life. Can you cite some examples from these two chapters to prove it?

Unit 8

David Copperfield

I. Introduction

1. The author

Charles Dickens (1812-1870) enjoyed a wider popularity than had any previous author during his lifetime. Much in his work could appeal to simple and sophisticated, to the poor and to the Queen, and technological developments as well as the qualities of his work enabled his fame to spread worldwide very quickly. His long career saw fluctuations in the reception and sales of individual novels, but none of them was negligible or uncharacteristic or disregarded, and, though he is now admired for aspects and phases of his work that were given less weight by his contemporaries, his popularity has never ceased and his present critical standing is higher than ever before. The most abundantly comic of English authors, he was much more than a great entertainer. The range, compassion, and intelligence of his apprehension of his society and its shortcomings enriched his novels and made him both one of the great forces in 19th-century literature and an influential spokesman of the conscience of his age.

2. The story

Copperfield is fatherless, and his gentle, guileless mother (who becomes victim in matrimony to Murdstone) is like an elder sister to the child; both are children to the motherly, protective servant, Clara Peggotty. She is replaced by the harsh and loveless Miss Murdstone who plays the role of cruel stepmother. Copperfield runs away, and takes refuge with his idiosyncratic aunt, Betsey Trotwood, who has shaped for herself an eccentric independence of men, retaining for a harmless lunatic (Mr. Dick) a compassionate tenderness which she now extends to her nephew, in spite of having rejected him at birth because he was a boy. Copperfield's first wife, Dora Spenlow, is a simulacrum of his mother - a child wife, on whom Ibsen seems to have based Nora in A Doll's House. Two other representatives of Victorian womanhood are Agnes Wickfield (whom he eventually marries), the type of defenceless womanly sanctity and nearly a victim of Heap's rapacity, and Little Emily who is first under the protection of Peggotty and then becomes 'the fallen woman' when she is seduced by Steefforth. Another very striking portrait is Rosa Dartle, companion to Steefforth's mother and poisoned by vindictive hatred of him because of his cool assumption of social and masculine privilege. Though not the richest and deepest of Dickens's novels, it is perhaps psychologically the most revealing, both of Dickens him self and of the society of his time.

II. Text

Chapter 5 I am Sent away from Home (partly)

We might have gone about half a mile, and my pocket-handkerchief was quite wet through, when the carrier stopped short. Looking out to ascertain for what, I saw, to MY amazement, Peggotty burst from a hedge and climb into the cart. She took me in both her arms, and squeezed me to her stays until the pressure on my nose was extremely painful, though I never thought of that till afterwards when I found it very tender. Not a single word did Peggotty speak. Releasing one of her arms, she put it down in her pocket to the elbow, and brought out some paper bags of cakes which she crammed into my pockets, and a purse which she put into my hand, but not one word did she say. After another and a final squeeze with both arms, she got down from the cart and ran away; and, my belief is, and has always been, without a solitary button on her gown. I picked up one, of several that were rolling about, and treasured it as a keepsake for a long time.

The carrier looked at me, as if to inquire if she were coming back. I shook my head, and said I thought not. "Then come up," said the carrier to the lazy horse; who came up accordingly.

Having by this time cried as much as I possibly could, I began to think it was of no use crying any more, especially as neither Roderick Random, nor that Captain in the Royal British Navy, had ever cried, that I could remember, in trying situations. The carrier, seeing me in this resolution, proposed that my pocket-handkerchief should be spread upon the horse's back to dry. I thanked him, and assented; and particularly small it looked, under those circumstances.

I had now leisure to examine the purse. It was a stiff leather purse, with a snap, and had three bright shillings in it, which Peggotty had evidently polished up with whitening, for my greater delight. But its most precious contents were two half-crowns folded together in a bit of paper, on which was written, in my mother's hand,"For Davy. With my love." I was so overcome by this, that I asked the carrier to be so good as to reach me my pocket-handkerchief again; but he said he thought I had better do without it, and I thought I really had, so I wiped my eyes on my sleeve and stopped myself.

For good, too; though, in consequence of my previous emotions, I was still occasionally seized with a stormy sob. After we had jogged on for some little time, I asked the carrier if he was going all the way.

"All the way where?" inquired the carrier.

"There," I said.

"Where's there?" inquired the carrier.

"Near London," I said.

"Why that horse," said the carrier, jerking the rein to point him out,"would be deader than pork afore he got over half the ground."

"Are you only going to Yarmouth then?" I asked.

"That's about it," said the carrier."And there I shall take you to the stage-cutch, and the stage-cutch that'll take you to— wherever it is."

As this was a great deal for the carrier (whose name was Mr. Barkis) to say— he being, as I observed in a former chapter, of a phlegmatic temperament, and not at all conversational—

I offered him a cake as a mark of attention, which he ate at one gulp, exactly like an elephant, and which made no more impression on his big face than it would have done on an elephant's.

"Did SHE make 'em, now?" said Mr. Barkis, always leaning forward, in his slouching way, on the footboard of the cart with an arm on each knee.

"Peggotty, do you mean, sir?"

"Ah!" said Mr. Barkis. "Her."

"Yes. She makes all our pastry, and does all our cooking."

"Do she though?" said Mr. Barkis. He made up his mouth as if to whistle, but he didn't whistle. He sat looking at the horse's ears, as if he saw something new there; and sat so, for a considerable time. By and by, he said:

"No sweethearts, I believe?"

"Sweetmeats did you say, Mr. Barkis?" For I thought he wanted something else to eat, and had pointedly alluded to that description of refreshment.

"Hearts," said Mr. Barkis."Sweet hearts; no person walks with her!"

"With Peggotty?"

"Ah!" he said. "Her."

"Oh, no. She never had a sweetheart."

"Didn't she, though!" said Mr. Barkis.

Again he made up his mouth to whistle, and again he didn't whistle, but sat looking at the horse's ears.

"So she makes," said Mr. Barkis, after a long interval of reflection,"all the apple parsties, and doos all the cooking, do she?"

I replied that such was the fact.

"Well. I'll tell you what," said Mr. Barkis. "Perhaps you might be writing to her?"

"I shall certainly write to her," I rejoined.

"Ah!" he said, slowly turning his eyes towards me. "Well! If you was writing to her, perhaps you'd recollect to say that Barkis wasb willin'; would you?"

"That Barkis is willing," I repeated, innocently. "Is that all the message?"

"Ye-es," he said, considering. "Ye-es. Barkis is willing."

"But you will be at Blunderstone again tomorrow, Mr. Barkis," I said, faltering a little at the idea of my being far away from it then, and could give your own message so much better."

As he repudiated this suggestion, however, with a jerk of his head, and once more confirmed his previous request by saying, with profound gravity,"Barkis is willing. That's the message," I readily undertook its transmission. While I was waiting for the coach in the hotel at Yarmouth that very afternoon, I procured a sheet of paper and an inkstand, and wrote a note to Peggotty, which ran thus: "My dear Peggotty. I have come here safe. Barkis is willing. My love to mama. Yours affectionately. P.S. He says he particularly wants you to know - BARKIS IS WILLING."

When I had taken this commission on myself prospectively, Mr. Barkis relapsed into perfect silence; and I, feeling quite worn out by all that had happened lately, lay down on a sack in the cart and fell asleep. I slept soundly until we got to Yarmouth; which was so entirely new and strange to me in the inn-yard to which we drove, that I at once abandoned a latent hope I had of meeting with some of Mr. Peggotty's family there, perhaps even with little Emily herself.

The coach was in the yard, shining very much all over, but without any horses to it as yet; and it looked in that state as if nothing was more unlikely than its ever going to London. I was thinking this, and wondering what would ultimately become of my box, which Mr. Barkis had put down on the yard-pavement by the pole (he having driven up the yard to turn his cart), and also what would ultimately become of me, when a lady looked out of a bow-window where some fowls and joints of meat were hanging up, and said:

"Is that the little gentleman from Blunderstone?"

"Yes, ma'am," I said.

"What name?" inquired the lady.

"Copperfield, ma'am," I said.

"That won't do," returned the lady. "Nobody's dinner is paid for here, in that name."

"Is it Murdstone, ma'am?" I said.

"If you're Master Murdstone," said the lady,"why do you go and give another name, first?"

I explained to the lady how it was, who than rang a bell, and called out, "William! show the coffee-room!" upon which a waiter came running out of a kitchen on the opposite side of the yard to show it, and seemed a good deal surprised when he was only to show it to me.

It was a large long room with some large maps in it. I doubt if I could have felt much stranger if the maps had been real foreign countries, and I cast away in the middle of them. I felt it was taking a liberty to sit down, with my cap in my hand, on the corner of the chair nearest the door; and when the waiter laid a cloth on purpose for me, and put a set of castors on it, I think I must have turned red all over with modesty.

He brought me some chops, and vegetables, and took the covers off in such a bouncing manner that I was afraid I must have given him some offence. But he greatly relieved my mind by putting a chair for me at the table, and saying, very affably, "Now, six-foot! come on!"

I thanked him, and took my seat at the board; but found it extremely difficult to handle my knife and fork with anything like dexterity, or to avoid splashing myself with the gravy, while he was standing opposite, staring so hard, and making me blush in the most dreadful manner every time I caught his eye. After watching me into the second chop, he said:

"There's half a pint of ale for you. Will you have it now?"

I thanked him and said,"Yes." Upon which he poured it out of a jug into a large tumbler, and held it up against the light, and made it look beautiful.

"My eye!" he said. "It seems a good deal, don't it?"

"It does seem a good deal," I answered with a smile. For it was quite delightful to me, to find him so pleasant. He was a twinkling-eyed, pimple-faced man, with his hair standing upright all over his head; and as he stood with one arm akimbo, holding up the glass to the light with the other hand, he looked quite friendly.

"There was a gentleman here, yesterday," he said—"a stout gentleman, by the name of Topsawyer—perhaps you know him?"

"No," I said,"I don't think—"

"In breeches and gaiters, broad-brimmed hat, grey coat, speckled choker," said the waiter.

"No," I said bashfully,"I haven't the pleasure—"

"He came in here," said the waiter, looking at the light through the tumbler,"ordered a glass of this ale—WOULD order it—I told him not—drank it, and fell dead. It was too old for him. It oughtn't to be drawn; that's the fact."

I was very much shocked to hear of this melancholy accident, and said I thought I had better have some water.

"Why you see," said the waiter, still looking at the light through the tumbler, with one of his eyes shut up,"our people don't like things being ordered and left. It offends 'em. But I'll drink it, if you like. I'm used to it, and use is everything. I don't think it'll hurt me, if I throw my head back, and take it off quick. Shall I?"

I replied that he would much oblige me by drinking it, if he thought he could do it safely, but by no means otherwise. When he did throw his head back, and take it off quick, I had a horrible fear, I confess, of seeing him meet the fate of the lamented Mr. Topsawyer, and fall lifeless on the carpet. But it didn't hurt him. On the contrary, I thought he seemed the fresher for it.

"What have we got here?" he said, putting a fork into my dish.

"Not chops?"

"Chops," I said.

"Lord bless my soul!" he exclaimed,"I didn't know they were chops. Why, a chop's the very thing to take off the bad effects of that beer! Ain't it lucky?"

So he took a chop by the bone in one hand, and a potato in the other, and ate away with a very good appetite, to my extreme satisfaction. He afterwards took another chop, and another potato; and after that, another chop and another potato. When we had done, he brought me a pudding, and having set it before me, seemed to ruminate, and to become absent in his mind for some moments.

"How's the pie?" he said, rousing himself.

"It's a pudding," I made answer.

"Pudding!" he exclaimed. "Why, bless me, so it is! What!" looking at it nearer. "You don't mean to say it's a batter-pudding!"

"Yes, it is indeed."

"Why, a batter-pudding," he said, taking up a table-spoon,"is my favourite pudding! Ain't that lucky? Come on, little 'un, and let's see who'll get most."

The waiter certainly got most. He entreated me more than once to come in and win, but what with his table-spoon to my tea-spoon, his dispatch to my dispatch, and his appetite to my appetite, I was left far behind at the first mouthful, and had no chance with him. I never saw anyone enjoy a pudding so much, I think; and he laughed, when it was all gone, as if his enjoyment of it lasted still.

Finding him so very friendly and companionable, it was then that I asked for the pen and ink and paper, to write to Peggotty. He not only brought it immediately, but was good enough to look over me while I wrote the letter. When I had finished it, he asked me where I was going to school.

I said,"Near London," which was all I knew.

"Oh! my eye!" he said, looking very low-spirited,"I am sorry for that."

"Why?" I asked him.

"Oh, Lord!" he said, shaking his head,"that's the school where they broke the boy's ribs—two ribs—a little boy he was. I should say he was—let me see—how old are you, about?"

I told him between eight and nine.

"That's just his age," he said. "He was eight years and six months old when they broke his first rib; eight years and eight months old when they broke his second, and did for him."

I could not disguise from myself, or from the waiter, that this was an uncomfortable coincidence, and inquired how it was done. His answer was not cheering to my spirits, for it consisted of two dismal words,"With whopping."

The blowing of the coach-horn in the yard was a seasonable diversion, which made me get up and hesitatingly inquire, in the mingled pride and diffidence of having a purse (which I took out of my pocket), if there were anything to pay.

"There's a sheet of letter-paper," he returned. "Did you ever buy a sheet of letter-paper?"

I could not remember that I ever had.

"It's dear," he said,"on account of the duty. Three pence. That's the way we're taxed in this country. There's nothing else, except the waiter. Never mind the ink. I lose by that."

"What should you—what should I—how much I ought to—what would it be right to pay the waiter, if you please?" I stammered, blushing.

"If I hadn't a family, and that family hadn't the cowpock," said the waiter,"I wouldn't take a sixpence. If I didn't support a aged pairint, and a lovely sister," —here the waiter was greatly agitated—"I wouldn't take a farthing. If I had a good place, and was treated well here, I should beg acceptance of a trifle, instead of taking of it. But I live on broken wittles—and I sleep on the coals" —here the waiter burst into tears.

I was very much concerned for his misfortunes, and felt that any recognition short of ninepence would be mere brutality and hardness of heart. Therefore I gave him one of my three bright shillings, which he received with much humility and veneration, and spun up with his thumb, directly afterwards, to try the goodness of.

It was a little disconcerting to me, to find, when I was being helped up behind the coach, that I was supposed to have eaten all the dinner without any assistance. I discovered this, from overhearing the lady in the bow-window say to the guard, "Take care of that child, George, or he'll burst!" and from observing that the women-servants who were about the place came out to look and giggle at me as a young phenomenon. My unfortunate friend the waiter, who had quite recovered his spirits, did not appear to be disturbed by this, but joined in the general admiration without being at all confused. If I had any doubt of him, I suppose this half awakened it; but I am inclined to believe that with the simple confidence of a child, and the natural reliance of a child upon superior years (qualities I am very sorry any children should prematurely change for worldly wisdom), I had no serious mistrust of him on the whole, even then.

I felt it rather hard, I must own, to be made, without deserving it, the subject of jokes between the coachman and guard as to the coach drawing heavy behind, on account of my sitting there, and as to the greater expediency of my travelling by wagon. The story of my supposed appetite getting wind among the outside passengers, they were merry upon it likewise; and asked me whether I was going to be paid for, at school, as two brothers or three, and whether I was contracted for, or went upon the regular terms; with other pleasant questions. But the worst of it was, that I knew I should be ashamed to eat anything, when an opportunity offered, and that, after a rather light dinner, I should remain hungry all night—for I had left my cakes behind, at the hotel, in my hurry. My apprehensions were realized. When we stopped for supper I couldn't muster courage to take any, though I should have liked it very much, but sat by the fire and said I didn't want anything. This did not save me from more jokes, either; for a husky-voiced gentleman with a rough face, who had been eating out of a sandwich-box nearly all the way, except when he had been drinking out of a bottle, said I was like a boa-constrictor who took enough at one meal to last him a long time; after which, he actually brought a rash out upon himself with boiled beef.

III. Questions for discussion

1. What kind of person is Mr Barkis? What did he want David help him to do?
2. Did David enjoy his dinner? Did he really know what was happening to him?
3. How would you explain David's innocence?

Unit 9

Wuthering Heights

I. Introduction

1. The Brontës

In many ways, the qualities of Romantic verse could be absorbed, rather than simply superseded, by the Victorian novel. This is suggested clearly by the work of the Brontë sisters. Growing up in a remote but cultivated vicarage in Yorkshire, they invented, as children, the imaginary kingdoms of Angria and Gondal. These inventions supplied the context for many of the poems in their first and pseudonymous publication, *Poems by Currer, Ellis and Acton Bell* (1846). Their Gothic plots and Byronic passions also informed the novels that began to be published in the following year. Charlotte Brontë, like her sisters, appears at first sight to have been writing a literal fiction of provincial life. In her first novel, *Jane Eyre* (1847), for example, the heroine's choice between sexual need and ethical duty belongs very firmly to the mode of moral realism. But her hair's-breadth escape from a bigamous marriage with her employer, and the death by fire of his mad first wife derive from the rather different tradition of the Gothic novel. In *Shirley* (1849) Charlotte Brontë strove to be, in her own words, "as unromantic as Monday morning." In *Villette* (1853) the distinctive Gothic elements return to lend this study of the limits of stoicism an unexpected psychological intensity and drama. Emily Brontë united these diverse traditions still more successfully in her only novel, *Wuthering Heights* (1847). Closely observed regional detail, precisely handled plot, and a sophisticated use of multiple internal narrators are combined with vivid imagery and an extravagantly Gothic theme. The result is a perfectly achieved study of elemental passions and the strongest possible refutation of the assumption that the age of the novel must also be an age of realism.

2. The story

The title of the book, *Wuthering Heights*, is the name of an old house, high up on the Yorkshire moors, occupied by the Earnshaw family. The period is the very end of 18th century. Because of their remoteness, the Earnshaws live in a style more traditional than that characteristic of households in more domesticated parts of England; the family and the servants base a kind of democratic equality with each other which accounts for the independent judgment of the housekeeper (Nelly Dean, who tells most of the story) and her freedom of intimacy with her employers. Into this house Mr Earnshaw brings a child who has been living the life of a wild animal in the slums of Liverpool. His parents are quite unknown, and Earnshaw adopts him, giving him the single name of Heathcliff. However, Mr Earnshaw treats him less like a human being than like an over-indulged pet animal; this arouses the fierce resentment of his son Hindley, and it is only with the daughter Catherine (Cathy) that Heathcliff has a human relationship, and then only on the moors outside the house. After Mr Earnshaw's death, Heathcliff is maltreated by Hindley, now master of the house and lives like a despised animal instead of a spoilt one; his strong bond with Cathy, however, remains. But Cathy marries Edgar Linton from the "civilized" household of Thrushcross Grange in the valley. Heathcliff runs away, and is heard of no more for three years. During this period Cathy and Edgar are contented together, though she has fits of depression. When Heathcliff returns, he has become a rich man, but is as socially excluded as ever, as deeply identified with Cathy, and full of hatred for the Linton and the Earnshaw families, which he sets about to destroy, especially after the death of Cathy in giving birth to a daughter. He nearly succeeds in doing so, but has to withhold harm from Hareton Ernshaw, the son of Hindley, and Catherine Linton, the daughter of Cathy, who are deeply in love. Heathcliff becomes detached from external reality and lives only for his union with Cathy in death. On the last page a weeping little boy declares that he has seen the ghosts of the dead Heathcliff and Cathy walking on the moor.

II. Text

Chapter 9

He entered, vociferating oaths dreadful to hear; and caught me in the act of stowing his son away in the kitchen cupboard. Hareton was impressed with a wholesome terror of encountering either his wild beast's fondness or his madman's rage; for in one he ran a chance of being squeezed and kissed to death, and in the other of being flung into the fire, or dashed against the wall; and the poor thing remained perfectly quiet wherever I chose to put him.

"There, I've found it out at last!" cried Hindley, pulling me back by the skin of my neck, like a dog."By heaven and hell, you've sworn between you to murder that child! I know how it is, now, that he is always out of my way. But, with the help of Satan, I shall make you swallow the carving-knife, Nelly! You needn't laugh; for I've just crammed Kenneth, head downmost, in the Blackhorse marsh; and two is the same as one—and I want to kill some of you: I shall have no rest till I do!"

"But I don't like the carving-knife, Mr Hindley," I answered, "it has been cutting red herrings. I'd rather be shot, if you please."

"You'd rather be damned!" he said, "and so you shall. No law in England can hinder a man from keeping his house decent, and mine's abominable! Open your mouth."

He held the knife in his hand, and pushed its point between my teeth: but, for my part, I was never much afraid of his vagaries. I spat out, and affirmed it tasted detestably—I would not take it on any account.

"Oh!" said he, releasing me,"I see that hideous little villain is not Hareton: I beg your pardon, Nell. If it be, he deserves flaying alive for not running to welcome me, and for screaming as if I were a goblin. Unnatural cub, come hither! I'll teach thee to impose on a good-hearted, deluded father. Now, don't you think the lad would be handsomer cropped? It makes a dog fiercer, and I love something fierce—get me a scissors—something fierce and trim! Besides, it's infernal affectation—devilish conceit it is, to cherish our ears—we're asses enough without them. Hush, child, hush! Well then, it is my darling! Whist, dry thy eyes—there's a joy; kiss me. What!It won't? Kiss me, Hareton! Damn thee, kiss me! By God, as if I would rear such a monster! As sure as I'm living, I'll break the brat's neck."

Poor Hareton was squalling and kicking in his father's arms with all his might, and redoubled his yells when he carried him upstairs and lifted him over the banister. I cried out that he would frighten the child into fits, and ran to rescue him. As I reached them, Hindley leant forward on the rails to listen to a noise below; almost forgetting what he had in his hands. "Who is that?" he asked, hearing someone approaching the stair's foot. I leant forward also, for the purpose of signing to Heathcliff, whose step I recognized, not to come farther; and, at the instant when my eye quitted Hareton, he gave a sudden spring, delivered himself from the careless grasp that held him, and fell.

There was scarcely time to experience a thrill of horror before we saw that the little wretch was safe. Heathcliff arrived underneath just at the critical moment; by a natural impulse, he arrested his descent, and setting him on his feet, looked up to discover the author of the accident. A miser who has parted with a lucky lottery ticket for five shillings, and finds next day he has lost in the bargain five thousand pounds, could not show a blanker countenance than he did on beholding the figure of Mr Earnshaw above. It expressed, plainer than words could do, the intense anguish at having made himself the instrument of thwarting his own revenge. Had it been dark, I dare say, he would have tried to remedy the mistake by smashing Hareton's skull on the steps; but we witnessed his salvation; and I was presently below with my precious charge pressed to my heart. Hindley descended more leisurely, sobered and abashed.

"It is your fault, Ellen," he said, "you should have kept him out of sight, you should have taken him from me! Is he injured anywhere?"

"Injured!" I cried angrily, "if he's not killed, he'll be an idiot! Oh! I wonder his mother does not rise from her grave to see how you use him. You're worse than a heathen—treating your own flesh and blood in that manner!"

He attempted to touch the child, who, on finding himself with me, sobbed off his terror directly. At the first finger his father laid on him, however, he shrieked again louder than before, and struggled as if he would go into convulsions.

"You shall not meddle with him!" I continued."He hates you—they all hate you—that's the truth! A happy family you have, and a pretty state you're come to!"

"I shall come to a prettier, yet, Nelly," laughed the misguided man, recovering his hardness."At present, convey yourself and him away. And, hark you, Heathcliff! clear you too, quite from my reach and hearing. I wouldn't murder you tonight; unless, perhaps, I set the house on fire: but that's as my fancy goes."

While saying this he took a pint bottle of brandy from the dresser, and poured some into a tumbler.

"Nay, don't!" I entreated."Mr Hindley, do take warning. Have mercy on this unfortunate boy, if you care nothing for yourself!"

"Anyone will do better for him than I shall," he answered.

"Have mercy on your own soul!" I said, endeavouring to snatch the glass from his hand.

"Not I! On the contrary, I shall have great pleasure in sending it to perdition to punish its Maker," exclaimed the blasphemer. 'Here's to its hearty damnation!"

He drank the spirits and impatiently bade us go, terminating his command with a sequel of horrid imprecations, too bad to repeat or remember.

"It's a pity he cannot kill himself with drink," observed Heathcliff, muttering an echo of curses back when the door was shut."He's doing his very utmost; but his constitution defies him. Mr Kenneth says he would wager his mare, that he'll outlive any man on this side Gimmerton, and go to the grave a hoary sinner, unless some happy chance out of the common course befall him."

I went into the kitchen, and sat down to lull my little lamb to sleep. Heathcliff, as I thought, walked through to the barn. It turned out afterwards that he only got as far as the other side the settle, when he flung himself on a bench by the wall, removed from the fire, and remained silent.

I was rocking Hareton on my knee, and humming a song that began:

"*It was far in the night, and the bairnies grat,*

The mither beneath the mools heard that—"

When Miss Cathy, who had listened to the hubbub from her room, put her head in, and whispered:

"Are you alone, Nelly?"

"Yes, miss," I replied.

She entered and approached the hearth. I, supposing she was going to say something, looked up. The expression of her face seemed disturbed and anxious. Her lips were half asunder, as if she meant to speak, and she drew a breath, but it escaped in a sigh instead of a sentence. I resumed my song, not having forgotten her recent behaviour.

"Where's Heathcliff?" she said, interrupting me.

"About his work in the stable," was my answer.

He did not contradict me, perhaps he had fallen into a doze. There followed another long pause, during which I perceived a drop or two trickle from Catherine's cheek to the flags. Is she sorry for her shameful conduct? I asked myself. That will be a novelty, but she may come to the point as she will—I shan't help her! No, she felt small trouble regarding any subject, save her own concerns.

"Oh, dear!" she cried at last."I'm very unhappy!"

"A pity," observed I."You're hard to please: so many friends and so few cares, and can't make yourself content!"

"Nelly, will you keep a secret for me?" she pursued, kneeling down by me, and lifting her winsome eyes to my face with that sort of look which turns off bad temper, even when one has all the right in the world to indulge it.

"Is it worth keeping?" I inquired, less sulkily.

"Yes, and it worries me, and I must let it out! I want to know what I should do. Today, Edgar Linton has asked me to marry him, and I've given him an answer. Now, before I tell you whether it was a consent or denial, you tell me which it ought to have been."

"Really, Miss Catherine, how can I know?" I replied."To be sure, considering the exhibition you performed in his presence this afternoon, I might say it would be wise to refuse him: since he asked you after that, he must either be hopelessly stupid or a venturesome fool."

"If you talk so, I won't tell you any more," she returned peevishly, rising to her feet."I accepted him, Nelly. Be quick, and say whether I was wrong!"

"You accepted him! then, what good is it discussing the matter? You have pledged your word, and cannot retract."

"But, say whether I should have done so—do!" she exclaimed in an irritated tone, chafing her hands together, and frowning.

"There are many things to be considered before that question can be answered properly," I said sententiously."First and fore-most, do you love Mr Edgar?"

"Who can help it? Of course I do," she answered.

Then I put her through the following catechism: for a girl of twenty-two it was not injudicious.

"Why do you love him, Miss Cathy?"

"Nonsense, I do—that's sufficient."

"By no means, you must say why?"

"Well, because he is handsome, and pleasant to be with."

"Bad!" was my commentary.

"And because he is young and cheerful."

"Bad, still."

"And because he loves me."

"Indifferent, coming there."

"And he will be rich, and I shall like to be the greatest woman of the neighbourhood, and I shall be proud of having such a husband."

"Worst of all. And now, say how you love him?"

"As everybody loves—You're silly, Nelly."

"Not at all—Answer."

"I love the ground under his feet, and the air over his head, and everything he touches, and every word he says. I love all his looks, and all his actions, and him entirely and altogether. There now!"

"And why?"

"Nay; you are making a jest of it; it is exceedingly ill-natured! It's no jest to me!" said the young lady, scowling, and turning her face to the fire.

"I'm very far from jesting, Miss Catherine," I replied."You love Mr Edgar because he is handsome, and young, and cheerful, and rich, and loves you. The last, however, goes for nothing: you would love him without that, probably; and with it you wouldn't, unless he possessed the four former attractions."

"No, to be sure not. I should only pity him—hate him, perhaps, if he was ugly, and a clown."

"But there are several other handsome, rich young men in the world: handsomer, possibly, and richer than he is. What should hinder you from loving them?"

"If there be any, they are out of my way! I've seen none like Edgar."

"You may see some; and he won't always be handsome, and young, and may not always be rich."

"He is now; and I have only to do with the present. I wish you would speak rationally."

"Well, that settles it: if you have only to do with the present, marry Mr Linton."

"I don't want your permission for that—I shall marry him, and yet you have not told me whether I'm right."

"Perfectly right; if people be right to marry only for the present. And now, let us hear what you are unhappy about. Your brother will be pleased; the old lady and gentleman will not object, I think; you will escape from a disorderly, comfortless home into a wealthy, respectable one; and you love Edgar, and Edgar loves you. All seems smooth and easy: where is the obstacle?"

"Here! and here!" replied Catherine, striking one hand on her forehead, and the other on her breast:"in whichever place the soul lives. In my soul and in my heart, I'm convinced I'm wrong!"

"That's very strange! I cannot make it out."

"It's my secret. But if you will not mock at me, I'll explain it: I can't do it distinctly: but I'll give you a feeling of how I feel."

She seated herself by me again: her countenance grew sadder and graver, and her clasped hands trembled.

"Nelly, do you never dream queer dreams?" she said, suddenly, after some minutes' reflection.

"Yes, now and then," I answered.

"And so do I. I've dreamt in my life dreams that have stayed with me ever after, and changed my ideas: they've gone through and through me, like wine through water, and altered the colour of my mind. And this is one; I'm going to tell it—but take care not to smile at any part of it."

"Oh! don't, Miss Catherine!" I cried."We're dismal enough without conjuring up ghosts and visions to perplex us. Come, come, be merry and like yourself! Look at little Hareton! he's dreaming nothing dreary. How sweetly he smiles in his sleep!"

"Yes, and how sweetly his father curses in his solitude! You remember him, I dare say, when he was just such another as that chubby thing: nearly as young and innocent. However, Nelly, I shall oblige you to listen: it's not long; and I've no power to be merry tonight."

"I won't hear it, I won't hear it!" I repeated hastily.

I was superstitious about dreams then, and am still; and Catherine had an unusual gloom in her aspect, that made me dread something from which I might shape a prophecy, and foresee a fearful catastrophe. She was vexed, but she did not proceed. Apparently taking up another subject, she recommenced in a short time.

"If I were in heaven, Nelly, I should be extremely miserable."

"Because you are not fit to go there," I answered."All sinners would be miserable in heaven."

"But it is not for that. I dreamt once that I was there."

"I tell you I won't hearken to your dreams, Miss Catherine! I'll go to bed," I interrupted again.

She laughed, and held me down; for I made a motion to leave my chair.

"This is nothing," cried she,"I was only going to say that heaven did not seem to be my home; and I broke my heart with weeping to come back to earth; and the angels were so angry that they flung me out into the middle of the heath on the top of Wuthering Heights; where I woke sobbing for joy. That will do to explain my secret, as well as the other. I've no more business to marry Edgar Linton than I have to be in heaven; and if the wicked man in there had not brought Heathcliff so low, I shouldn't have thought of it. It would degrade me to marry Heathcliff now; so he shall never know how I love him: and that, not because he's handsome, Nelly, but because he's more myself than I am. Whatever our souls are made of, his and mine are the same; and Linton's is as different as a moonbeam from lightning, or frost from fire."

Ere this speech ended, I became sensible of Heathcliff's presence. Having noticed a slight movement, I turned my head, and saw him rise from the bench, and steal out noiselessly. He had listened till he heard Catherine say it would degrade her to marry him, and then he stayed to hear no further. My companion, sitting on the ground, was prevented by the back of the settle from remarking his presence or departure; but I started, and bade her hush!

"Why?" she asked, gazing nervously round.

"Joseph is here," I answered, catching opportunely the roll of his cart-wheels up the road;"and Heathcliff will come in with him. I'm not sure whether he were not at the door this moment."

"Oh, he couldn't overhear me at the door!" said she."Give me Hareton, while you get the supper, and when it is ready ask me to sup with you. I want to cheat my uncomfortable conscience, and be convinced that Heathcliff has no notion of these things. He has not, has he? He does not know what being in love is?"

"I see no reason that he should not know, as well as you," I returned, "and if you are his choice, he will be the most unfortunate creature that ever was born! As soon as you become Mrs Linton, he loses friend, and love, and all! Have you considered how you'll bear the separation, and how he'll be deserted in the world? Because, Miss Catherine—"

"He quite deserted! we separated!" she exclaimed, with an accent of indignation."Who is to separate us, pray? They'll meet the fate of Milo! Not as long as I live, Ellen: for no mortal creature. Every Linton on the face of the earth might melt into nothing, before I could consent to forsake Heathcliff. Oh, that's not what I intend—that's not what I mean! I shouldn't be Mrs Linton were such a price demanded! He'll be as much to me as he has been all his lifetime. Edgar must shake off his antipathy, and tolerate him, at least. He will, when he learns my true feelings towards him. Nelly, I see now, you think me a selfish wretch; but did it never strike you that if Heathcliff and I married, we should be beggars? whereas, if I marry Linton, I can aid Heathcliff to rise, and place him out of my brother's power."

"With your husband's money, Miss Catherine?" I asked."You'll find him not so pliable as you calculate upon: and, though I'm hardly a judge, I think that's the worst motive you've given yet for being the wife of young Linton."

"It is not," retorted she, "it is the best! The others were the satisfaction of my whims: and for Edgar's sake, too, to satisfy him. This is for the sake of one who comprehends in his person my feelings to Edgar and myself. I cannot express it; but surely you and everybody have a notion that there is or should be an existence of yours beyond you. What were the use of my creation, if I were entirely contained here? My great miseries in this world have been Heathcliff's miseries, and I watched and felt each from the beginning: my great thought in living is himself. If all else perished, and he remained, I should still continue to be; and if all else remained, and he were annihilated, the universe would turn to a mighty stranger: I should not seem a part of it. My love for Linton is like the foliage in the woods: time will change it, I'm well aware, as winter changes the trees. My love for Heathcliff resembles the eternal rocks beneath: a source of little visible delight, but necessary. Nelly, I am Heathcliff! He's always, always in my mind: not as a pleasure, any more than I am always a pleasure to myself, but as my own being. So don't talk of our separation again: it is impracticable; and—"

She paused, and hid her face in the folds of my gown; but I jerked it forcibly away. I was out of patience with her folly!

"If I can make any sense of your nonsense, miss," I said,"it only goes to convince me that you are ignorant of the duties you undertake in marrying; or else that you are a wicked, unprincipled girl. But trouble me with no more secrets: I'll not promise to keep them."

"You'll keep that?" she asked eagerly.

"No, I'll not promise," I repeated.

She was about to insist, when the entrance of Joseph finished our conversation; and Catherine removed her seat to a corner, and nursed Hareton, while I made the supper. After it was cooked, my fellow-servant and I began to quarrel who should carry some to Mr Hindley; and we didn't settle it till all was nearly cold. Then we came to the agreement that we would let him ask, if he wanted any; for we feared particularly to go into his presence when he had been some time alone.

"Und hah isn't that nowt comed in frough the field, be this time? What is he abaht? girt eedle seeght![1]" demanded the old man, looking round for Heathcliff.

"I'll call him," I replied."He's in the barn, I've no doubt."

I went and called, but got no answer. On returning, I whispered to Catherine that he had heard a good part of what she said, I was sure; and told how I saw him quit the kitchen just as she complained of her brother's conduct regarding him. She jumped up in a fine fright, flung Hareton on to the settle, and ran to seek for her friend herself; not taking leisure to consider why she was so flurried, or how her talk would have affected him. She was absent such a while that Joseph proposed we should wait no longer. He cunningly conjectured they were staying away in order to avoid hearing his protracted blessing. They were "ill eneugh for ony fahl manners", he affirmed. And on their behalf he added that night a special prayer to the usual quarter of an hour's supplication before meat, and would have tacked another to the end of the grace, had not his young mistress broken in upon him with a hurried command that he must run down the road, and wherever Heathcliff had rambled, find and make him re-enter directly!

"I want to speak to him, and I must, before I go upstairs," she said."And the gate is open: he is somewhere out of hearing; for he would not reply, though I shouted at the top of the fold as loud as I could."

Joseph objected at first; she was too much in earnest, however, to suffer contradiction; and at last he placed his hat on his head, and walked grumbling forth. Meantime, Catherine paced up and down the floor, exclaiming:

"I wonder where he is—I wonder where he can be? What did I say, Nelly? I've forgotten. Was he vexed at my bad humour this afternoon? Dear! tell me what I've said to grieve him? I do wish he'd come. I do wish he would!"

"What a noise for nothing!" I cried, though rather uneasy myself."What a trifle scares you! It's surely no great cause of alarm that Heathcliff should take a moonlight saunter on the moors, or even lie too sulky to speak to us in the hay-loft. I'll engage he's lurking there. See if I don't ferret him out!"

I departed to renew my search; its result was disappointment, and Joseph's quest ended in the same.

"Yon lads gets war un war!" observed he on re-entering."He's left th' yate ut t' full swing, and Miss's pony has trodden dahn two rigs uh corn, un plottered through, raight o'er intuh t'

1. girt eedle seeght = great idle sight.

meadow! Hahsomdiver, t' maister 'ull play t' devil tomorn, and he'll do weel. He's patience itsseln wi' sich careless, offald craters—patience itsseln he is! Bud he'll nut be soa allus—yah's see, all on ye! Yah mum'nt drive him aht uf his heead for nowt!"

"Have you found Heathcliff, you ass?" interrupted Catherine."Have you been looking for him, as I ordered?"

"Aw sud more likker look for th' horse," he replied."It 'ud be tuh more sense. Bud, Aw can look for norther horse nur man uf a neeght loike this—as black as t' chimbley! und Hathecliff's noan t' chap to coom at maw whistle—happen he'll be less hard uh hearing wi' ye!"

It was a very dark evening for summer: the clouds appeared inclined to thunder, and I said we had better all sit down; the approaching rain would be certain to bring him home without further trouble. However, Catherine would not be persuaded into tranquillity. She kept wandering to and fro, from the gate to the door, in a state of agitation which permitted no repose; and at length took up a permanent situation on one side of the wall, near the road: where, heedless of my expostulations and the growling thunder, and the great drops that began to plash around her, she remained, calling at intervals, and then listening, and then crying outright. She beat Hareton, or any child, at a good passionate fit of crying.

About midnight, while we still sat up, the storm came rattling over the Heights in full fury. There was a violent wind, as well as thunder, and either one or the other split a tree off at the corner of the building: a huge bough fell across the roof, and knocked down a portion of the east chimney-stack, sending a clatter of stones and soot into the kitchen fire. We thought a bolt had fallen in the middle of us; and Joseph swung on to his knees beseeching the Lord to remember the patriarchs Noah and Lot, and, as in former times, spare the righteous, though He smote the ungodly. I felt some sentiment that it must be a judgment on us also. The Jonah, in my mind, was Mr Earnshaw; and I shook the handle of his den that I might ascertain if he were yet living. He replied audibly enough, in a fashion which made my companion vociferate, more clamorously than before, that a wide distinction might be drawn between saints like himself and sinners like his master. But the uproar passed away in twenty minutes, leaving us all unharmed; excepting Cathy, who got thoroughly drenched for her obstinacy in refusing to take shelter, and standing bonnetless and shawl-less to catch as much water as she could with her hair and clothes. She came in and lay down on the settle, all soaked as she was, turning her face to the back, and putting her hands before it.

"Well, miss!" I exclaimed, touching her shoulder;"you are not bent on getting your death, are you? Do you know what o'clock it is? Half past twelve. Come, come to bed! there's no use waiting longer on that foolish boy: he'll be gone to Gimmetton, and he'll stay there now. He guesses we shouldn't wait for him till this late hour: at least, he guesses that only Mr Hindley would be up; and he'd rather avoid having the door opened by the master."

"Nay, nay, he's noan at Gimmerton," said Joseph."Aw's niver wonder, bud he's at t' bothom uf a bog-hoile. This visitation worn't for nowt, and I wod hev ye to look out, miss--yah muh be t' next. Thank Hiven for all! All warks togither for gooid to them as is chozzen, and piked out fro' th' rubbidge! Yah knaw whet t' Scripture ses." And he began quoting several texts, referring us to the chapters and verses where we might find them.

I, having vainly begged the wilful girl to rise and remove her wet things, left him preaching and her shivering, and betook myself to bed with little Hareton, who slept as fast as if everyone had been sleeping round him. I heard Joseph read on a while afterwards; then I distinguished his slow step on the ladder, and then I dropped asleep.

Coming down somewhat later than usual, I saw, by the sunbeams piercing the chinks of the shutters, Miss Catherine still seated near the fireplace. The house door was ajar, too; light entered from its unclosed windows; Hindley had come out, and stood on the kitchen hearth, haggard and drowsy.

"What ails you, Cathy?" he was saying when I entered, "you look as dismal as a drowned whelp. Why are you so damp and pale, child?"

"I've been wet," she answered reluctantly,"and I'm cold, that's all."

"Oh, she is naughty!" I cried, perceiving the master to be tolerably sober."She got steeped in the shower of yesterday evening, and there she has sat the night through, and I couldn't prevail on her to stir."

Mr Earnshaw stared at us in surprise."The night through," he repeated."What kept her up? not fear of the thunder, surely? That was over hours since."

Neither of us wished to mention Heathcliff's absence, as long as we could conceal it; so I replied, I didn't know how she took it into her head to sit up; and she said nothing. The morning was fresh and cool; I threw back the lattice, and presently the room filled with sweet scents from the garden; but Catherine called peevishly to me,"Ellen, shut the window. I'm starving!" And her teeth chattered as she shrunk closer to the almost extinguished embers.

"She's ill," said Hindley, taking her wrist. "I suppose that's the reason she would not go to bed. Damn it! I don't want to be troubled with more sickness here. What took you into the rain!"

"Running after t' lads, as usuald!" croaked Joseph, catching an opportunity, from our hesitation, to thrust in his evil tongue."If I war yah, maister, I'd just slam t' boards i' their faces all on 'em, gentle and simple! Never a day ut yah're off, but yon cat o' Linton comes sneaking hither; and Miss Nelly, shoo's a fine lass! shoo sits watching for ye i' t' kitchen; and as yah're in at one door, he's out at t'other; and, then, wer grand lady goes a coorting of her side! It's bonny behaviour, lurking amang t' fields, after twelve o' t' night, wi' that fahl, flaysome divil of a gipsy, Heathcliff! They think I'm blind; but I'm noan: nowt ut t' soart! — I seed young Linton boath coming and going, and I seed yah" (directing his discourse to me),"yah gooid fur nowt, slattenly witch! nip up and bolt into th' house, t' minute yah heard t' maister's horse fit clatter up t' road."

"Silence, eavesdropper!" cried Catherine;"none of your insolence before me! Edgar Linton came yesterday by chance, Hindley; and it was I who told him to be off: because I knew you would not like to have met him as you were."

"You lie, Cathy, no doubt," answered her brother,"and you are a confounded simpleton! But never mind Linton at present: tell me, were you not with Heathcliff last night? Speak the truth, now. You need not be afraid of harming him: though I hate him as much as ever, he did me a good turn a short time since, that will make my conscience tender of breaking his neck. To prevent it, I shall send him about his business, this very morning; and after he's gone, I'd advise you all to look sharp: I shall only have the more humour for you."

"I never saw Heathcliff last night," answered Catherine, beginning to sob bitterly, "and if you do turn him out of doors, I'll go with him. But, perhaps, you'll never have an opportunity: perhaps he's gone." Here she burst into uncontrollable grief, and the remainder of her words were inarticulate.

Hindley lavished on her a torrent of scornful abuse, and bade her get to her room immediately, or she shouldn't cry for nothing! I obliged her to obey; and I shall never forget what a scene she acted when we reached her chamber: it terrified me. I thought she was going mad, and I begged Joseph to run for the doctor. It proved the commencement of delirium: Mr Kenneth, as soon as he saw her, pronounced her dangerously ill; she had a fever. He bled her, and he told me to let her live on whey and water gruel, and take care she did not throw herself downstairs or out of the window; and then he left: for he had enough to do in the parish, where two or three miles was the ordinary distance between cottage and cottage.

Though I cannot say I made a gentle nurse, and Joseph and the master were no better; and though our patient was as wearisome and headstrong as a patient could be, she weathered it

through. Old Mrs Linton paid us several visits, to be sure, and set things to rights, and scolded and ordered us all; and when Catherine was convalescent, she insisted on conveying her to Thrushcross Grange: for which deliverance we were very grateful. But the poor dame had reason to repent of her kindness: she and her husband both took the fever, and died within a few days of each other.

Our young lady returned to us, saucier and more passionate, and haughtier than ever. Heathcliff had never been heard of since the evening of the thunder-storm; and one day I had the misfortune, when she had provoked me exceedingly, to lay the blame of his disappearance on her: where indeed it belonged, as she well knew. From that period, for several months, she ceased to hold any communication with me, save in the relation of a mere servant. Joseph fell under a ban also: he would speak his mind, and lecture her all the same as if she were a little girl; and she esteemed herself a woman, and our mistress, and thought that her recent illness gave her a claim to be treated with consideration. Then the doctor had said that she would not bear crossing much; she ought to have her own way; and it was nothing less than murder in her eyes for anyone to presume to stand up and contradict her. From Mr Earnshaw and his companions she kept aloof; and tutored by Kenneth, and serious threats of a fit that often attended her rages, her brother allowed her whatever she pleased to demand, and generally avoided aggravating her fiery temper. He was rather too indulgent in humouring her caprices; not from affection, but from pride: he wished earnestly to see her bring honour to the family by an alliance with the Lintons, and as long as she let him alone she might trample us like slaves, for aught he cared! Edgar Linton, as multitudes have been before and will be after him, was infatuated; and believed himself the happiest man alive on the day he led her to Gimmerton Chapel, three years subsequent to his father's death.

Much against my inclination, I was persuaded to leave Wuthering Heights and accompany her here. Little Hareton was nearly five years old, and I had just begun to teach him his letters. We made a sad parting; but Catherine's tears were more powerful than ours. When I refused to go, and when she found her entreaties did not move me, she went lamenting to her husband and brother. The former offered me munificent wages; the latter ordered me to pack up: he wanted no women in the house, he said, now that there was no mistress; and as to Hareton, the curate should take him in hand, by and by. And so I had but one choice left: to do as I was ordered. I told the master he got rid of all decent people only to run to ruin a little faster; I kissed Hareton goodbye; and since then he has been a stranger: and it's very queer to think it, but I've no doubt he has completely forgotten all about Ellen Dean, and that he was ever more than all the world to her, and she to him!

At this point of the housekeeper's story, she chanced to glance towards the timepiece over the chimney; and was in amazement on seeing the minute hand measure half past one. She would not hear of staying a second longer: in truth, I felt rather disposed to defer the sequel of her narrative myself. And now that she is vanished to her rest, and I have meditated for another hour or two, I shall summon courage to go, also, in spite of aching laziness of head and limbs.

III. Reading Tasks

1. Who was the narrator? What was her status in the novel?
2. What coincidence helps build the basic plot of this chapter? Try to explain its function.
3. What obstacles stood in Heathcliff and Catharine's way to love.
4. What was the ultimate reason for Heathclif's departure from Wuthering Heights?

Unit 10

Tess of the D'Urbervilles

I. Introduction

1. The author

Thomas Hardy (1840-1928), whose continuing popularity of novels owes much to their richly varied yet always accessible style and their combination of romantic plots with convincingly presented characters. Equally important—particularly in terms of their suitability to film and television adaptation—is their nostalgic evocation of a vanished rural world through the creation of highly particularized regional settings. Hardy's verse has been slower to win full acceptance, but his unique status as a major 20th-century poet as well as a major 19th-century novelist is now universally recognized.

2. The story

Tess is a poor peasant girl. Sent by her mother to claim kindred with a more prosperous branch of the D'UrberviUe family, she is seduced by the young master of the house, Alec, and bas to return home in disgrace. After giving birth to a child who dies in infancy, she goes to work as wage-labourer at a dairy farm at Talbothays. There she meets Angel Clare, son of a clergyman, and he falls in love with her and marries her. On their wedding night Tess and Clare tell each other about their past, and Clare, after hearing Tess' confession, leaves her abruptly for Brazil. Poverty forces Tess to seek for work and she works for a time at a capitalist farm at Flintcomb-Ash where she is insulted and oppressed by the master. Then the news of her father's death and the expulsion of her family from their cottage drive her to seek for assistance from Alec and the latter, now a preacher, soon resumes his former illicit relations with her. Angel Clare returns repentant and ready to be reconciled to Tess, but the girl finds that her living with Alec hinders her from returning to Clare. She kills Alec and then is speedily arrested, tried and hanged.

II. Text

PHASE THE FIFTH

The Woman Pays

Chapter 35

Her narrative ended; even its re-assertions and secondary explanations were done. Tess's voice throughout had hardly risen higher than its opening tone; there had been no exculpatory phrase of any kind, and she had not wept.

But the complexion even of external things seemed to suffer transmutation as her announcement progressed. The fire in the grate looked impish—demoniacally funny, as if it did not care in the least about her strait. The fender grinned idly, as if it too did not care. The light from the water-bottle was merely engaged in a chromatic problem. All material objects around announced their irresponsibility with terrible iteration. And yet nothing had changed since the moments when he had been kissing her; or rather, nothing in the substance of things. But the essence of things had changed.

When she ceased the auricular impressions from their previous endearments seemed to hustle away into the corners of their brains, repeating themselves as echoes from a time of supremely purblind foolishness.

Clare performed the irrelevant act of stirring the fire; the intelligence had not even yet got to the bottom of him. After stirring the embers he rose to his feet; all the force of her disclosure had imparted itself now. His face had withered. In the strenuousness of his concentration he treadled fitfully on the floor. He could not, by any contrivance, think closely enough; that was the meaning of his vague movement. When he spoke it was in the most inadequate, commonplace voice of the many varied tones she had heard from him.

"Tess!"

"Yes, dearest."

"Am I to believe this? From your manner I am to take it as true. O, you cannot be out of your mind! You ought to be! Yet you are not... . My wife, my Tess—nothing in you warrants such a supposition as that?"

"I am not out of my mind," she said.

"And yet—" He looked vacantly at her, to resume with dazed senses, "Why didn't you tell me before? Ah, yes, you would have told me, in a way—but I hindered you, I remember!"

These and other of his words were nothing but the perfunctory babble of the surface while the depths remained paralyzed. He turned away, and bent over a chair. Tess followed him to the middle of the room where he was, and stood there staring at him with eyes that did not weep. Presently she slid down upon her knees beside his foot, and from this position she crouched in a heap.

"In the name of our love, forgive me!" she whispered with a dry mouth."I have forgiven you for the same!"

And, as he did not answer, she said again—

"Forgive me as you are forgiven! I forgive you, Angel."

"You—yes, you do."

"But you do not forgive me?"

"O, Tess, forgiveness does not apply to the case! You were one person; now you are another. My God—how can forgiveness meet such a grotesque-prestidigitation as that!"

He paused, contemplating this definition; then suddenly broke into horrible laughter—as unnatural and ghastly as a laugh in hell.

"Don't—don't! It kills me quite, that!" she shrieked."O have mercy upon me—have mercy!"

He did not answer; and, sickly white, she jumped up.

"Angel, Angel! What do you mean by that laugh?" she cried out.

"Do you know what this is to me?"

He shook his head.

"I have been hoping, longing, praying, to make you happy! I have thought what joy it will be to do it, what an unworthy wife I shall be if I do not! That's what I have felt, Angel!"

"I know that."

"I thought, Angel, that you loved me—me, my very self! If it is I you do love, O how can it be that you look and speak so? It frightens me! Having begun to love you, I love you for ever—in all changes, in all disgraces, because you are yourself. I ask no more. Then how can you, O my own husband, stop loving me?"

"I repeat, the woman I have been loving is not you."

"But who?"

"Another woman in your shape."

She perceived in his words the realization of her own apprehensive foreboding in former times. He looked upon her as a species of impostor; a guilty woman in the guise of an innocent one. Terror was upon her white face as she saw it; her cheek was flaccid, and her mouth had almost the aspect of a round little hole. The horrible sense of his view of her so deadened her that she staggered; and he stepped forward, thinking she was going to fall.

"Sit down, sit down," he said gently."You are ill; and it is natural that you should be."

She did sit down, without knowing where she was, that strained look still upon her face, and her eyes such as to make his flesh creep.

"I don't belong to you any more, then; do I, Angel?" she asked helplessly."It is not me, but another woman like me that he loved, he says."

The image raised caused her to take pity upon herself as one who was ill-used. Her eyes filled as she regarded her position further; she turned round and burst into a flood of self-sympathetic tears.

Clare was relieved at this change, for the effect on her of what had happened was beginning to be a trouble to him only less than the woe of the disclosure itself. He waited patiently, apathetically, till the violence of her grief had worn itself out, and her rush of weeping had lessened to a catching gasp at intervals.

"Angel," she said suddenly, in her natural tones, the insane, dry voice of terror having left her now."Angel, am I too wicked for you and me to live together?"

"I have not been able to think what we can do."

"I shan't ask you to let me live with you, Angel, because I have no right to! I shall not write to mother and sisters to say we be married, as I said I would do; and I shan't finish the good-hussif I cut out and meant to make while we were in lodgings."

"Shan't you?"

"No, I shan't do anything, unless you order me to; and if you go away from me I shall not follow 'ee; and if you never speak to me any more I shall not ask why, unless you tell me I may."

"And if I do order you to do anything?"

"I will obey you like your wretched slave, even if it is to lie down and die."

"You are very good. But it strikes me that there is a want of harmony between your present mood of self-sacrifice and your past mood of self-preservation."

These were the first words of antagonism. To fling elaborate sarcasms at Tess, however, was much like flinging them at a dog or cat. The charms of their subtlety passed by her unappreciated, and she only received them as inimical sounds which meant that anger ruled. She remained mute, not knowing that he was smothering his affection for her. She hardly observed that a tear descended slowly upon his cheek, a tear so large that it magnified the pores of the skin over which it rolled, like the object lens of a microscope. Meanwhile reillumination as to the terrible and total change that her confession had wrought in his life, in his universe, returned to him, and he tried desperately to advance among the new conditions in which he stood. Some consequent action was necessary; yet what?

"Tess," he said, as gently as he could speak,"I cannot stay in this room just now. I will walk out a little way."

He quietly left the room, and the two glasses of wine that he had poured out for their supper — one for her, one for him — remained on the table untasted. This was what their Agape had come to. At tea, two or three hours earlier, they had, in the freakishness of affection, drunk from one cup.

The closing of the door behind him, gently as it had been pulled to, roused Tess from her stupor. He was gone; she could not stay. Hastily flinging her cloak around her she opened the door and followed, putting out the candles as if she were never coming back. The rain was over and the night was now clear.

She was soon close at his heels, for Clare walked slowly and without purpose. His form beside her light gray figure looked black, sinister, and forbidding, and she felt as sarcasm the touch of the jewels of which she had been momentarily so proud. Clare turned at hearing her footsteps, but his recognition of her presence seemed to make no difference in him, and he went on over the five yawning arches of the great bridge in front of the house.

The cow and horse tracks in the road were full of water, the rain having been enough to charge them, but not enough to wash them away. Across these minute pools the reflected stars flitted in a quick transit as she passed; she would not have known they were shining overhead if she had not seen them there — the vastest things of the universe imaged in objects so mean.

The place to which they had travelled today was in the same valley as Talbothays, but some miles lower down the river; and the surroundings being open she kept easily in sight of him. Away from the house the road wound through the meads, and along these she followed Clare without any attempt to come up with him or to attract him, but with dumb and vacant fidelity.

At last, however, her listless walk brought her up alongside him, and still he said nothing. The cruelty of fooled honesty is often great after enlightenment, and it was mighty in Clare now. The outdoor air had apparently taken away from him all tendency to act on impulse; she knew that he saw her without irradiation — in all her bareness; that Time was chanting his satiric psalm at her then—

Behold, when thy face is made bare, he that loved thee shall hate;
Thy face shall be no more fair at the fall of thy fate.
For thy life shall fall as a leaf and be shed as the rain;
And the veil of thine head shall be grief, and the crown shall be pain.

He was still intently thinking, and her companionship had now insufficient power to break or divert the strain of thought. What a weak thing her presence must have become to him! She could not help addressing Clare.

"What have I done — what have I done! I have not told of anything that interferes with or belies my love for you. You don't think I planned it, do you? It is in your own mind what you are angry at, Angel; it is not in me. O, it is not in me, and I am not that deceitful woman you think me!"

"H'm - well. Not deceitful, my wife; but not the same. No, not the same. But do not make me reproach you. I have sworn that I will not; and I will do everything to avoid it."

But she went on pleading in her distraction; and perhaps said things that would have been better left to silence.

"Angel! Angel! I was a child — a child when it happened! I knew nothing of men."

"You were more sinned against than sinning, that I admit."

"Then will you not forgive me?"

"I do forgive you, but forgiveness is not all."

"And love me?"

To this question he did not answer.

"O, Angel, my mother says that it sometimes happens so! she knows several cases where they were worse than I, and the husband has not minded it much — has got over it at least.

And yet the woman has not loved him as I do you!"

"Don't, Tess; don't argue. Different societies, different manners. You almost make me say you are an unapprehending peasant woman, who have never been initiated into the proportions of social things. You don't know what you say."

"I am only a peasant by position, not by nature!"

She spoke with an impulse to anger, but it went as it came.

"So much the worse for you. I think that parson who unearthed your pedigree would have done better if he had held his tongue. I cannot help associating your decline as a family with this other fact — of your want of firmness. Decrepit families imply decrepit wills, decrepit conduct. Heaven, why did you give me a handle for despising you more by informing me of your descent! Here was I thinking you a new-sprung child of nature; there were you, the belated seedling of an effete aristocracy!"

"Lots of families are as bad as mine in that! Retty's family were once large landowners, and so were Dairyman Billett's. And the Debbyhouses, who now are carters, were once the De Bayeux family. You find such as I everywhere; 'tis a feature of our county, and I can't help it."

"So much the worse for the county."

She took these reproaches in their bulk simply, not in their particulars; he did not love her as he had loved her hitherto, and to all else she was indifferent.

They wandered on again in silence. It was said afterwards that a cottager of Wellbridge, who went out late that night for a doctor, met two lovers in the pastures, walking very slowly, without converse, one behind the other, as in a funeral procession, and the glimpse that he obtained of their faces seemed to denote that they were anxious and sad. Returning later, he passed them again in the same field, progressing just as slowly, and as regardless of the hour and of the cheerless night as before. It was only on account of his preoccupation with his own affairs, and the illness in his house, that he did not bear in mind the curious incident, which, however, he recalled a long while after.

During the interval of the cottager's going and coming, she had said to her husband—

"I don't see how I can help being the cause of much misery to you all your life. The river is down there. I can put an end to myself in it. I am not afraid."

"I don't wish to add murder to my other follies," he said.

"I will leave something to show that I did it myself — on account of my shame. They will not blame you then."

"Don't speak so absurdly — I wish not to hear it. It is nonsense to have such thoughts in this kind of case, which is rather one for satirical laughter than for tragedy. You don't in the least understand the quality of the mishap. It would be viewed in the light of a joke by nine-tenths of the world if it were known. Please oblige me by returning to the house, and going to bed."

"I will," said she dutifully.

They had rambled round by a road which led to the well-known ruins of the Cistercian abbey behind the mill, the latter having, in centuries past, been attached to the monastic establishment. The mill still worked on, food being a perennial necessity; the abbey had perished, creeds being transient. One continually sees the ministration of the temporary outlasting the ministration of the eternal. Their walk having been circuitous they were still not far from the house, and in obeying his direction she only had to reach the large stone bridge across the main river, and follow the road for a few yards. When she got back everything remained as she had left it, the fire being still burning. She did not stay downstairs for more than a minute, but proceeded to her chamber, whither the luggage had been taken. Here she sat down on the edge of the bed, looking blankly around, and presently began to undress. In removing the light towards the bedstead its rays fell upon the tester of white dimity; something was hanging beneath it, and she lifted the candle to see what it was. A bough of mistletoe. Angel had put it there; she knew that in an instant. This was the explanation of that mysterious parcel which it had been so difficult to pack and bring; whose contents he would not explain to her, saying that time would soon show her the purpose there of. In his zest and his gaiety he had hung it there. How foolish and inopportune that mistletoe looked now.

Having nothing more to fear, having scarce anything to hope, for that he would relent there seemed no promise whatever, she lay down dully. When sorrow ceases to be speculative sleep sees her opportunity. Among so many happier moods which forbid repose this was a mood which welcomed it, and in a few minutes the lonely Tess forgot existence, surrounded by the aromatic illness of the chamber that had once, possibly, been the bride-chamber of her own ancestry.

Later on that night Clare also retraced his steps to the house. Entering softly to the sitting-room he obtained a light, and with the manner of one who had considered his course he spread his rugs upon the old horse-hair sofa which stood there, and roughly shaped it to a sleeping-couch. Before lying down he crept shoeless upstairs, and listened at the door of her apartment. Her measured breathing told that she was sleeping profoundly.

"Thank God!" murmured Clare; and yet he was conscious of a pang of bitterness at the thought — approximately true, though not wholly so—that having shifted the burden of her life to his shoulders she was now reposing without care.

He turned away to descend; then, irresolute, faced round to her door again. In the act he caught sight of one of the d'Urberville dames, whose portrait was immediately over the entrance to Tess's bedchamber. In the candlelight the painting was more than unpleasant. Sinister design lurked in the woman's features, a concentrated purpose of revenge on the other sex—so it seemed to him then. The Caroline bodice of the portrait was low—precisely as Tess's had been when he tucked it in to show the necklace; and again he experienced the distressing sensation of a resemblance between them.

The check was sufficient. He resumed his retreat and descended.

His air remained calm and cold, his small compressed mouth indexing his powers of selfcontrol; his face wearing still that terribly sterile expression which had spread thereon since her disclosure. It was the face of a man who was no longer passion's slave, yet who found no advantage in his enfranchisement. He was simply regarding the harrowing contingencies of human experience, the unexpectedness of things. Nothing so pure, so sweet, so virginal as Tess had seemed possible all the long while that he had adored her, up to an hour ago; but The little less, and what worlds away!

He argued erroneously when he said to himself that her heart was not indexed in the honest freshness of her face; but Tess had no advocate to set him right. Could it be possible, he continued, that eyes which as they gazed never expressed any divergence from what the tongue was telling, were yet ever seeing another world behind her ostensible one, discordant and contrasting.

He reclined on his couch in the sitting-room, and extinguished the light. The night came in, and took up its place there, unconcerned and indifferent the night which had already swallowed up his happiness, and was now digesting it listlessly; and was ready to swallow up the happiness of a thousand other people with as little disturbance or change of mien.

III. Reading Tasks

1. How do you understand Angel's statement:"I repeat, the woman I have been loving is not you...Another woman in your shape." What was Angel's ideal of love?

2. What can you learn about Tess's moral concept from her decisive forgiveness of Angel's past faults?

3. Which, in Angel's mind, came first, morality or sensation?

Unit 11

The Mark on the Wall

I. Introduction

1. The author

Virginia Woolf (1882-1941), British novelist, also distinguished feminist essayist, critic, and a central figure of the Bloomsbury group. She was born on January 25, 1882 in London, as the daughter of Julia Jackson Duckworth, a member of the Duckworth publishing family, and Leslie Stephen, a literary critic and the founder of the *Dictionary of National Biography*. Woolf was educated at home by her father, and grew up at the family home at Hyde Park Gate. Her mother died when she was in her early teens. Stella Duckworth, her half sister, took her mother's place, but died two years later. Leslie Stephen, her father, suffered a slow death from cancer. When her brother Toby died in 1906, she had a prolonged mental breakdown. Following the death of her father in 1904, Woolf moved with her sister Vanessa and two brothers to the house in Bloomsbury, which would become central to activities of the Bloomsbury group.

From 1905 Woolf began to write for the *Times Literary Supplement*. In 1912 she married the political theorist Leonard Woolf and published her first book, *The Voyage Out* in 1915. In 1919 appeared *Night and Day*, a realistic novel set in London, contrasting the lives of two friends, Katherine and Mary. *Jacob's Room* (1922) was based upon the life and death of her brother Toby.

With *To The Lighthouse* (1927) and *The Waves* (1931) Woolf established herself as one of the leading writers of modernism. In these works Woolf developed innovative literary techniques in order to reveal women's experience and find an alternative to the male-dominated views of reality. *Mrs. Dalloway* (1925) is formed of a giant web of thoughts of several groups of people during the course of a single day.

Virginia Woolf's concern with feminist thematics are dominant in *A Room of One's Own* (1929), which deals with the obstacles and prejudices that have hindered women writers, and explores in the last chapter the possibility of an androgynous mind. *Three Guineas* (1938) examined the necessity for women to make a claim for their own history and literature. *Orlando* (1928), a fantasy novel, traced the career of the androgynous protagonist from a masculine identity within the Elizabethan court to a feminine identity in 1928. Woolf was also prolific as an essayist, publishing some 500 essays in periodicals and collections, beginning 1905.

After her final attack of mental illness Woolf loaded her pockets with stones and drowned herself in the River Ouse near her Sussex home on March 28, 1941.

2. The stream of consciousness

Narrative technique in nondramatic fiction intended to render the flow of myriad impressions—visual, auditory, physical, associative, and subliminal—that impinge on the consciousness of an individual and form part of his awareness along with the trend of his rational thoughts. The term was first used by the psychologist William James in *The Principles of Psychology* (1890). As the psychological novel developed in the 20th century, some writers attempted to capture the total flow of their characters' consciousness, rather than limit themselves to rational thoughts. To represent the full richness, speed, and subtlety of the mind at work, the writer incorporates snatches of incoherent thought, ungrammatical constructions, and free association of ideas, images, and words at the pre-speech level. The stream-of-consciousness novel commonly uses the narrative techniques of interior monologue. Probably the most famous example is James Joyce's *Ulysses* (1922), a complex evocation of the inner states of the characters Leopold and Molly Bloom and Stephen Daedalus. Other notable examples include William Faulkner's *The Sound and the Fury* (1929), which records the fragmentary and impressionistic responses in the minds of three members of the Compson family to events that are immediately being experienced or events that are being remembered.

II. Text

The Mark on the Wall

Perhaps it was the middle of January in the present year that I first looked up and saw the mark on the wall. In order to fix a date it is necessary to remember what one saw. So now I think of the fire; the steady film of yellow light upon the page of my book; the three chrysanthemums in the round glass bowl on the mantelpiece. Yes, it must have been the winter time, and we had just finished our tea, for I remember that I was smoking a cigarette when I looked up and saw the mark on the wall for the first time. I looked up through the smoke of my cigarette and my eyes lodged for a moment upon the burning coals, and that old fancy of the crimson flag flapping from the castle tower came into my mind, and I thought of the cavalcade of red knights riding up the side of the black rock. Rather to my relief the sight of the mark interrupted the fancy, for it is an old fancy, an automatic fancy, made as a child perhaps. The mark was a small round mark, black upon the white wall, about six or seven inches above the mantelpiece.

How readily our thoughts swarm upon a new object, lifting it a little way, as ants carry a blade of straw so feverishly, and then leave it.... If that mark was made by a nail, it can't have been for a picture, it must have been for a miniature—the miniature of a lady with white powdered curls, powder-dusted cheeks, and lips like red carnations. A fraud of course, for the people who had this house before us would have chosen pictures in that way—an old picture for an old room. That is the sort of people they were—very interesting people, and I think of them so often, in such queer places, because one will never see them again, never know what happened next. They wanted to leave this house because they wanted to change their style of furniture, so he said, and he was in process of saying that in his opinion art should have ideas behind it when we were torn asunder, as one is torn from the old lady about to pour out tea and the young man about to hit the tennis ball in the back garden of the suburban villa as one rushes past in the train.

But as for that mark, I'm not sure about it; I don't believe it was made by a nail after all; it's too big, too round, for that. I might get up, but if I got up and looked at it, ten to one I shouldn't be able to say for certain; because once a thing's done, no one ever knows how it happened. Oh! dear me, the mystery of life; The inaccuracy of thought! The ignorance of humanity! To show how very little control of our possessions we have—what an accidental affair this living is after all our civilization—let me just count over a few of the things lost in one lifetime, beginning, for that seems always the most mysterious of losses—that cat would gnaw, what rat would nibble—three pale blue canisters of book-binding tools? Then there were the bird cages, the iron hoops, the steel skates, the Queen Anne coal-scuttle, the bagatelle board, the hand organ—all gone, and jewels, too. Opals and emeralds, they lie about the roots of turnips. What a scraping paring affair it is to be sure! The wonder is that I've any clothes on my back, that I sit surrounded by solid furniture at this moment. Why, if one wants to compare life to anything, one must liken it to being blown through the Tube at fifty miles an hour—landing at the other end without a single hairpin in one's hair! Shot out at the feet of God entirely naked! Tumbling head over heels in the asphodel meadows like brown paper parcels pitched down a shoot in the post office! With one's hair flying back like the tail of a race-horse. Yes, that seems to express the rapidity of life, the perpetual waste and repair; all so casual, all so haphazard....

But after life. The slow pulling down of thick green stalks so that the cup of the flower, as it turns over, deluges one with purple and red light. Why, after all, should one not be born there as one is born here, helpless, speechless, unable to focus one's eyesight, groping at the roots of the grass, at the toes of the Giants? As for saying which are trees, and which are men and women, or whether there are such things, that one won't be in a condition to do for fifty years or so. There will be nothing but spaces of light and dark, intersected by thick stalks, and rather higher up perhaps, rose-shaped blots of an indistinct colour—dim pinks and blues—which will, as time goes on, become more definite, become—I don't know what....

And yet that mark on the wall is not a hole at all. It may even be caused by some round black substance, such as a small rose leaf, left over from the summer, and I, not being a very vigilant housekeeper—look at the dust on the mantelpiece, for example, the dust which, so they say, buried Troy three times over, only fragments of pots utterly refusing annihilation, as one can believe.

The tree outside the window taps very gently on the pane.... I want to think quietly, calmly, spaciously, never to be interrupted, never to have to rise from my chair, to slip easily from one thing to another, without any sense of hostility, or obstacle. I want to sink deeper and deeper, away from the surface, with its hard separate facts. To steady myself, let me catch hold of the first idea that passes.... Shakespeare.... Well, he will do as well as another. A man who sat himself solidly in an arm-chair, and looked into the fire, so— A shower of ideas fell perpetually from some very high Heaven down through his mind. He leant his forehead on his hand, and people, looking in through the open door, —for this scene is supposed to take place on a summer's evening—But how dull this is, this historical fiction! It doesn't interest me at all. I wish I could hit upon a pleasant track of thought, a track indirectly reflecting credit upon myself, for those are the pleasantest thoughts, and very frequent even in the minds of modest mouse-coloured people, who believe genuinely that they dislike to hear their own praises. They are not thoughts directly praising oneself; that is the beauty of them; they are thoughts like this:

"And then I came into the room. They were discussing botany. I said how I'd seen a flower growing on a dust heap on the site of an old house in Kingsway. The seed, I said, must have been sown in the reign of Charles the First. What flowers grew in the reign of Charles the First?" I asked—(But I don't remember the answer). Tall flowers with purple tassels to them perhaps. And so it goes on. All the time I'm dressing up the figure of myself in my own mind, lovingly, stealthily, not openly adoring it, for if I did that, I should catch myself out, and stretch my hand at once for a book in self-protection. Indeed, it is curious how instinctively one protects the image of oneself from idolatry or any other handling that could make it ridiculous, or too unlike the original to be believed in any longer. Or is it not so very curious after all? It is a matter of great importance. Suppose the looking glass smashes, the image disappears, and the romantic figure with the green of forest depths all about it is there no longer, but only that shell of a person which is seen by other people—what an airless, shallow, bald, prominent world it becomes! A world not to be lived in. As we face each other in omnibuses and underground railways we are looking into the mirror; that accounts for the vagueness, the gleam of glassiness, in our eyes. And the novelists in future will realize more and more the importance of these reflections, for of course there is not one reflection but an almost infinite number; those are the depths they will explore, those the phantoms they will pursue, leaving the description of reality more and more out of their stories, taking a knowledge of it for granted, as the Greeks did and Shakespeare perhaps—but these generalizations are very worthless. The military sound of the word is enough. It recalls leading articles, cabinet ministers—a whole class of things indeed which as a child one thought the thing itself, the standard thing, the real thing, from which one could not depart save at the risk of nameless damnation. Generalizations bring back somehow Sunday in London, Sunday afternoon walks, Sunday luncheons, and also ways of speaking of the dead, clothes, and habits—like the habit of sitting all together in one room until a certain hour, although nobody liked it. There was a rule for everything. The rule for tablecloths at that particular period was that they should be made of tapestry with little yellow compartments marked upon them, such as you may see in photographs of the carpets in the corridors of the royal palaces. Tablecloths of a different kind were not real tablecloths. How shocking, and yet how wonderful it was to discover that these real things, Sunday luncheons, Sunday walks, country houses, and tablecloths were not entirely real, were indeed half phantoms, and the damnation which visited the disbeliever in them was only a sense of illegitimate freedom. What now takes the place of those things I wonder, those real standard things? Men perhaps, should you be a woman; the masculine point of view which governs our lives, which sets the standard, which establishes Whitaker's Table of Precedency, which has become, I suppose, since the war half a phantom to many men and women, which soon, one may hope, will be laughed into the dustbin where the phantoms go, the mahogany sideboards and the Landseer prints, Gods and Devils, Hell and so forth, leaving us all with an intoxicating sense of illegitimate freedom—if freedom exists....

In certain lights that mark on the wall seems actually to project from the wall. Nor is it entirely circular. I cannot be sure, but it seems to cast a perceptible shadow, suggesting that if I ran my finger down that strip of the wall it would, at a certain point, mount and descend a small tumulus, a smooth tumulus like those barrows on the South Downs which are, they say, either tombs or camps. Of the two I should prefer them to be tombs, desiring melancholy like most English people, and finding it natural at the end of a walk to think of the bones stretched beneath the turf.... There must be some book about it. Some antiquary must have dug up those bones and given them a name.... What sort of a man is an antiquary, I wonder? Retired Colonels for the most part, I daresay, leading parties of aged labourers to the top here, examining clods of earth and stone, and getting into correspondence with the neighbouring clergy, which, being opened at breakfast time, gives them a feeling of importance, and the comparison of arrow-heads necessitates cross-country journeys to the county towns, an agreeable necessity both to them and to their elderly wives, who wish to make plum jam or to clean out the study, and have every reason for keeping that great question of the camp or the tomb in perpetual suspension, while the Colonel himself feels agreeably philosophic in accumulating evidence on both sides of the question. It is true that he does finally incline to believe in the camp; and, being opposed, indites a pamphlet which he is about to read at the quarterly meeting of the local society when a stroke lays him low, and his last conscious thoughts are not of wife or child, but of the camp and that arrowhead there, which is now in the case at the local museum, together with the foot of a Chinese murderess, a handful of Elizabethan nails, a great many Tudor clay pipes, a piece of Roman pottery, and the wine-glass that Nelson drank out of—proving I really don't know what.

No, no, nothing is proved, nothing is known. And if I were to get up at this very moment and ascertain that the mark on the wall is really—what shall we say? —the head of a gigantic old nail, driven in two hundred years ago, which has now, owing to the patient attrition of many generations of housemaids, revealed its head above the coat of paint, and is taking its first view of modern life in the sight of a white-walled fire-lit room, what should I gain? —Knowledge? Matter for further speculation? I can think sitting still as well as standing up. And what is knowledge? What are our learned men save the descendants of witches and hermits who crouched in caves and in woods brewing herbs, interrogating shrew-mice and writing down the language of the stars? And the less we honour them as our superstitions dwindle and our respect for beauty and health of mind increases.... Yes, one could imagine a very pleasant world. A quiet, spacious world, with the flowers so red and blue in the open fields. A world without professors or specialists or house-keepers with the profiles of policemen, a world which one could slice with one's thought as a fish slices the water with his fin, grazing the stems of the water-lilies, hanging suspended over nests of white sea eggs.... How peaceful it is down here, rooted in the centre of the world and gazing up through the grey waters, with their sudden gleams of light, and their reflections—if it were not for Whitaker's Almanack—if it were not for the Table of Precedency!

I must jump up and see for myself what that mark on the wall really is—a nail, a rose-leaf, a crack in the wood?

Here is nature once more at her old game of self-preservation. This train of thought, she perceives, is threatening mere waste of energy, even some collision with reality, for who will ever be able to lift a finger against Whitaker's Table of Precedency? The Archbishop of Canterbury is followed by the Lord High Chancellor; the Lord High Chancellor is followed by the Archbishop of York. Everybody follows somebody, such is the philosophy of Whitaker; and the great thing is to know who follows whom. Whitaker knows, and let that, so Nature counsels, comfort you, instead of enraging you; and if you can't be comforted, if you must shatter this hour of peace, think of the mark on the wall.

I understand Nature's game—her prompting to take action as a way of ending any thought that threatens to excite or to pain. Hence, I suppose, comes our slight contempt for men of action—men, we assume, who don't think. Still, there's no harm in putting a full stop to one's disagreeable thoughts by looking at a mark on the wall.

Indeed, now that I have fixed my eyes upon it, I feel that I have grasped a plank in the sea; I feel a satisfying sense of reality which at once turns the two Archbishops and the Lord High Chancellor to the shadows of shades. Here is something definite, something real. Thus, waking from a midnight dream of horror, one hastily turns on the light and lies quiescent, worshipping the chest of drawers, worshipping solidity, worshipping reality, worshipping the impersonal world which is a proof of some existence other than ours. That is what one wants to be sure of.... Wood is a pleasant thing to think about. It comes from a tree; and trees grow, and we don't know how they grow. For years and years they grow, without paying any attention to us, in meadows, in forests, and by the side of river—all things one likes to think about. The cows swish their tails beneath them on hot afternoons; they paint rivers so green that when a moorhen dives one expects to see its feathers all green when it comes up again. I like to think of the fish balanced against the stream like flags blown out; and of water-beetles slowly raising domes of mud upon the bed of the river. I like to think of the tree itself: first the close dry sensation of being wood; then the grinding of the storm; then the slow, delicious ooze of sap. I like to think of it, too, on winter's nights standing in the empty field with all leaves close-furled, nothing tender exposed to the iron bullets of the moon, a naked mast upon an earth that goes tumbling, tumbling, all night long. The song of birds must sound very loud and strange in June; and how cold the feet of insects must feel upon it, as they make laborious progresses up the creases of the bark, or sun themselves upon the thin green awning of the leaves, and look straight in front of them with diamond-cut red eyes.... One by one the fibres snap beneath the immense cold pressure of the earth, then the last storm comes and, falling, the highest branches drive deep into the ground again. Even so, life isn't done with; there are a million patient, watchful lives still for a tree, all over the world, in bedrooms, in ships, on the pavement, lining rooms, where men and women sit after tea, smoking cigarettes. It is full of peaceful thoughts, happy thoughts, this tree. I should like to take each one separately—but something is getting in the way.... Where was I? What has it all been about? A tree? A river? The Downs? Whitaker's Almanack? The fields of asphodel? I can't remember a thing. Everything's moving, falling, slipping, vanishing.... There is a vast upheaval of matter. Someone is standing over me and saying?

"I'm going out to buy a newspaper." "Yes?"

"Though it's no good buying newspapers.... Nothing ever happens. Curse this war; God damn this war! All the same, I don't see why we should have a snail on our wall."

Ah, the mark on the wall! It was a snail.

III. Reading Tasks

1. Name the things that the author thought of as many as possible. Explain how the things were related to the mark on the wall?

2. What is the thread that goes through the whole article? How is the article structured and organized?

3. How imagination as a literary approach is applied in this article?

4. Is there a plot in this piece of writing? How do you define the genre of this article?

Unit 12

Araby

I. Introduciton

1. The author

James Joyce (1882-1941) whose subtle yet frank portrayal of human nature, coupled with his mastery of language and brilliant development of new literary forms, made him one of the most commanding influences on novelists of the 20th century. *Ulysses* has come to be accepted as a major masterpiece, two of its characters, Leopold Bloom and his wife, Molly, being portrayed with a fullness and warmth of humanity unsurpassed in fiction. Joyce's *A Portrait of the Artist as a Young Man* is also remarkable for the intimacy of the reader's contact with the central figure and contains some astonishingly vivid passages. The 15 short stories collected in *Dubliners* mainly focused upon Dublin life's sordidness, but "The Dead" is one of the world's great short stories. Critical opinion remains divided over Joyce's last work, *Finnegans Wake*, a universal dream about an Irish family, composed in a multilingual style on many levels and aiming at a multiplicity of meanings; but, although seemingly unintelligible at first reading, the book is full of poetry and wit, containing passages of great beauty. Joyce's other works — some verse (*Chamber Music*, 1907; *Pomes*

Penyeach, 1927; *Collected Poems*, 1936) and a play, *Exiles* (1918)—though competently written, added little to his international stature.

II. Text

Araby

North Richmond Street, being blind, was a quiet street except at the hour when the Christian Brothers' School set the boys free. An uninhabited house of two storeys stood at the blind end, detached from its neighbours in a square ground. The other houses of the street, conscious of decent lives within them, gazed at one another with brown imperturbable faces.

The former tenant of our house, a priest, had died in the back drawing-room. Air, musty from having been long enclosed, hung in all the rooms, and the waste room behind the kitchen was littered with old useless papers. Among these I found a few paper-covered books, the pages of which were curled and damp: *The Abbot*, by Walter Scott, *The Devout Communicant*, and *The Memoirs of Vidocq*. I liked the last best because its leaves were yellow. The wild garden behind the house contained a central apple-tree and a few straggling bushes, under one of which I found the late tenant's rusty bicycle-pump. He had been a very charitable priest; in his will he had left all his money to institutions and the furniture of his house to his sister.

When the short days of winter came, dusk fell before we had well eaten our dinners. When we met in the street the houses had grown sombre. The space of sky above us was the colour of ever-changing violet and towards it the lamps of the street lifted their feeble lanterns. The cold air stung us and we played till our bodies glowed. Our shouts echoed in the silent street. The career of our play brought us through the dark muddy lanes behind the houses, where we ran the gauntlet of the rough tribes from the cottages, to the back doors of the dark dripping gardens where odours arose from the ashpits, to the dark odorous stables where a coachman smoothed and combed the horse or shook music from the buckled harness. When we returned to the street, light from the kitchen windows had filled the areas. If my uncle was seen turning the corner, we hid in the shadow until we had seen him safely housed. Or if Mangan's sister came out on the doorstep to call her brother in to his tea, we watched her from our shadow peer up and down the street. We waited to see whether she would remain or go in and, if she remained, we left our shadow and walked up to Mangan's steps resignedly. She was waiting for us, her figure defined by the light from the half-opened door. Her brother always teased her before he obeyed, and I stood by the railings looking at her. Her dress swung as she moved her body, and the soft rope of her hair tossed from side to side.

Every morning I lay on the floor in the front parlour watching her door. The blind was pulled down to within an inch of the sash so that I could not be seen. When she came out on the doorstep my heart leaped. I ran to the hall, seized my books and followed her. I kept her brown figure always in my eye and, when we came near the point at which our ways diverged, I quickened my pace and passed her. This happened morning after morning. I had never spoken to her, except for a few casual words, and yet her name was like a summons to all my foolish blood.

Her image accompanied me even in places the most hostile to romance. On Saturday evenings when my aunt went marketing I had to go to carry some of the parcels. We walked through the flaring streets, jostled by drunken men and bargaining women, amid the curses of labourers, the shrill litanies of shop-boys who stood on guard by the barrels of pigs' cheeks, the nasal chanting of street-singers, who sang a come-all-you about O'Donovan Rossa, or a ballad about the troubles in our native land. These noises converged in a single sensation of life for me: I imagined that I bore my chalice safely through a throng of foes. Her name sprang to my lips at moments in strange prayers and praises which I myself did not understand. My eyes were often full of tears (I could not tell why) and at times a flood from my heart seemed to pour itself out into my bosom. I thought little of the future. I did not know whether I would ever speak to her or not, if I spoke to her, how I could tell her of my confused adoration. But my body was like a harp and her words and gestures were like fingers running upon the wires.

One evening I went into the back drawing-room in which the priest had died. It was a dark rainy evening and there was no sound in the house. Through one of the broken panes I heard the rain impinge upon the earth, the fine incessant needles of water playing in the sodden beds. Some distant lamp or lighted window gleamed below me. I was thankful that I could see so little. All my senses seemed to desire to veil themselves and, feeling that I was about to slip from them, I pressed the palms of my hands together until they trembled, murmuring:"O, love! O, love!" many times.

At last she spoke to me. When she addressed the first words to me I was so confused that I did not know what to answer. She asked me was I going to Araby. I forgot whether I answered yes or no. It would be a splendid bazaar; she said she would love to go.

"And why can't you?" I asked.

While she spoke she turned a silver bracelet round and round her wrist. She could not go, she said, because there would be a retreat that week in her convent. Her brother and two other boys were fighting for their caps, and I was alone at the railings. She held one of the spikes, bowing her head towards me. The light from the lamp opposite our door caught the white curve of her neck, lit up her hair that rested there and, falling, lit up the hand upon the railing. It fell over one side of her dress and caught the white border of a petticoat, just visible as she stood at ease.

"It's well for you," she said.

"If I go," I said,"I will bring you something."

What innumerable follies laid waste my waking and sleeping thoughts after that evening! I wished to annihilate the tedious intervening days. I chafed against the work of school. At night in my bedroom and by day in the classroom her image came between me and the page I strove to read. The syllables of the word Araby were called to me through the silence in which my soul luxuriated and cast an Eastern enchantment over me. I asked for leave to go to the bazaar on Saturday night. My aunt was surprised, and hoped it was not some Freemason affair. I answered few questions in class. I watched my master's face pass from amiability to sternness; he hoped I was not beginning to idle. I could not call my wandering thoughts together. I had hardly any patience with the serious work of life which, now that it stood between me and my desire, seemed to me child's play, ugly monotonous child's play.

On Saturday morning I reminded my uncle that I wished to go to the bazaar in the evening. He was fussing at the hallstand, looking for the hat-brush, and answered me curtly:

"Yes, boy, I know."

As he was in the hall I could not go into the front parlour and lie at the window. I felt the house in bad humour and walked slowly towards the school. The air was pitilessly raw and already my heart misgave me.

When I came home to dinner my uncle had not yet been home. Still it was early. I sat staring at the clock for some time and, when its ticking began to irritate me, I left the room. I mounted the staircase and gained the upper part of the house. The high, cold, empty, gloomy rooms liberated me and I went from room to room singing. From the front window I saw my companions playing below in the street. Their cries reached me weakened and indistinct and, leaning my forehead against the cool glass, I looked over at the dark house where she lived. I may have stood there for an hour, seeing nothing but the brown-clad figure cast by my imagination, touched discreetly by the lamplight at the curved neck, at the hand upon the railings and at the border below the dress.

When I came downstairs again I found Mrs Mercer sitting at the fire. She was an old, garrulous woman, a pawnbroker's widow, who collected used stamps for some pious purpose.

I had to endure the gossip of the tea-table. The meal was prolonged beyond an hour and still my uncle did not come. Mrs Mercer stood up to go: she was sorry she couldn't wait any longer, but it was after eight o'clock and she did not like to be out late, as the night air was bad for her. When she had gone I began to walk up and down the room, clenching my fists. My aunt said:

"I'm afraid you may put off your bazaar for this night of our Lord."

At nine o'clock I heard my uncle's latchkey in the hall door. I heard him talking to himself and heard the hallstand rocking when it had received the weight of his overcoat. I could interpret these signs. When he was midway through his dinner I asked him to give me the money to go to the bazaar. He had forgotten.

"The people are in bed and after their first sleep now," he said.

I did not smile. My aunt said to him energetically:

"Can't you give him the money and let him go? You've kept him late enough as it is."

My uncle said he was very sorry he had forgotten. He said he believed in the old saying:"All work and no play makes Jack a dull boy." He asked me where I was going and, when I told him a second time, he asked me did I know *The Arab's Farewell to his Steed*. When I left the kitchen he was about to recite the opening lines of the piece to my aunt.

I held a florin tightly in my hand as I strode down Buckingham Street towards the station. The sight of the streets thronged with buyers and glaring with gas recalled to me the purpose of my journey. I took my seat in a third-class carriage of a deserted train. After an intolerable delay the train moved out of the station slowly. It crept onward among ruinous houses and over the twinkling river. At Westland Row Station a crowd of people pressed to the carriage doors; but the porters moved them back, saying that it was a special train for the bazaar. I remained alone in the bare carriage. In a few minutes the train drew up beside an improvised wooden platform. I passed out on to the road and saw by the lighted dial of a clock that it was ten minutes to ten. In front of me was a large building which displayed the magical name.

I could not find any sixpenny entrance and, fearing that the bazaar would be closed, I passed in quickly through a turnstile, handing a shilling to a weary-looking man. I found myself in a big hall girded at half its height by a gallery. Nearly all the stalls were closed and the greater part of the hall was in darkness. I recognized a silence like that which pervades a church after a service. I walked into the centre of the bazaar timidly. A few people were gathered about the stalls which were still open. Before a curtain, over which the words Café Chantant were written in coloured lamps, two men were counting money on a salver. I listened to the fall of the coins.

Remembering with difficulty why I had come, I went over to one of the stalls and examined porcelain vases and flowered tea-sets. At the door of the stall a young lady was talking and laughing with two young gentlemen. I remarked their English accents and listened vaguely to their conversation.

"O, I never said such a thing!"

"O, but you did!"

"O, but I didn't!"

"Didn't she say that?"

"Yes. I heard her."

"O, there's a... fib!"

Observing me, the young lady came over and asked me did I wish to buy anything. The tone of her voice was not encouraging; she seemed to have spoken to me out of a sense of duty. I looked humbly at the great jars that stood like eastern guards at either side of the dark entrance to the stall and murmured:

"No, thank you."

The young lady changed the position of one of the vases and went back to the two young men. They began to talk of the same subject. Once or twice the young lady glanced at me over her shoulder.

I lingered before her stall, though I knew my stay was useless, to make my interest in her wares seem the more real. Then I turned away slowly and walked down the middle of the bazaar. I allowed the two pennies to fall against the sixpence in my pocket. I heard a voice call from one end of the gallery that the light was out. The upper part of the hall was now completely dark.

Gazing up into the darkness I saw myself as a creature driven and derided by vanity; and my eyes burned with anguish and anger.

III. Reading Tasks

1. What atmosphere is suggested by its setting?

2. Does the story make use of symbols? If so, what do they represent?

3. Do you know the legend of the Holy Grail? Can you see any hint of it in this story?

4. It seems the protagonist was questing for something. What was he looking for? Did he find it?

Unit 13

The Happy Prince

I. Introduction

1. The author

Oscar Wilde (1854-1900), was Irish writer, poet, and dramatist whose reputation rests on his comic masterpieces *Lady Windermere's Fan* (1892) and *The Importance of Being Earnest* (1895). He was a spokesman for the late 19th-century Aesthetic movement in England, which advocated art for art's sake. In the final decade of his life, Wilde wrote and published nearly all of his major works. In his only novel, *The Picture of Dorian Gray* , Wilde combined the supernatural elements of the Gothic novel with the unspeakable sins of French decadent fiction. Critics charged immorality despite Dorian's self-destruction; Wilde, however, insisted on the amoral nature of art regardless of an apparently moral ending. *Intentions* (1891), consisting of previously published essays, restated his aesthetic attitude toward art by borrowing ideas from the French poets Théophile Gautier and Charles Baudelaire and the American painter James McNeill Whistler. In the same year, two volumes of stories and fairy tales also appeared, testifying to his extraordinary creative inventiveness: *Lord Arthur Savile's Crime*, and *Other Stories* and *A House of Pomegranates*.

II. Text

The Happy Prince

High above the city, on a tall column, stood the statue of the Happy Prince. He was gilded all over with thin leaves of fine gold, for eyes he had two bright sapphires, and a large red ruby glowed on his sword-hilt.

He was very much admired indeed. "He is as beautiful as a weathercock," remarked one of the Town Councillors who wished to gain a reputation for having artistic tastes; "only not quite so useful," he added, fearing lest people should think him unpractical, which he really was not.

"Why can't you be like the Happy Prince?" asked a sensible mother of her little boy who was crying for the moon. "The Happy Prince never dreams of crying for anything."

"I am glad there is some one in the world who is quite happy," muttered a disappointed man as he gazed at the wonderful statue.

"He looks just like an angel," said the Charity Children as they came out of the cathedral in their bright scarlet cloaks and their clean white pinafores.

"How do you know?" said the Mathematical Master, "you have never seen one."

"Ah! but we have, in our dreams," answered the children; and the Mathematical Master frowned and looked very severe, for he did not approve of children dreaming.

One night there flew over the city a little Swallow. His friends had gone away to Egypt six weeks before, but he had stayed behind, for he was in love with the most beautiful Reed. He had met her early in the spring as he was flying down the river after a big yellow moth, and had been so attracted by her slender waist that he had stopped to talk to her.

"Shall I love you?" said the Swallow, who liked to come to the point at once, and the Reed made him a low bow. So he flew round and round her, touching the water with his wings, and making silver ripples. This was his courtship, and it lasted all through the summer.

"It is a ridiculous attachment," twittered the other Swallows; "she has no money, and far too many relations"; and indeed the river was quite full of Reeds. Then, when the autumn came they all flew away.

After they had gone he felt lonely, and began to tire of his lady-love. "She has no conversation," he said, "and I am afraid that she is a coquette, for she is always flirting with the wind." And certainly, whenever the wind blew, the Reed made the most graceful curtseys. "I admit that she is domestic," he continued, "but I love travelling, and my wife, consequently, should love traveling also."

"Will you come away with me?" he said finally to her; but the Reed shook her head, she was so attached to her home.

"You have been trifling with me," he cried. "I am off to the Pyramids. Good-bye!" and he flew away.

All day long he flew, and at night-time he arrived at the city.

"Where shall I put up?" he said; "I hope the town has made preparations."

Then he saw the statue on the tall column.

"I will put up there," he cried; "it is a fine position, with plenty of fresh air." So he alighted just between the feet of the Happy Prince.

"I have a golden bedroom," he said softly to himself as he looked round, and he prepared to go to sleep; but just as he was putting his head under his wing a large drop of water fell on him. "What a curious thing!" he cried; "there is not a single cloud in the sky, the stars are quite clear and bright, and yet it is raining. The climate in the north of Europe is really dreadful. The Reed used to like the rain, but that was merely her selfishness." Then another drop fell.

"What is the use of a statue if it cannot keep the rain off?" he said; "I must look for a good chimney-pot," and he determined to fly away.

But before he had opened his wings, a third drop fell, and he looked up, and saw - Ah! what did he see? The eyes of the Happy Prince were filled with tears, and tears were running down his golden cheeks. His face was so beautiful in the moonlight that the little Swallow was filled with pity.

"Who are you?" he said.

"I am the Happy Prince."

"Why are you weeping then?" asked the Swallow; "you have quite drenched me."

"When I was alive and had a human heart," answered the statue, "I did not know what tears were, for I lived in the Palace of Sans-Souci, where sorrow is not allowed to enter. In the daytime I played with my companions in the garden, and in the evening I led the dance in the Great Hall. Round the garden ran a very lofty wall, but I never cared to ask what lay beyond it, everything about me was so beautiful. My courtiers called me the Happy Prince, and happy indeed I was, if pleasure be happiness. So I lived, and so I died. And now that I am dead they have set me up here so high that I can see all the ugliness and all the misery of my city, and though my heart is made of lead yet I cannot choose but weep."

"What! is he not solid gold?" said the Swallow to himself. He was too polite to make any personal remarks out loud.

"Far away," continued the statue in a low musical voice, "far away in a little street there is a poor house. One of the windows is open, and through it I can see a woman seated at a table. Her face is thin and worn, and she has coarse, red hands, all pricked by the needle, for she is a seamstress. She is embroidering passion-flowers on a satin gown for the loveliest of the Queen's maids-of-honour to wear at the next Court-ball. In a bed in the corner of the room her little boy is lying ill. He has a fever, and is asking for oranges. His mother has nothing to give him but river water, so he is crying. Swallow, Swallow, little Swallow, will you not bring her the ruby out of my sword-hilt? My feet are fastened to this pedestal and I cannot move."

"I am waited for in Egypt," said the Swallow. "My friends are flying up and down the Nile, and talking to the large lotus-flowers. Soon they will go to sleep in the tomb of the great King. The King is there himself in his painted coffin. He is wrapped in yellow linen, and embalmed with spices. Round his neck is a chain of pale green jade, and his hands are like withered leaves."

"Swallow, Swallow, little Swallow," said the Prince, "will you not stay with me for one night, and be my messenger? The boy is so thirsty, and the mother so sad."

"I don't think I like boys," answered the Swallow. "Last summer, when I was staying on the river, there were two rude boys, the miller's sons, who were always throwing stones at me. They never hit me, of course; we swallows fly far too well for that, and besides, I come of a family famous for its agility; but still, it was a mark of disrespect." But the Happy Prince looked so sad that the little allow was sorry. "It is very cold here," he said; "but I will stay with you for one night, and be your messenger."

"Thank you, little Swallow," said the Prince.

So the Swallow picked out the great ruby from the Prince's sword, and flew away with it in his beak over the roofs of the town.

He passed by the cathedral tower, where the white marble angels were sculptured. He passed by the palace and heard the sound of dancing. A beautiful girl came out on the balcony with her lover.

"How wonderful the stars are," he said to her, "and how wonderful is the power of love!"

"I hope my dress will be ready in time for the State-ball," she answered; "I have ordered passion-flowers to be embroidered on it; but the seamstresses are so lazy."

He passed over the river, and saw the lanterns hanging to the masts of the ships. He passed over the Ghetto, and saw the old Jews bargaining with each other, and weighing out money in copper scales. At last he came to the poor house and looked in. The boy was tossing feverishly on his bed, and the mother had fallen asleep, she was so tired. In he hopped, and laid the great ruby on the table beside the woman's thimble. Then he flew gently round the bed, fanning the boy's forehead with his wings.

"How cool I feel," said the boy, "I must be getting better"; and he sank into a delicious slumber.

Then the Swallow flew back to the Happy Prince, and told him what he had done. "It is curious," he remarked, "but I feel quite warm now, although it is so cold."

"That is because you have done a good action," said the Prince.

And the little Swallow began to think, and then he fell asleep. Thinking always made him sleepy.

When day broke he flew down to the river and had a bath. "What a remarkable phenomenon," said the Professor of Ornithology as he was passing over the bridge. "A swallow in winter!" And he wrote a long letter about it to the local newspaper. Every one quoted it, and it was full of so many words that they could not understand.

"To-night I go to Egypt," said the Swallow, and he was in high spirits at the prospect. He visited all the public monuments, and sat a long time on top of the church steeple. Wherever he went the Sparrows chirruped, and said to each other, "What a distinguished stranger!" so he enjoyed himself very much.

When the moon rose he flew back to the Happy Prince. "Have you any commissions for Egypt?" he cried; "I am just starting."

"Swallow, Swallow, little Swallow," said the Prince, "will you not stay with me one night longer?"

"I am waited for in Egypt," answered the Swallow. "To-morrow my friends will fly up to the Second Cataract. The river-horse couches there among the bulrushes, and on a great granite throne sits the God Memnon. All night long he watches the stars, and when the morning star shines he utters one cry of joy, and then he is silent. At noon the yellow lions come down to the water's edge to drink. They have eyes like green beryls, and their roar is louder than the roar of the cataract."

"Swallow, Swallow, little Swallow," said the Prince, "far away across the city I see a young man in a garret. He is leaning over a desk covered with papers, and in a tumbler by his side there is a bunch of withered violets. His hair is brown and crisp, and his lips are red as a pomegranate, and he has large and dreamy eyes. He is trying to finish a play for the Director of the Theatre, but he is too cold to write any more. There is no fire in the grate, and hunger has made him faint."

"I will wait with you one night longer," said the Swallow, who really had a good heart. "Shall I take him another ruby?"

"Alas! I have no ruby now," said the Prince; "my eyes are all that I have left. They are made of rare sapphires, which were brought out of India a thousand years ago. Pluck out one of them and take it to him. He will sell it to the jeweller, and buy food and firewood, and finish his play."

"Dear Prince," said the Swallow, "I cannot do that"; and he began to weep.

"Swallow, Swallow, little Swallow," said the Prince, "do as I command you."

So the Swallow plucked out the Prince's eye, and flew away to the student's garret. It was easy enough to get in, as there was a hole in the roof. Through this he darted, and came into the room.

The young man had his head buried in his hands, so he did not hear the flutter of the bird's wings, and when he looked up he found the beautiful sapphire lying on the withered violets.

"I am beginning to be appreciated," he cried; "this is from some great admirer. Now I can finish my play," and he looked quite happy.

The next day the Swallow flew down to the harbour. He sat on the mast of a large vessel and watched the sailors hauling big chests out of the hold with ropes. "Heave a-hoy!" they shouted as each chest came up. "I am going to Egypt"! cried the Swallow, but nobody minded, and when the moon rose he flew back to the Happy Prince.

"I am come to bid you good-bye," he cried.

"Swallow, Swallow, little Swallow," said the Prince, "will you not stay with me one night longer?"

"It is winter," answered the Swallow, "and the chill snow will soon be here. In Egypt the sun is warm on the green palm-trees, and the crocodiles lie in the mud and look lazily about them. My companions are building a nest in the Temple of Baalbec, and the pink and white doves are watching them, and cooing to each other. Dear Prince, I must leave you, but I will never forget you, and next spring I will bring you back two beautiful jewels in place of those you have given away. The ruby shall be redder than a red rose, and the sapphire shall be as blue as the great sea."

"In the square below," said the Happy Prince, "there stands a little match-girl. She has let her matches fall in the gutter, and they are all spoiled. Her father will beat her if she does not bring home some money, and she is crying. She has no shoes or stockings, and her little head is bare. Pluck out my other eye, and give it to her, and her father will not beat her."

"I will stay with you one night longer," said the Swallow, "but I cannot pluck out your eye. You would be quite blind then."

"Swallow, Swallow, little Swallow," said the Prince, "do as I command you."

So he plucked out the Prince's other eye, and darted down with it. He swooped past the match-girl, and slipped the jewel into the palm of her hand. "What a lovely bit of glass," cried the little girl; and she ran home, laughing. Then the Swallow came back to the Prince.

"You are blind now," he said, "so I will stay with you always."

"No, little Swallow," said the poor Prince, "you must go away to Egypt."

"I will stay with you always," said the Swallow, and he slept at the Prince's feet.

All the next day he sat on the Prince's shoulder, and told him stories of what he had seen in strange lands. He told him of the red ibises, who stand in long rows on the banks of the Nile, and catch gold-fish in their beaks; of the Sphinx, who is as old as the world itself, and lives in the desert, and knows everything; of the merchants, who walk slowly by the side of their camels, and carry amber beads in their hands; of the King of the Mountains of the Moon, who is as black as ebony, and worships a large crystal; of the great green snake that sleeps in a palm-tree, and has twenty priests to feed it with honey-cakes; and of the pygmies who sail over a big lake on large flat leaves, and are always at war with the butterflies.

"Dear little Swallow," said the Prince, "you tell me of marvelous things, but more marvellous than anything is the suffering of men and of women. There is no Mystery so great as Misery. Fly over my city, little Swallow, and tell me what you see there."

So the Swallow flew over the great city, and saw the rich making merry in their beautiful houses, while the beggars were sitting at the gates. He flew into dark lanes, and saw the white faces of starving children looking out listlessly at the black streets. Under the archway of a bridge two little boys were lying in one another's arms to try and keep themselves warm. "How hungry we are!" they said. "You must not lie here," shouted the Watchman, and they wandered out into the rain. Then he flew back and told the Prince what he had seen.

"I am covered with fine gold," said the Prince, "you must take it off, leaf by leaf, and give it to my poor; the living always think that gold can make them happy."

Leaf after leaf of the fine gold the Swallow picked off, till the Happy Prince looked quite dull and grey. Leaf after leaf of the fine gold he brought to the poor, and the children's faces grew rosier, and they laughed and played games in the street. "We have bread now!" they cried.

Then the snow came, and after the snow came the frost. The streets looked as if they were made of silver, they were so bright and glistening; long icicles like crystal daggers hung down from the eaves of the houses, everybody went about in furs, and the little boys wore scarlet caps and skated on the ice.

The poor little Swallow grew colder and colder, but he would not leave the Prince, he loved him too well. He picked up crumbs outside the baker's door when the baker was not looking and tried to keep himself warm by flapping his wings. But at last he knew that he was going to die. He had just strength to fly up to the Prince's shoulder once more.

"Good-bye, dear Prince!" he murmured, "will you let me kiss your hand?"

"I am glad that you are going to Egypt at last, little Swallow," said the Prince, "you have stayed too long here; but you must kiss me on the lips, for I love you."

"It is not to Egypt that I am going," said the Swallow. "I am going to the House of Death. Death is the brother of Sleep, is he not?"

And he kissed the Happy Prince on the lips, and fell down dead at his feet. At that moment a curious crack sounded inside the statue, as if something had broken. The fact is that the leaden heart had snapped right in two. It certainly was a dreadfully hard frost.

Early the next morning the Mayor was walking in the square below in company with the Town Councillors. As they passed the column he looked up at the statue: "Dear me! how shabby the Happy Prince looks!" he said.

"How shabby indeed!" cried the Town Councillors, who always agreed with the Mayor; and they went up to look at it.

"The ruby has fallen out of his sword, his eyes are gone, and he is golden no longer," said the Mayor in fact, "he is litttle better than a beggar!"

"Little better than a beggar," said the Town Councillors.

"And here is actually a dead bird at his feet!" continued the Mayor. "We must really issue a proclamation that birds are not to be allowed to die here." And the Town Clerk made a note of the suggestion.

So they pulled down the statue of the Happy Prince. "As he is no longer beautiful he is no longer useful," said the Art Professor at the University.

Then they melted the statue in a furnace, and the Mayor held a meeting of the Corporation to decide what was to be done with the metal. "We must have another statue, of course," he said, "and it shall be a statue of myself."

"Of myself," said each of the Town Councillors, and they quarrelled. When I last heard of them they were quarrelling still.

"What a strange thing!" said the overseer of the workmen at the foundry. "This broken lead heart will not melt in the furnace. We must throw it away." So they threw it on a dust-heap where the dead Swallow was also lying.

"Bring me the two most precious things in the city," said God to one of His Angels; and the Angel brought Him the leaden heart and the dead bird.

"You have rightly chosen," said God, "for in my garden of Paradise this little bird shall sing for evermore, and in my city of gold the Happy Prince shall praise me."

III. Reading Tasks

1. What fables do you like best? What are the characteristics of fables?
2. Was the happy prince really happy? Why?
3. What is your opinion on "Art's for art's sake"?

Unit 14

The Horse Dealer's Daughter

I. Introduction

1. The author

David Herbert Lawrence (1885-1930), son of a coal miner, was born at the colliery village of Eastwood, Nottinghamshire. At 13, he entered Nottingham High school with a scholarship. Leaving at 16, he was a clerk for a short time and then worked as a pupil teacher. Two years later, he entered the University College of Nottingham. Meanwhile he had begun to write verse. With the publication of his first novel *The White Peacock* in 1911, he decided to live by literature. His second novel *The Trespasser* appeared in 1912 and his first collection of poems and another novel *Sons and Lovers* in 1913. In 1914, he married the wife of Professor Ernest Weekley of Nottingham, who was a German. During the First World War, they lived a nomadic, gypsying life, wandering restlessly about England and Europe as objects of deep suspicion. But in this period, Lawrence did a good deal of work and made the literary acquaintance with John Middleton Murry, Katherine Mansfield, Herbert Asquith, etc. In 1914, he published a book of short stories *The Prussian Officer*; in 1915 appeared *The Rainbow* which was banned as obscene. After that followed a travel book, a volume of verse and a series of other novels, among which were *Aaron's Rod*(1922), *Kangaroo* (1923), and *The Plumed Serpent* (1926). In these novels he tried to search for his solution to the capitalist chaos by eulogying the primitivism of the Mexican Indians and the mysticism of the ancient world untouched by bourgeois civilization. In 1928, he finished *Lady Chatterley's Lover*, an account of sexual relations of a high born lady with a gamekeeper. The book was prohibited in both England and the United States. Only after his death did its expurgated edition appeared (1932). But the full text did not come out until around the end of the sixties, when it was the subject of a sensational court case on the justification of the use of sex words in the novel. The manuscript of his poems *Pansies* was confiscated on the same account. After a desperate struggle for life for several years, he died of tuberculosis at Vence in France at the age of 44.

D. H. Lawrence was an important and controversial 20th-century English novelist. He attacked capitalism but also negated socialism. He was criticized for his insistence on the physical aspects of sex in his writings, but his powers as a novelist of deep psychological insight and minute descriptions are apparent.

II. Text

The Horse Dealer's Daughter

"Well, Mabel, and what are you going to do with yourself?" asked Joe, with foolish flippancy. He felt quite safe himself. Without listening for an answer, he turned aside, worked a grain of tobacco to the tip of his tongue, and spat it out. He did not care about anything, since he felt safe himself.

The three brothers and the sister sat round the desolate breakfast table, attempting some sort of desultory consultation. The morning's post had given the final tap to the family fortunes, and all was over. The dreary dining-room itself, with its heavy mahogany furniture, looked as if it were waiting to be done away with.

But the consultation amounted to nothing. There was a strange air of ineffectuality about the three men, as they sprawled at table, smoking and reflecting vaguely on their own condition. The girl was alone, a rather short, sullen-looking young woman of twenty-seven. She did not share the same life as her brothers. She would have been good-looking, save for the impassive fixity of her face, "bull-dog", as her brothers called it.

There was a confused tramping of horses' feet outside. The three men all sprawled round in their chairs to watch. Beyond the dark holly-bushes that separated the strip of lawn from the highroad, they could see a cavalcade of shire horses swinging out of their own yard, being taken for exercise. This was the last time. These were the last horses that would go through their hands. The young men watched with critical, callous look. They were all frightened at the collapse of their lives, and the sense of disaster in which they were involved left them no inner freedom.

Yet they were three fine, well-set fellows enough. Joe, the eldest, was a man of thirty-three, broad and handsome in a hot, flushed way. His face was red, he twisted his black moustache over a thick finger, his eyes were shallow and restless. He had a sensual way of uncovering his teeth when he laughed, and his bearing was stupid. Now he watched the horses with a glazed look of helplessness in his eyes, a certain stupor of downfall.

The great draught-horses swung past. They were tied head to tail, four of them, and they heaved along to where a lane branched off from the highroad, planting their great hoofs floutingly in the fine black mud, swinging their great rounded haunches sumptuously, and trotting a few sudden steps as they were led into the lane, round the corner. Every movement showed a massive, slumberous strength, and a stupidity which held them in subjection. The groom at the head looked back, jerking the leading rope. And the cavalcade moved out of sight up the lane, the tail of the last horse, bobbed up light and stiff, held out taut from the swinging great haunches as they rocked behind the hedges in a motion - like sleep.

Joe watched with glazed hopeless eyes. The horses were almost like his own body to him. He felt he was done for now. Luckily he was engaged to a woman as old as himself, and therefore her father, who was steward of a neighbouring estate, would provide him with a job. He would marry and go into harness. His life was over, he would be a subject animal now.

He turned uneasily aside the retreating steps of the horses echoing in his ears. Then, with foolish restlessness, he reached for the scraps of bacon-rind from the plates, and making a faint whistling sound, flung them to the terrier that lay against the fender. He watched the dog swallow them, and waited till the creature looked into his eyes. Then a faint grin came on his face, and in a high, foolish voice he said:

"You won't get much more bacon, shall you, you little b-?"

The dog faintly and dismally wagged its tail, then lowered its haunches, circled round, and lay down again.

There was another helpless silence at the table. Joe sprawled uneasily in his seat, not willing to go till the family conclave was dissolved. Fred Henry, the second brother, was erect, clean-limbed, alert. He had watched the passing of the horses with more sang-froid. If he was an animal, like Joe, he was an animal which controls, not one which is controlled. He was master of any horse, and he carried himself with a well-tempered air of mastery. But he was not master of the situations of life. He pushed his coarse brown moustache upwards, off his lip, and glanced irritably at his sister, who sat impassive and inscrutable.

"You'll go and stop with Lucy for a bit, shan't you?" he asked. The girl did not answer.

"I don't see what else you can do," persisted Fred Henry.

"Go as a skivvy," Joe interpolated laconically.

The girl did not move a muscle.

"If I was her, I should go in for training for a nurse," said Malcolm, the youngest of them all. He was the baby of the family, a young man of twenty-two, with a fresh, jaunty museau.

But Mabel did not take any notice of him. They had talked at her and round her for so many years, that she hardly heard them at all.

The marble clock on the mantel-piece softly chimed the half-hour, the dog rose uneasily from the hearthrug and looked at the party at the breakfast table. But still they sat on in ineffectual conclave.

"Oh, all right," said Joe suddenly, apropos of nothing. "I'll get a move on."

He pushed back his chair, straddled his knees with a downward jerk, to get them free, in horsy fashion, and went to the fire. Still he did not go out of the room; he was curious to know what the others would do or say. He began to charge his pipe, looking down at the dog and saying, in a high, affected voice:

"Going wi' me? Going wi' me are ter? Tha'rt goin' further than tha counts on just now, dost hear?"

The dog faintly wagged its tail, the man stuck out his jaw and covered his pipe with his hands, and puffed intently, losing himself in the tobacco, looking down all the while at the dog with an absent brown eye. The dog looked up at him in mournful distrust. Joe stood with his knees stuck out, in real horsy fashion.

"Have you had a letter from Lucy?" Fred Henry asked of his sister.

"Last week," came the neutral reply.

"And what does she say?"

There was no answer.

"Does she ask you to go and stop there?" persisted Fred Henry.

"She says I can if I like."

"Well, then, you'd better. Tell her you'll come on Monday."

This was received in silence.

"That's what you'll do then, is it?" said Fred Henry, in some exasperation.

But she made no answer. There was a silence of futility and irritation in the room. Malcolm grinned fatuously.

"You'll have to make up your mind between now and next Wednesday," said Joe loudly, "or else find yourself lodgings on the curbstone."

The face of the young woman darkened, but she sat on immutable.

"Here's Jack Fergusson!" exclaimed Malcolm, who was looking aimlessly out of the window.

"Where?" exclaimed Joe, loudly.

"Just gone past."

"Coming in?"

Malcolm craned his neck to see the gate.

"Yes," he said.

There was a silence. Mabel sat on like one condemned, at the head of the table. Then a whistle was heard from the kitchen. The dog got up and barked sharply. Joe opened the door and shouted:

"Come on."

After a moment a young man entered. He was muffled up in overcoat and a purple woollen scarf, and his tweed cap, which he did not remove, was pulled down on his head. He was of medium height, his face was rather long and pale, his eyes looked tired.

"Hello, Jack! Well, Jack!" exclaimed Malcolm and Joe. Fred Henry merely said, "Jack."

"What's doing?" asked the newcomer, evidently addressing Fred Henry.

"Same. We've got to be out by Wednesday. Got a cold?"

"I have — got it bad, too."

"Why don't you stop in?"

"Me slop in? When I can't stand on my legs, perhaps I shall have a chance." The young man spoke huskily. He had a slight Scotch accent.

"It's a knock-out, isn't it," said Joe, boisterously, "if a doctor goes round croaking with a cold. Looks bad for the patients, doesn't it?"

The young doctor looked at him slowly.

"Anything the matter with you, then?" he asked sarcastically.

"Not as I know of. Damn your eyes, I hope not. Why?"

"I thought you were very concerned about the patients, wondered if you might be one yourself."

"Damn it, no, I've never been patient to no flaming doctor, and hope I never shall be," returned Joe.

At this point Mabel rose from the table, and they all seemed to become aware of her existence. She began putting the dishes together. The young doctor looked at her, but did not address her. He had not greeted her. She went out of the room with the tray, her face impassive and unchanged.

"When are you off then, all of you?" asked the doctor.

"I'm catching the eleven-forty," replied Malcolm.

"Are you goin' down wi' th' trap, Joe?"

"Yes, I've told you I'm going down wi' th' trap, haven't I?"

"We'd better be getting her in then. So long, Jack, if I don't see you before I go," said Malcolm, shaking hands.

He went out, followed by Joe, who seemed to have his tail between his legs.

"Well, this is the devil's own," exclaimed the doctor, when he was left alone with Fred Henry. "Going before Wednesday, are you?"

"That's the orders," replied the other.

"Where, to Northampton?"

"The devil!" exclaimed Fergusson, with quiet chagrin.

And there was silence between the two.

"All settled up, are you?" asked Fergusson.

"About."

There was another pause.

"Well, I shall miss you, Freddy, boy," said the young doctor.

"And I shall miss thee. Jack," returned the other.

"Miss you like hell," mused the doctor.

Fred Henry turned aside. There was nothing to say. Mabel came in again, to finish clearing the table.

"What are you going to do, then. Miss Pervin? " asked Fergusson. "Going to your sister's, are you?"

Mabel looked at him with her steady, dangerous eyes, that always made him uncomfortable, unsettling his superficial ease.

"No," she said.

"Well, what in the name of fortune are you going to do? Say what you mean to do," cried Fred Henry, with futile intensity.

But she only averted her head, and continued her work. She folded the white table-cloth, and put on the chenille cloth.

"The sulkiest bitch that ever trod!" muttered her brother.

But she finished her task with perfectly impassive face, the young doctor watching her interestedly all the while. Then she went out.

Fred Henry stared after her, clenching his lips, his blue eyes fixing in sharp antagonism, as he made a grimace of sour exasperation.

"You could bray her into bits, and that's all you'd get out of her," he said, in a small, narrowed tone.

The doctor smiled faintly.

"What's she going to do, then?" he asked.

"Strike me if I know!" returned the other.

There was a pause. Then the doctor stirred.

"I'll be seeing you tonight, shall I?" he said to his friend.

"Ay — where's it to be? Are we going over to Jessdale?"

"I don't know. I've got such a cold on me. I'll come round to the Moon and Stars, anyway."

"Let Lizzie and May miss their night for once, eh?"

"That's it — if I feel as I do now."

"All's one — "

The two young men went through the passage and down to the back door together. The house was large, but it was servantless now, and desolate. At the back was a small bricked house-yard, and beyond that a big square, graveled fine and red, and having stables on two sides. Sloping, dank, winter-dark fields stretched away on the open sides.

But the stables were empty. Joseph Pervin, the father of the family, had been a man of no education, who had become a fairly large horse dealer. The stables had been full of horses, there was a great turmoil and come-and-go of horses and of dealers and grooms. Then the kitchen was full of servants. But of late things had declined. The old man had married a second time, to retrieve his fortunes. Now he was dead and everything was gone to the dogs, there was nothing but debt and threatening.

For months, Mabel had been servantless in the big house, keeping the home together in penury for her ineffectual brothers. She had kept house for ten years. But previously, it was with unstinted means. Then, however brutal and coarse everything was, the sense of money had kept her proud, confident. The men might be foul-mouthed, the women in the kitchen might have bad reputations, her brothers might have illegitimate children. But so long as there was money, the girl fell herself established, and brutally proud, reserved.

No company came to the house, save dealers and coarse men. Mabel had no associates of her own sex, after her sister went away. But she did not mind. She went regularly to church, she attended to her father. And she lived in the memory of her mother, who had died when she was fourteen, and whom she had loved. She had loved her father, too, in a different way, depending upon him, and feeling secure in him, until at the age of fifty-four he married again. And then she had set hard against him. Now he had died and left them all hopelessly in debt.

She had suffered badly during the period of poverty. Nothing, however, could shake the curious sullen, animal pride that dominated each member of the family. Now, for Mabel, the end had come. Still she would not cast about her. She would follow her own way just the same. She would always hold the keys of her own situation. Mindless and persistent, she endured from day to day. Why should she think? Why should she answer anybody? It was enough that this was the end, and there was no way out. She need not pass any more darkly along the main street of the small town, avoiding every eye. She need not demean herself any more, going into the shops and buying the cheapest food. This was at an end. She thought of nobody, not even of herself. Mindless and persistent, she seemed in a sort of ecstasy to be coming nearer to her fulfillment, her own glorification, approaching her dead mother, who was glorified.

In the afternoon she took a little bag, with shears and sponge and a small scrubbing brush, and went out. It was a grey, wintry day, with saddened, dark-green fields and an atmosphere blackened by the smoke of foundries not far off. She went quickly, darkly along the causeway, heeding nobody, through the town to the churchyard.

There she always felt secure, as if no one could see her, although as a matter of fact she was exposed to the stare of everyone who passed along under the churchyard wall. Nevertheless, once under the shadow of the great looming church, among the graves, she felt immune from the world, reserved within the thick churchyard wall as in another country.

Carefully she clipped the grass from the grave, and arranged the pinky-white, small chrysanthemums in the tin cross. When this was done, she took an empty jar from a neighbouring grave, brought water, and carefully, most scrupulously sponged the marble headstone and the coping-stone.

It gave her sincere satisfaction to do this. She felt in immediate contact with the world of her mother. She took minute pains, went through the park in a state bordering on pure happiness, as if in performing this task she came into a subtle, intimate connexion with her mother. For the life she followed here in the world was far less real than the world of death she inherited from her mother.

The doctor's house was just by the church. Fergusson, being a mere hired assistant, was slave to the countryside.

As he hurried now to attend to the outpatients in the surgery, glancing across the graveyard with his quick eye, he saw the girl at her task at the grave. She seemed so intent and remote, it was like looking into another world. Some mystical element was touched in him. He slowed down as he walked, watching her as if spell-bound.

She lifted her eyes, feeling him looking. Their eyes met. And each looked again at once, each feeling, in some way, found out by the other. He lifted his cap and passed on down the road. There remained distinct in his consciousness, like a vision, the memory of her face, lifted from the tombstone in the churchyard, and looking at him with slow, large, portentous eyes. It was portentous, her face. It seemed to mesmerize him. There was a heavy power in her eyes which laid hold of his whole being, as if he had drunk some powerful drug. He had been feeling weak and done before. Now the life came back into him, he felt delivered from his own fretted, daily self.

He finished his duties at the surgery as quickly as might be, hastily filling up the bottles of the waiting people with cheap drugs. Then, in perpetual haste, he set off again to visit several cases in another part of his round, before teatime. At all times he preferred to walk, if he could, but particularly when he was not well. He fancied the motion restored him.

The afternoon was falling. It was grey, deadened, and wintry, with a slow, moist, heavy coldness sinking in and deadening all the faculties. But why should he think or notice? He hastily climbed the hill and turned across the dark-green fields, following the black cinder-tract. In the distance, across a shallow dip in the country, the small town was clustered like smouldering ash, a tower, a spire, a heap of low, raw, extinct houses. And on the nearest fringe of the town, sloping into the dip, was Oldmeadow, the Pervins' house. He could see the stables and the outbuildings distinctly, as they lay towards him on the slope. Well, he would not go there many more times! Another resource would be lost to him, another place gone: the only company he cared for in the alien, ugly little town he was losing. Nothing but work, drudgery, constant hastening from dwelling to dwelling among the colliers and the iron-workers. It wore him out, but at the same time he had a craving for it. It was a stimulant to him to be in the homes of the working people, moving as it were through the innermost body of their life. His nerves were excited and gratified. He could come so near, into the very lives of the rough, inarticulate, powerfully emotional men and women. He grumbled, he said he hated the hellish hole. But as a matter of fact it excited him, the contact with the rough, strongly-feeling people was a stimulant applied direct to his nerves.

Below Oldmeadow, in the green, shallow, soddened hollow of fields, lay a square, deep pond. Roving across the landscape, the doctor's quick eye detected a figure in black passing through the gate of the field, down towards the pond. He looked again. It would be Mabel Pervin. His mind suddenly became alive and attentive.

Why was she going down there? He pulled up on the path on the slope above, and stood staring. He could just make sure of the small black figure moving in the hollow of the failing day. He seemed to see her in the midst of such obscurity, that he was like a clairvoyant, seeing rather with the mind's eye than with ordinary sight. Yet he could see her positively enough, whilst he kept his eye attentive. He felt, if he looked away from her, in the thick, ugly falling dusk, he would lose her altogether.

He followed her minutely as she moved, direct and intent, like something transmitted rather than stirring in voluntary activity, straight down the field towards the pond. There she stood on the bank for a moment. She never raised her head. Then she waded slowly into the water.

He stood motionless as the small black figure walked slowly and deliberately towards the centre of the pond, very slowly, gradually moving deeper into the motionless water, and still moving forward as the water got up to her breast. Then he could see her no more in the dusk of the dead afternoon.

"There!" he exclaimed. "Would you believe it?"

And he hastened straight down, running over the wet, soddened fields, pushing through the hedges, down into the depression of callous wintry obscurity. It took him several minutes to come to the pond. He stood on the bank, breathing heavily. He could see nothing. His eyes seemed to penetrate the dead water. Yes, perhaps that was the dark shadow of her black clothing beneath the surface of the water.

He slowly ventured into the pond. The bottom was deep, soft clay, he sank in, and the water clasped dead cold round his legs. As he stirred he could smell the cold, rotten clay that fouled up into the water. It was objectionable in his lungs. Still, repelled and yet not heeding, he moved deeper into the pond. The cold water rose over his thighs, over his loins, upon his abdomen. The lower part of his body was all sunk in the hideous cold element. And the bottom was so deeply soft and uncertain, he was afraid of pitching with his mouth underneath. He could not swim, and was afraid.

He crouched a little, spreading his hands under the water and moving them round, trying to feel for her. The dead cold pond swayed upon his chest. He moved again, a little deeper, and again, with his hands underneath, he felt all around under the water. And he touched her clothing. But it evaded his fingers. He made a desperate effort to grasp it.

And so doing he lost his balance and went under, horribly, suffocating in the foul earthy water, struggling madly for a few moments. At last, after what seemed an eternity, he got his footing, rose again into the air and looked around. He gasped, and knew he was in the world. Then he looked at the water. She has risen near him. He grasped her clothing, and drawing her nearer, turned to take his way to land again.

He went very slowly, carefully, absorbed in the slow progress. He rose higher, climbing out of the pond. The water was now only about his legs; he was thankful, full of relief to be out of the clutches of the pond. He lifted her and staggered on to the bank, out of the horror of wet, grey clay.

He laid her down on the bank. She was quite unconscious and running with water. He made the water come from her mouth, he worked to restore her. He did not have to work very long before he could feel the breathing begin again in her; she was breathing naturally. He worked a little longer. He could feel her live beneath his hands; she was coming back. He wiped her face, wrapped her in his overcoat, looked round into the dim, dark-grey world, then lifted her and staggered down the bank and across the fields.

It seemed an unthinkably long way, and his burden so heavy he felt he would never get to the house. But at last he was in the stable-yard, and then in the house-yard. He opened the door and went into the house. In the kitchen he laid her down on the hearthrug, and called. The house was empty. But the fire was burning in the grate.

Then again he kneeled to attend to her. She was breathing regularly, her eyes were wide open and as if conscious, but there seemed something missing in her look. She was conscious in herself, but unconscious of her surroundings. He ran upstairs, took blankets from a bed, and put them before the fire to warm. Then he removed her saturated, earthy-smelling clothing, rubbed her dry with a towel, and wrapped her naked in the blankets. Then he went into the dining-room, to look for spirits. There was a little whisky. He drank a gulp himself, and put some into her mouth.

The effect was instantaneous. She looked full into his face, as if she had been seeing him for some time, and yet had only just become conscious of him.

"Dr. Fergusson?" she said.

"What?" he answered.

He was divesting himself of his coat, intending to find some dry clothing upstairs. He could not bear the smell of the dead, clayey water, and he was mortally afraid for his own health.

"What did I do?" she asked.

"Walked into the pond," he replied. He had begun to shudder like one sick, and could hardly attend to her. Her eyes remained full on him, he seemed to be going dark in his mind, looking back at her helplessly. The shuddering became quieter in him, his life came back in him, dark and unknowing, but strong again.

"Was I out of my mind?" she asked, while her eyes were fixed on him all the time.

"Maybe, for the moment," he replied. He fell quiet, because his strength had come back. The strange fretful strain had left him.

"Am I out of my mind now?" she asked.

"Are you?" he reflected a moment. "No," he answered truthfully, "I don't see that you are." He turned his face aside. He was afraid now, because he felt dazed, and felt dimly that her power was stronger than his, in this issue.

And she continued to look at him fixedly all the time. "Can you tell me where I shall find some dry things to put on?" he asked.

"Did you dive into the pond for me?" she asked.

"No," he answered. "I walked in. But I went in overhead as well."

There was silence for a moment. He hesitated. He very much wanted to go upstairs to get into dry clothing. But there was another desire in him. And she seemed to hold him. His will seemed to have gone to sleep, and left him, standing there slack before her. But he fell warm inside himself. He did not shudder at all, though his clothes were sodden on him.

"Why did you?" she asked.

"Because I didn't want you to do such a foolish thing," he said.

"It wasn't foolish," she said, still gazing at him as she lay on the floor, with a sofa cushion under her head. "It was the right thing to do. I knew best, then."

"I'll go and shift these wet things," he said. But still he had not the power to move out of her presence, until she sent him. It was as if she had the life of his body in her hands, and he could not extricate himself. Or perhaps he did not want to.

Suddenly she sat up. Then she became aware of her own immediate condition. She felt the blankets about her, she knew her own limbs. For a moment it seemed as if her reason were going. She looked round, with wild eye, as if seeking something. He stood still with fear. She saw her clothing lying scattered.

"Who undressed me? " she asked, her eyes resting full and inevitable on his face.

"I did," he replied, "to bring you round."

For some moments she sat and gazed at him awfully, her lips parted.

"Do you love me then?" she asked.

He only stood and stared at her, fascinated. His soul seemed to melt.

She shuffled forward on her knees, and put her arms round him, round his legs, as he stood there, pressing her breasts against his knees and thighs, clutching him with strange, convulsive certainly, pressing his thighs against her, drawing him to her face, her throat, as she looked up at him with flaring, humble eyes, of transfiguration, triumphant in first possession.

"You love me," she murmured, in strange transport, yearning and triumphant and confident. "You love me. I know you love me, I know."

And she was passionately kissing his knees, through the wet clothing, passionately and indiscriminately kissing his knees, his legs, as if unaware of everything.

He looked down at the tangled wet hair, the wild, bare, animal shoulders. He was amazed, bewildered, and afraid. He had never thought of loving her. He had never wanted to love her. When he rescued her and restored her, he was a doctor, and she was a patient. He had had no single personal thought other. Nay, this introduction of the personal element was very distasteful to him, a violation of his professional honour. It was horrible to have her there embracing his knees. It was horrible. He revolted from it, violently. And yet — and yet — he had not the power to break away.

She looked at him again, with the same supplication of powerful love, and that same transcendent, frightening light of triumph. In view of the delicate flame which seemed to come from her face like a light, he was powerless. And yet he had never intended to love her. He had never intended. And something stubborn in him could not give way.

"You love me," she repeated, in a murmur of deep, rhapsodic assurance. "You love me."

Her hands were drawing him, drawing him down to her. He was afraid, even a little horrified. For he had, really, no intention of loving her. Yet her hands were drawing him towards her. He put out his hand quickly to steady himself, and grasped her bare shoulder. A flame seemed to burn the hand that grasped her soft shoulder. He had no intention of loving her: his whole will was against his yielding. It was horrible. And yet wonderful was the touch of her shoulders, beautiful the shining of her face. Was she perhaps mad? He had a horror of yielding to her. Yet something in him ached also.

He had been staring away at the door, away from her. But his hand remained on her shoulder. She had gone suddenly very still. He looked down at her. Her eyes were now wide with fear, with doubt, the light was dying from her face, a shadow of terrible greyness was returning. He could not bear the touch of her eyes' question upon him, and the look of death behind the question.

With an inward groan he gave way, and let his heart yield towards her. A sudden gentle smile came on his face. And her eyes, which never left his face, slowly, slowly filled with tears. He watched the strange water rise in her eyes, like some slow fountain coiming up. And his heart seemed to burn and melt away in his breast.

He could not bear to look at her any more. He dropped on his knees and caught her head with his arms and pressed her face against his throat. She was very still. His heart, which seemed to have broken, was burning with a kind of agony in his breast. And he felt her slow, hot tears wetting his throat. But he could not move.

He felt the hot tears wet his neck and the hollows of his neck, and he remained motionless, suspended through one of man's eternities. Only now it had become indispensable to him to have her face pressed close to him; he could never let her go again. He could never let her head go away from the close clutch of his arm. He wanted to remain like that for ever, with his heart hurting him in a pain that was also life to him. Without knowing, he was looking down on her damp, soft brown hair.

Then, as it were suddenly, he smelt the horrid stagnant smell of that water. And at the same moment she drew away from him and looked at him. Her eyes were wistful and unfathomable. He was afraid of them, and he fell to kissing her, not knowing what he was doing. He wanted her eyes not to have that terrible, wistful, unfathomable look.

When she turned her face to him again, a faint delicate flush was glowing, and there was again dawning that terrible shining of joy in her eyes, which really terrified him, and yet which he now wanted to see, because he feared the look of doubt still more.

"You love me?" she said, rather faltering.

"Yes." The word cost him a painful effort. Not because it wasn't true. But because it was too newly true, the saying seemed to tear open again his newly-torn heart.

She lifted her face to him, and he bent forward and kissed her on the mouth, gently, with the one kiss that is an eternal pledge. And as he kissed her his heart strained again in his breast. He never intended to love her. But now it was over. He had crossed over the gulf to her, and all that he had left behind had shriveled and become void.

After the kiss, her eyes again slowly filled with tears. She sat still, away from him, with her face drooped aside, and her hands folded in her lap. The tears fell very slowly. There was complete silence. He too sat there motionless and silent on the hearthrug. The strange pain of his heart that was broken seemed to consume him. That he should love her? That this was love! That he should be ripped open in this way! — Him, a doctor! — How they would all jeer if they knew! — It was agony to him to think they might know.

In the curious naked pain of the thought he looked again to her. She was sitting there drooped into a muse. He saw a tear fall, and his heart flared hot. He saw for the first time that one of her shoulders was quite uncovered, one arm bare, he could see one of her small breasts; dimly, because it had become almost dark in the room.

"Why are you crying?" he asked, in an altered voice.

She looked up at him, and behind her tears the consciousness of her situation for the first time brought a dark look of shame to her eyes.

"I'm not crying, really," she said, watching him half frightened.

He reached his hand, and softly closed it on her bare arm.

"I love you! I love you!" he said in a soft, low vibrating voice, unlike himself.

She shrank, and dropped her head. The soft, penetrating grip of his hand on her arm distressed her. She looked up at him.

"I want to go," she said. "I want to go and get you some dry things."

"Why?" he said. "I'm all right."

"But I want to go," she said. "And I want you to change your things."

He released her arm, and she wrapped herself in the blanket, looking at him rather frightened. And still she did not rise.

"Kiss me," she said wistfully.

He kissed her, but briefly, half in anger.

Then, after a second, she rose nervously, all mixed up in the blanket. He watched her in her confusion, as she tried to extricate herself and wrap herself up so that she could walk. He watched her relentlessly, as she knew. And as she went, the blanket trailing, and as he saw a glimpse of her feet and her white leg, he tried to remember her as she was when he had wrapped her in the blanket. But then he didn't want to remember, because she had been nothing to him then, and his nature revolted from remembering her as she was when she was nothing to him.

A tumbling, muffled noise from within the dark house startled him. Then he heard her voice: — "There are clothes." He rose and went to the foot of the stairs, and gathered up the garments she had thrown down. Then he came back to the fire, to rub himself down and dress. He grinned at his own appearance when he had finished.

The fire was sinking, so he put on coat. The house was now quite dark, save for the light of a street-lamp that shone in faintly from beyond the holly trees. He lit the gas with matches he found on the mantel-piece. Then he emptied the pockets of his own clothes, and threw all his wet things in a heap into the scullery. After which he gathered up her sodden clothes, gently, and put them in a separate heap on the copper-top in the scullery.

It was six o'clock on the clock. His own watch had stopped. He ought to go back to the surgery. He waited, and still she did not come down. So he went to the foot of the stairs and called:

"I shall have to go."

Almost immediately he heard her coming down. She had on her best dress of black voile, and her hair was tidy, but still damp. She looked at him — and in spite of herself, smiled.

"I don't like you in those clothes," she said.

"Do I look a sight?" he answered.

They were shy of one another.

"I'll make yon some tea," she said.

"No, I must go."

"Must you?" And she looked at him again with the wide, strained, doubtful eyes. And again, from the pain of his breast, he knew how he loved her. He went and bent to kiss her, gently, passionately, with his heart's painful kiss.

"And my hair smells so horrible," she murmured in distraction. "And I'm so awful, I'm so awful! Oh, no, I'm too awful." And she broke into bitter, heart-broken sobbing. "You can't want to love me, I'm horrible."

"Don't be silly, don't be silly," he said, trying to comfort her, kissing her, holding her in his arms. "I want you, I want to marry you, we're going to be married, quickly, quickly — tomorrow if I can."

But she only sobbed terribly, and cried:

"I feel awful. I feel awful. I feel I'm horrible to you."

"No, I want you, I want you," was all he answered, blindly, with that terrible intonation which frightened her almost more than her horror lest he should not want her.

III. Reading Tasks

1. Why was Mabel silent and indifferent? What actually led her to suicide?

2. What means does the writer adopt to reveal Mabel's indifference? Cite some examples from the story and explain their effects.

3. Do you think the love between Mabel and Fergusson was well-founded? Which was more in Fergusson, sympathy or affection on Mabel?

Unit 15

Harry Potter and the Sorcerer's Stone

I. Introduction

1. The author

J.K. Rowling, born at Yate, England on 31 July 1965, is best known as the author of the seven Harry Potter books, which were published between 1997 and 2007. The enduringly popular adventures of Harry, Ron and Hermione have gone on to sell over 500 million copies, be translated into over 80 languages and made into eight blockbuster films. The Harry Potter books have gained recognition for sparking an interest in reading among the young at a time when children were thought to be abandoning books for computers and television, although the series' overall impact on children's reading habits has been questioned. Alongside the Harry Potter series, she also wrote three short companion volumes for charity: *Quidditch Through the Ages* and *Fantastic Beasts and Where to Find Them*, in aid of Comic Relief and Lumos, and *The Tales of Beedle the Bard*, in aid of Lumos. J.K. Rowling collaborated with playwright Jack Thorne and director John Tiffany to continue Harry's story in a stage play, *Harry Potter and the Cursed Child*, which opened in London in 2016 and is now playing worldwide. In the same year, she made her debut as a screenwriter with the film *Fantastic Beasts and Where to Find Them*, the first in a series featuring Magizoologist Newt Scamander, which was inspired by the original companion volume. J.K. Rowling has also written a standalone novel, *The Casual Vacancy*, and is the author of the Strike crime series under the pseudonym Robert Galbraith. Both have been adapted for television. In 2020 J.K. Rowling returned to publishing for younger children with the fairy tale *The Ickabog*, the royalties from which she is donating to groups affected by the Covid-19 pandemic. Her latest children's novel *The Christmas Pig*, a standalone adventure story, was published in 2021. She has received many awards and honours, including an OBE and a Companion of Honour for services to literature and philanthropy. She lives in Scotland with her family.

Harry Potter books include:

1. Harry Potter and the Sorcerer's Stone (1997)
2. Harry Potter and the Chamber of Secrets (1998)
3. Harry Potter and the Prisoner of Azkaban (1999)
4. Harry Potter and the Goblet of Fire (2000)
5. Harry Potter and the Order of the Phoenix (2003)
6. Harry Potter and the Half-Blood Prince (2005)
7. Harry Potter and the Deathly Hallows (2007)
8. Harry Potter and the Cursed Child (2016)

2. The story

The novels revolve around Harry Potter, an orphan who discovers at the age of eleven that he is a wizard, living within the ordinary world of non-magical, or Muggle, people. His ability is inborn and such children are invited to attend a school that teaches the necessary skills to succeed in the wizarding world. Harry becomes a student at Hogwarts School of

Witchcraft and Wizardry and it is in here where most of the novels' events take place. As Harry develops through his adolescence, he learns to overcome the problems that face him: magical, social and emotional, including ordinary teenage challenges such as friendships and exams, and the greater test of preparing himself for the confrontation that lies ahead. Each book chronicles one year in Harry's life with the main narrative being set in the years 1991–1998. The books also contain many flashbacks, which are usually described by characters viewing memories in a device called a Pensieve.

II. Text

CHAPTER ONE THE BOY WHO LIVED

Mr. and Mrs. Dursley, of number four, Privet Drive, were proud to say that they were perfectly normal, thank you very much. They were the last people you'd expect to be involved in anything strange or mysterious, because they just didn't hold with such nonsense.

Mr. Dursley was the director of a firm called Grunnings, which made drills. He was a big, beefy man with hardly any neck, although he did have a very large mustache. Mrs. Dursley was thin and blonde and had nearly twice the usual amount of neck, which came in very useful as she spent so much of her time craning over garden fences, spying on the neighbors. The Dursleys had a small son called Dudley and in their opinion there was no finer boy anywhere.

The Dursleys had everything they wanted, but they also had a secret, and their greatest fear was that somebody would discover it. They didn't think they could bear it if anyone found out about the Potters. Mrs. Potter was Mrs. Dursley's sister, but they hadn't met for several years; in fact, Mrs. Dursley pretended she didn't have a sister, because her sister and her good-for-nothing husband were as unDursleyish as it was possible to be. The Dursleys shuddered to think what the neighbors would say if the Potters arrived in the street. The Dursleys knew that the Potters had a small son, too, but they had never even seen him. This boy was another good reason for keeping the Potters away; they didn't want Dudley mixing with a child like that.

When Mr. and Mrs. Dursley woke up on the dull, gray Tuesday our story starts, there was nothing about the cloudy sky outside to suggest that strange and mysterious things would soon be happening all over the country. Mr. Dursley hummed as he picked out his most boring tie for work, and Mrs. Dursley gossiped away happily as she wrestled a screaming Dudley into his high chair.

None of them noticed a large, tawny owl flutter past the window.

At half past eight, Mr. Dursley picked up his briefcase, pecked Mrs. Dursley on the cheek, and tried to kiss Dudley good-bye but missed, because Dudley was now having a tantrum and throwing his cereal at the walls. "Little tyke," chortled Mr. Dursley as he left the house. He got into his car and backed out of number four's drive.

It was on the corner of the street that he noticed the first sign of something peculiar — a cat reading a map. For a second, Mr. Dursley didn't realize what he had seen — then he jerked his head around to look again. There was a tabby cat standing on the corner of Privet Drive, but there wasn't a map in sight. What could he have been thinking of? It must have been a trick of the light. Mr. Dursley blinked and stared at the cat. It stared back. As Mr. Dursley drove around the corner and up the road, he watched the cat in his mirror. It was now reading the sign that said Privet Drive — no, looking at the sign; cats couldn't read maps or signs. Mr. Dursley gave himself a little shake and put the cat out of his mind. As he drove toward town he thought of nothing except a large order of drills he was hoping to get that day.

But on the edge of town, drills were driven out of his mind by something else. As he sat in the usual morning traffic jam, he couldn't help noticing that there seemed to be a lot of strangely dressed people about. People in cloaks. Mr. Dursley couldn't bear people who dressed in funny clothes — the getups you saw on young people! He supposed this was some stupid new fashion. He drummed his fingers on the steering wheel and his eyes fell on a huddle of these weirdos standing quite close by. They were whispering excitedly together. Mr. Dursley was enraged to see that a couple of them weren't young at all; why, that man had to be older than he was, and wearing an emerald-green cloak! The nerve of him! But then it struck Mr. Dursley that this was probably some silly stunt — these people were obviously collecting for something... yes, that would be it. The traffic moved on and a few minutes later, Mr. Dursley arrived in the Grunnings parking lot, his mind back on drills.

Mr. Dursley always sat with his back to the window in his office on the ninth floor. If he hadn't, he might have found it harder to concentrate on drills that morning. He didn't see the owls swooping past in broad daylight, though people down in the street did; they pointed and gazed open-mouthed as owl after owl sped overhead. Most of them had never seen an owl even at nighttime. Mr. Dursley, however, had a perfectly normal, owl-free morning. He yelled at five different people. He made several important telephone calls and shouted a bit more. He was in a very good mood until lunchtime, when he thought he'd stretch his legs and walk across the road to buy himself a bun from the bakery.

He'd forgotten all about the people in cloaks until he passed a group of them next to the baker's. He eyed them angrily as he passed. He didn't know why, but they made him uneasy. This bunch were whispering excitedly, too, and he couldn't see a single collecting tin. It was on his way back past them, clutching a large doughnut in a bag, that he caught a few words of what they were saying.

"The Potters, that's right, that's what I heard yes, their son, Harry."

Mr. Dursley stopped dead. Fear flooded him. He looked back at the whisperers as if he wanted to say something to them, but thought better of it.

He dashed back across the road, hurried up to his office, snapped at his secretary not to disturb him, seized his telephone, and had almost finished dialing his home number when he changed his mind. He put the receiver back down and stroked his mustache, thinking... no, he was being stupid. Potter wasn't such an unusual name. He was sure there were lots of people called Potter who had a son called Harry. Come to think of it, he wasn't even sure his nephew was called Harry. He'd never even seen the boy. It might have been Harvey. Or Harold. There was no point in worrying Mrs. Dursley; she always got so upset at any mention of her sister. He didn't blame her — if he'd had a sister like that... but all the same, those people in cloaks...

He found it a lot harder to concentrate on drills that afternoon and when he left the building at five o'clock, he was still so worried that he walked straight into someone just outside the door.

"Sorry," he grunted, as the tiny old man stumbled and almost fell. It was a few seconds before Mr. Dursley realized that the man was wearing a violet cloak. He didn't seem at all upset at being almost knocked to the ground. On the contrary, his face split into a wide smile and he said in a squeaky voice that made passersby stare, "Don't be sorry, my dear sir, for nothing could upset me today! Rejoice, for You-Know-Who has gone at last! Even Muggles like yourself should be celebrating, this happy, happy day!"

And the old man hugged Mr. Dursley around the middle and walked off.

Mr. Dursley stood rooted to the spot. He had been hugged by a complete stranger. He also thought he had been called a Muggle, whatever that was. He was rattled. He hurried to his car and set off for home, hoping he was imagining things, which he had never hoped before, because he didn't approve of imagination.

As he pulled into the driveway of number four, the first thing he saw — and it didn't improve his mood — was the tabby cat he'd spotted that morning. It was now sitting on his garden wall. He was sure it was the same one; it had the same markings around its eyes.

"Shoo!" said Mr. Dursley loudly. The cat didn't move. It just gave him a stern look. Was this normal cat behavior? Mr. Dursley wondered. Trying to pull himself together, he let himself into the house. He was still determined not to mention anything to his wife.

Mrs. Dursley had had a nice, normal day. She told him over dinner all about Mrs. Next

Door's problems with her daughter and how Dudley had learned a new word ("Won't!"). Mr. Dursley tried to act normally. When Dudley had been put to bed, he went into the living room in time to catch the last report on the evening news:

"And finally, bird-watchers everywhere have reported that the nation's owls have been behaving very unusually today. Although owls normally hunt at night and are hardly ever seen in daylight, there have been hundreds of sightings of these birds flying in every direction since sunrise. Experts are unable to explain why the owls have suddenly changed their sleeping pattern." The newscaster allowed himself a grin. "Most mysterious. And now, over to Jim McGuffin with the weather. Going to be any more showers of owls tonight, Jim?"

"Well, Ted," said the weatherman, "I don't know about that, but it's not only the owls that have been acting oddly today. Viewers as far apart as Kent, Yorkshire, and Dundee have been phoning in to tell me that instead of the rain I promised yesterday, they've had a downpour of shooting stars! Perhaps people have been celebrating Bonfire Night early — it's not until next week, folks! But I can promise a wet night tonight."

Mr. Dursley sat frozen in his armchair. Shooting stars all over Britain? Owls flying by daylight? Mysterious people in cloaks all over the place? And a whisper, a whisper about the Potters...

Mrs. Dursley came into the living room carrying two cups of tea. It was no good. He'd have to say something to her. He cleared his throat nervously. "Er — Petunia, dear — you haven't heard from your sister lately, have you?"

As he had expected, Mrs. Dursley looked shocked and angry. After all, they normally pretended she didn't have a sister.

"No," she said sharply. "Why?"

"Funny stuff on the news," Mr. Dursley mumbled. "Owls... shooting stars... and there were a lot of funny-looking people in town today..."

"So?" snapped Mrs. Dursley.

"Well, I just thought... maybe... it was something to do with... you know... her crowd."

Mrs. Dursley sipped her tea through pursed lips. Mr. Dursley wondered whether he dared tell her he'd heard the name "Potter." He decided he didn't dare. Instead he said, as casually as he could, "Their son — he'd be about Dudley's age now, wouldn't he?"

"I suppose so," said Mrs. Dursley stiffly.

"What's his name again? Howard, isn't it?"

"Harry. Nasty, common name, if you ask me."

"Oh, yes," said Mr. Dursley, his heart sinking horribly. "Yes, I quite agree."

He didn't say another word on the subject as they went upstairs to bed. While Mrs. Dursley was in the bathroom, Mr. Dursley crept to the bedroom window and peered down into the front garden. The cat was still there. It was staring down Privet Drive as though it were waiting for something.

Was he imagining things? Could all this have anything to do with the Potters? If it did... if it got out that they were related to a pair of — well, he didn't think he could bear it.

The Dursleys got into bed. Mrs. Dursley fell asleep quickly but Mr. Dursley lay awake, turning it all over in his mind. His last, comforting thought before he fell asleep was that even if the Potters were involved, there was no reason for them to come near him and Mrs. Dursley. The Potters knew very well what he and Petunia thought about them and their kind.... He couldn't see how he and Petunia could get mixed up in anything that might be going on — he yawned and turned over — it couldn't affect them....

How very wrong he was.

Mr. Dursley might have been drifting into an uneasy sleep, but the cat on the wall outside was showing no sign of sleepiness. It was sitting as still as a statue, its eyes fixed unblinkingly on the far corner of Privet Drive. It didn't so much as quiver when a car door slammed on the next street, nor when two owls swooped overhead. In fact, it was nearly midnight before the cat moved at all.

A man appeared on the corner the cat had been watching, appeared so suddenly and silently you'd have thought he'd just popped out of the ground. The cat's tail twitched and its eyes narrowed.

Nothing like this man had ever been seen on Privet Drive. He was tall, thin, and very old, judging by the silver of his hair and beard, which were both long enough to tuck into his belt. He was wearing long robes, a purple cloak that swept the ground, and high-heeled, buckled boots. His blue eyes were light, bright, and sparkling behind half-moon spectacles and his nose was very long and crooked, as though it had been broken at least twice. This man's name was Albus Dumbledore.

Albus Dumbledore didn't seem to realize that he had just arrived in a street where everything from his name to his boots was unwelcome. He was busy rummaging in his cloak, looking for something. But he did seem to realize he was being watched, because he looked up suddenly at the cat, which was still staring at him from the other end of the street. For some reason, the sight of the cat seemed to amuse him. He chuckled and muttered, "I should have known."

He found what he was looking for in his inside pocket. It seemed to be a silver cigarette lighter. He flicked it open, held it up in the air, and clicked it. The nearest street lamp went out with a little pop. He clicked it again — the next lamp flickered into darkness. Twelve times he clicked the Put-Outer, until the only lights left on the whole street were two tiny pinpricks in the distance, which were the eyes of the cat watching him. If anyone looked out of their window now, even beady-eyed Mrs. Dursley, they wouldn't be able to see anything that was happening down on the pavement. Dumbledore slipped the Put-Outer back inside his cloak and set off down the street toward number four, where he sat down on the wall next to the cat. He didn't look at it, but after a moment he spoke to it.

"Fancy seeing you here, Professor McGonagall."

He turned to smile at the tabby, but it had gone. Instead he was smiling at a rather severe-looking woman who was wearing square glasses exactly the shape of the markings the cat had had around its eyes. She, too, was wearing a cloak, an emerald one. Her black hair was drawn into a tight bun. She looked distinctly ruffled.

"How did you know it was me?" she asked.

"My dear Professor, I 've never seen a cat sit so stiffly."

"You'd be stiff if you'd been sitting on a brick wall all day," said Professor McGonagall.

"All day? When you could have been celebrating? I must have passed a dozen feasts and parties on my way here."

Professor McGonagall sniffed angrily.

"Oh yes, everyone's celebrating, all right," she said impatiently. "You'd think they'd be a bit more careful, but no — even the Muggles have noticed something's going on. It was on their news." She jerked her head back at the Dursleys' dark living-room window. "I heard it. Flocks of owls... shooting stars.... Well, they're not completely stupid. They were bound to notice something. Shooting stars down in Kent — I'll bet that was Dedalus Diggle. He never had much sense."

"You can't blame them," said Dumbledore gently. "We've had precious little to celebrate for eleven years."

"I know that," said Professor McGonagall irritably. "But that's no reason to lose our heads. People are being downright careless, out on the streets in broad daylight, not even dressed in Muggle clothes, swapping rumors."

She threw a sharp, sideways glance at Dumbledore here, as though hoping he was going to tell her something, but he didn't, so she went on. "A fine thing it would be if, on the very day You-Know-Who seems to have disappeared at last, the Muggles found out about us all. I suppose he really has gone, Dumbledore?"

"It certainly seems so," said Dumbledore. "We have much to be thankful for. Would you care for a lemon drop?"

"A what?"

"A lemon drop. They're a kind of Muggle sweet I'm rather fond of."

"No, thank you," said Professor McGonagall coldly, as though she didn't think this was the moment for lemon drops. "As I say, even if You-Know-Who has gone."

"My dear Professor, surely a sensible person like yourself can call him by his name? All this 'You- Know-Who' nonsense — for eleven years I have been trying to persuade people to call him by his proper name: Voldemort." Professor McGonagall flinched, but Dumbledore, who was unsticking two lemon drops, seemed not to notice. "It all gets so confusing if we keep saying 'You-Know-Who.' I have never seen any reason to be frightened of saying Voldemort's name."

"I know you haven't," said Professor McGonagall, sounding half exasperated, half admiring. "But you're different. Everyone knows you're the only one You-Know- oh, all right, Voldemort, was frightened of."

"You flatter me," said Dumbledore calmly. "Voldemort had powers I will never have."

"Only because you're too — well — noble to use them."

"It's lucky it's dark. I haven't blushed so much since Madam Pomfrey told me she liked my new earmuffs."

Professor McGonagall shot a sharp look at Dumbledore and said, "The owls are nothing next to the rumors that are flying around. You know what everyone's saying? About why he's disappeared? About what finally stopped him?"

It seemed that Professor McGonagall had reached the point she was most anxious to discuss, the real reason she had been waiting on a cold, hard wall all day, for neither as a cat nor as a woman had she fixed Dumbledore with such a piercing stare as she did now. It was plain that whatever "everyone" was saying, she was not going to believe it until Dumbledore told her it was true. Dumbledore, however, was choosing another lemon drop and did not answer.

"What they're saying," she pressed on, "is that last night Voldemort turned up in Godric's Hollow. He went to find the Potters. The rumor is that Lily and James Potter are — are — that they're — dead. "

Dumbledore bowed his head. Professor McGonagall gasped.

"Lily and James... I can't believe it... I didn't want to believe it... Oh, Albus..."

Dumbledore reached out and patted her on the shoulder. "I know... I know..." he said heavily.

Professor McGonagall's voice trembled as she went on. "That's not all. They're saying he tried to kill the Potter's son, Harry. But — he couldn't. He couldn't kill that little boy. No one knows why, or how, but they're saying that when he couldn't kill Harry Potter, Voldemort's power somehow broke — and that's why he's gone.

Dumbledore nodded glumly.

"It's — it's true?" faltered Professor McGonagall. "After all he's done... all the people he's killed... he couldn't kill a little boy? It's just astounding... of all the things to stop him... but how in the name of heaven did Harry survive?"

"We can only guess," said Dumbledore. "We may never know."

Professor McGonagall pulled out a lace handkerchief and dabbed at her eyes beneath her spectacles. Dumbledore gave a great sniff as he took a golden watch from his pocket and examined it. It was a very odd watch. It had twelve hands but no numbers; instead, little planets were moving around the edge. It must have made sense to Dumbledore, though, because he put it back in his pocket and said, "Hagrid's late. I suppose it was he who told you I'd be here, by the way?"

"Yes," said Professor McGonagall. "And I don't suppose you're going to tell me why you're here, of all places?"

"I've come to bring Harry to his aunt and uncle. They're the only family he has left now."

"You don't mean — you can't mean the people who live here?" cried Professor McGonagall, jumping to her feet and pointing at number four. "Dumbledore — you can't. I've been watching them all day. You couldn't find two people who are less like us. And they've got this son — I saw him kicking his mother all the way up the street, screaming for sweets. Harry Potter come and live here!"

"It's the best place for him," said Dumbledore firmly. "His aunt and uncle will be able to explain everything to him when he's older. I've written them a letter."

"A letter?" repeated Professor McGonagall faintly, sitting back down on the wall. "Really, Dumbledore, you think you can explain all this in a letter? These people will never understand him! He'll be famous — a legend — I wouldn't be surprised if today was known as Harry

Potter day in the future — there will be books written about Harry — every child in our world will know his name!"

"Exactly," said Dumbledore, looking very seriously over the top of his half-moon glasses. "It would be enough to turn any boy's head. Famous before he can walk and talk! Famous for something he won't even remember! Can't you see how much better off he'll be, growing up away from all that until he's ready to take it?"

Professor McGonagall opened her mouth, changed her mind, swallowed, and then said, "Yes — yes, you're right, of course. But how is the boy getting here, Dumbledore?" She eyed his cloak suddenly as though she thought he might be hiding Harry underneath it.

"Hagrid's bringing him."

"You think it — wise — to trust Hagrid with something as important as this?"

"I would trust Hagrid with my life," said Dumbledore.

"I'm not saying his heart isn't in the right place," said Professor McGonagall grudgingly, "but you can't pretend he's not careless. He does tend to — what was that?"

A low rumbling sound had broken the silence around them. It grew steadily louder as they looked up and down the street for some sign of a headlight; it swelled to a roar as they both looked up at the sky — and a huge motorcycle fell out of the air and landed on the road in front of them.

If the motorcycle was huge, it was nothing to the man sitting astride it. He was almost twice as tall as a normal man and at least five times as wide. He looked simply too big to be allowed, and so wild - long tangles of bushy black hair and beard hid most of his face, he had hands the size of trash can lids, and his feet in their leather boots were like baby dolphins. In his vast, muscular arms he was holding a bundle of blankets.

"Hagrid," said Dumbledore, sounding relieved. "At last. And where did you get that motorcycle?"

"Borrowed it, Professor Dumbledore, sit," said the giant, climbing carefully off the motorcycle as he spoke. "Young Sirius Black lent it to me. I've got him, sir."

"No problems, were there?"

"No, sir — house was almost destroyed, but I got him out all right before the Muggles started swarmin' around. He fell asleep as we was flying over Bristol."

Dumbledore and Professor McGonagall bent forward over the bundle of blankets. Inside, just visible, was a baby boy, fast asleep. Under a tuft of jet-black hair over his forehead they could see a curiously shaped cut, like a bolt of lightning.

"Is that where -?" whispered Professor McGonagall.

"Yes," said Dumbledore. "He'll have that scar forever."

"Couldn't you do something about it, Dumbledore?"

"Even if I could, I wouldn't. Scars can come in handy. I have one myself above my left knee that is a perfect map of the London Underground. Well — give him here, Hagrid — we'd better get this over with."

Dumbledore took Harry in his arms and turned toward the Dursleys' house.

"Could I — could I say good-bye to him, sir?" asked Hagrid. He bent his great, shaggy head over Harry and gave him what must have been a very scratchy, whiskery kiss. Then, suddenly, Hagrid let out a howl like a wounded dog.

"Shhh!" hissed Professor McGonagall, "you'll wake the Muggles!"

"S-s-sorry," sobbed Hagrid, taking out a large, spotted handkerchief and burying his face in it. "But I c-c-can't stand it — Lily and James dead — and poor little Harry off ter live with Muggles -"

"Yes, yes, it's all very sad, but get a grip on yourself, Hagrid, or we'll be found," Professor McGonagall whispered, patting Hagrid gingerly on the arm as Dumbledore stepped over the low garden wall and walked to the front door. He laid Harry gently on the doorstep, took a letter out of his cloak, tucked it inside Harry's blankets, and then came back to the other two. For a full minute the three of them stood and looked at the little bundle; Hagrid's shoulders shook, Professor McGonagall blinked furiously, and the twinkling light that usually shone from Dumbledore's eyes seemed to have gone out.

"Well," said Dumbledore finally, "that's that. We've no business staying here. We may as well go and join the celebrations."

"Yeah," said Hagrid in a very muffled voice, "I'll be taking Sirius his bike back. G'night, Professor McGonagall — Professor Dumbledore, sir."

Wiping his streaming eyes on his jacket sleeve, Hagrid swung himself onto the motorcycle and kicked the engine into life; with a roar it rose into the air and off into the night.

"I shall see you soon, I expect, Professor McGonagall," said Dumbledore, nodding to her. Professor McGonagall blew her nose in reply.

Dumbledore turned and walked back down the street. On the corner he stopped and took out the silver Put-Outer. He clicked it once, and twelve balls of light sped back to their street lamps so that Privet Drive glowed suddenly orange and he could make out a tabby cat slinking around the corner at the other end of the street. He could just see the bundle of blankets on the step of number four.

"Good luck, Harry," he murmured. He turned on his heel and with a swish of his cloak, he was gone.

A breeze ruffled the neat hedges of Privet Drive, which lay silent and tidy under the inky sky, the very last place you would expect astonishing things to happen. Harry Potter rolled over inside his blankets without waking up. One small hand closed on the letter beside him and he slept on, not knowing he was special, not knowing he was famous, not knowing he would be woken in a few hours' time by Mrs. Dursley's scream as she opened the front door to put out the milk bottles, nor that he would spend the next few weeks being prodded and pinched by his cousin Dudley... He couldn't know that at this very moment, people meeting in secret all over the country were holding up their glasses and saying in hushed voices: "To Harry Potter — the boy who lived!"

III. Reading Tasks

1. What was the relationship between the Dursleys and the Potters? How did the Dursleys feel about the Potters?

2. What do you think of the Dursleys? Were they kind-hearted to others? How do you consider their son Dudley? Was he really finer than any boy as in his parents' opinion?

3. Why did Albus Dumbledore, Professor McGonagall and Hagrid gather at Previt Drive that night? Who was the tabby cat actually?

4. How did Harry Potter get the scar in the shape of a bold lightening on his forehead? What had happened to his parents? Was he an orphan now?

英国文学经典名篇选读

Selected Readings from British Literary Classics

Part B

Vocabulary and Text Translation

B

第一单元

坎特伯雷故事

词汇

abstemious [æb'sti:mɪəs] adj. 节约的

Aries ['eəri:z] n. 白羊座，白羊宫

beaver ['bi:və(r)] n. 海狸（毛皮）

buckled ['bʌk(ə)ld] adj. 有扣子的

consonant ['kɔnsənənt] adj. 一致的

devout [dɪ'vaʊt] adj. 虔敬的，诚恳的

dignified ['dɪgnɪfaɪd] adj. 有威严的，有品格的

ecclesiastical [ɪkli:zɪ'æstɪk(ə)l] adj. 教会的，牧师的，神职的

emaciated [ɪ'meɪʃɪeɪtɪd] adj. 瘦弱的

fiddle ['fɪd(ə)l] n. 小提琴

Flemish ['flemɪʃ] n. 佛兰德人（语）adj. 佛兰德的，佛兰德人（语）的

formality [fɔ:'mælɪtɪ] n. 形式

fowl [faʊl] n. 鸟，禽

heed [hi:d] n. 注意，take heed of 留意

hostelry ['hɔstəlrɪ] n. 旅馆

incite [ɪn'saɪt] vt. 激发

interlinear [ɪntə'lɪnɪə(r)] adj. 写在行间的，隔一行书写原文和译文的

martyr ['mɑ:tə(r)] n. 殉教者

parti-coloured adj. 杂色的，斑驳的

psaltery ['sɔ:ltərɪ] n. 八弦琴

rake [reɪk] n. 耙子

robe [rəʊb] n. 长袍，罩衣，礼服，制服

shire ['ʃaɪə(r)] n. 郡

shrine [ʃraɪn] n. 神殿，圣地

strongbox ['strɔŋbɔks] n. 保险箱

Tabard ['tæbəd] n. 泰巴旅店

threadbare ['θredbeə(r)] adj. 穿破旧衣服的

wherewithal ['weəwɪðɔ:l] n.（常做 the ...）必要的资金

译文

坎特伯雷故事

总引
坎特伯雷故事由此开始

当四月带来它那甘美的骤雨，
让三月里的干旱湿到根子里，
让浆汁滋润每棵草木的茎脉，
凭其催生的力量使花开出来；
当和风甜美的气息挟着生机，
吹进树林和原野上的嫩芽里，
年轻的太阳也已进入白羊座，
已把白羊座一半的路程走过，
而小鸟小雀唱着各自的曲调——
整夜里它们都睁着眼睛睡觉——
（这是大自然拨弄出它们心声）；
这时候人们也就渴望去朝圣，
游方僧也就渴望去异地他乡，
去各地知名于世的神龛圣堂。
无论英格兰各郡的东西南北，
人们尤其要去的是坎特伯雷，
去拜谢恩泽万民的殉难圣徒，
因为人们有病时他给予救助。

就在这时节，就在其中的一天，
我正住在萨瑟克的泰巴旅店，
已经满心虔诚地准备好登程，
专诚去坎特伯雷那地方朝圣。
在那天傍晚，
有二十九位旅客来到了这客店，
他们形形色色，
全都是在路上彼此萍水相逢，
全都是跨着坐骑要前去朝圣，
而坎特伯雷是他们去的地方。
旅店的房间和马厩都很宽敞，
把我们个个安顿得十分舒适。
不久后太阳从地平线上消失，
我同他们每个人都作了交谈，
很快就成了他们当中的一员。
大家约定来日上路要起个早，
而路上的情形，下面我会说到。

但是既然我有很充裕的时间，
在我进一步细述这故事之前，
我觉得比较合情合理的做法
是根据我对他们各人的观察，
把我看到的情况全告诉你们：
他们是什么人，属于哪个阶层，
甚至还要说说他们穿的衣裳——
现在我就从一位骑士开始讲。

骑士：
……

商人：

他胡须一半朝右而一半朝左——
这商人身穿花色衣，骑着大马。
做他帽子的，是佛兰德水獭；
他的靴子扣得又牢靠又美观。
他发表他的见解时颇为庄严，
总在强调他如何使利润增长。
米德尔堡和奥威尔之间通航，
他认为应不惜代价确保安全。
他善于买卖外汇，用外币赚钱。
这个体面人很会用他那天分；
没有人知道他还有债务在身，
尽管他又做买卖又向人借债，
但言谈举止还有那么点气派。
不管怎么讲，他确实是个人物；
可是说实话，他大名我没记住。

学士：
这一位是牛津来的饱学之人，
多年来他研究逻辑这门学问。
他的马瘦骨嶙峋像是个草耙，
而要说胖却怎么也轮不到他。
我说，看上去他瘦削而又严肃，
一件短短的外套已经经纬毕露，
因为至今还不曾拿到过薪水——
他不识时务，得不到教会职位。
他不爱提琴、竖琴或华丽衣服，
宁可在床头放上二十来本书——
书中的哲学出自亚里士多德，
书外的封皮做成黑色或红色。
然而尽管对哲理他非常精通，
钱箱里却没金子可供他使用；
从朋友那里得到的所有接济
他已全部都用于学术和书籍；
对于给他钱、支持他研究的人，
他热心祈祷，祝福他们的灵魂。
他的心思大部分用在学问上，
不是必要的话他一个字不讲，
讲起来则头头是道，提纲挈领，
而见解之精到令人肃然起敬。
他讲的内容多是道德和道义，
他爱做的事不外施教与学习。

（黄杲炘　译）

第二单元

莎士比亚的诗歌

词汇

audacious [ɔː'deɪʃəs] adj. 大胆创新的

carnage ['kɑːnɪdʒ] n.（尤指在战场上的）残杀，大屠杀，流血

contrive [kən'traɪv] v. 设计

crudity ['kruːdɪtɪ] n. 原始，生硬，不成熟

ensue [ɪn'sjuː; (*US*) ɪn'suː] vi. 跟着发生，继起

feign [feɪn] vt. 假装

hypocrite ['hɪpəkrɪt] n. 伪君子，伪善者

impersonation [imˌpəːsə'neiʃən] n. 扮演

intelligible [ɪn'telɪdʒɪb(ə)l] adj. 可理解的

mirth [mɜːθ] n. 欢笑，高兴

pathos ['peɪθɔs] n. 痛苦，感伤，悲怅，哀婉

pompous ['pɔmpəs] adj. 华而不实的

quarto ['kwɔːtəʊ] n. 四开，四开大的书本

repertory ['repətərɪ] n. 仓库，常备剧目

theatrical [θɪ'ætrɪk(ə)l] adj. 戏剧性的

unnerve [ʌn'nɜːv] vt. 使失去勇气，使身心交疲，使失常

vicarious [vɪ'keərɪəs] adj. 产生同感（共鸣）的

译文

1. 哈姆雷特独白

活着还是不活，这是个问题：
究竟哪样更高贵，
去忍受那狂暴的命运的摧残，
还是挺身去反抗那无边的烦恼，
把它扫一个干净？
去死，去睡——就结束了。

如果睡眠能够结束我们心灵的创伤
和肉体所承受的千百种痛苦，
那真是求之不得的天大的好事。
去死，去睡……去睡，
也许会做梦！唉，这就麻烦了。
即使摆脱了这尘世，
可在这死的睡眠里又会做什么梦呢？
真得想一想。
就这点顾虑使人受着终身的折磨。
谁甘心忍受那鞭打和嘲弄，受人压迫，
受尽诬蔑和轻视，忍受那失恋的痛苦。
法庭的拖延，衙门的横征暴敛，
默默无闻的劳碌却只换来多少凌辱；
当他自己用把尖刀就能解脱了。
谁甘心，呻吟，流汗，拖着这残生；
可对死后又感到恐惧，
又从来没有任何人从死亡的国度里回来，
因此动摇了，
宁愿忍受着目前的苦难，
而不愿投奔向另一种苦难。
顾虑就使我们都成了懦夫，
使那果断的本色蒙上一层思虑的惨白的容颜。
本来可以做出伟大的事业，
由于思虑就化为乌有了，
丧失了行动的能力。

（卞之琳　陈叙一　译）

2. 十四行诗第 18 首

能不能让我来把你比作夏日？
你可是更加可爱，更加温婉，
狂风会吹落五月里开的好花儿，
夏季租出的日子又未免太短暂：
有时候苍天的巨眼照得太灼热，
他那金彩的脸色也会被遮暗，
每一样美呀，总会离开美而凋落，
被时机或者自然的代谢所摧残，
但是你永久的夏天决不会凋枯，
你永远不会失去你美的形相，
死神夸不着你在他影子里踯躅，
你将在不朽的诗中与时间同长，
只要人类在呼吸，眼睛看得见，
我这诗就活着，使你的生命绵延。

（屠岸　译）

3. 十四行诗第 29 首

我一旦失去了幸福，又遭人白眼，
就独自哭泣，怨人家把我抛弃，
白白地用哭喊来麻烦聋耳的苍天，
又看看自己，只痛恨时运不济，
愿自己像人家那样：或前程远大，
或一表人才，或胜友如云广交谊，
想有这人的权威，那人的才华，
于自己平素最得意的，倒最不满意，
但在这几乎是看轻自己的思想里，
我偶尔想到了你呵，——我的心怀

顿时像破晓的云雀从阴郁的大地
冲上了天门，歌唱起赞美诗来，

我记着你的甜爱，就是珍宝，
教我不屑把处境跟帝王对调。

（屠岸　译）

第三单元

论读书

词汇

affectation [æfek'teɪʃ(ə)n] n. 矫饰
confer [kən'fəː] vt. 交换意见
contemn [kən'tem] vt. 蔑视
contend [kən'tend] v. 能言善辩
contradict [kɔntrə'dɪkt] vt. 同……矛盾
confute [kən'fjuːt] vt. 驳斥，驳倒
counsel ['kaʊns(ə)l] n. 讨论，商议
discourse [dis'kɔːs, 'diskɔːs] n. 演讲
deputy ['depjʊtɪ] n. 代理人
disposition [dispə'ziʃən] n. 处置，部署
distill [dɪ'stɪl] vt. 蒸馏，提取 vi. 滴下
execute ['eksɪkjuːt] vt. 执行，实行，完成
flashy ['flæʃɪ] adj. 浮华的
impediment [ɪm'pedɪmənt] n. 阻碍，障碍物
marshal ['mɑːʃ(ə)l] vt. 管理，整顿
nay [neɪ] adv.〈古〉否，不
proyn = prune [pruːn] v. 剪除
receipt [rɪ'siːt]= recipe ['resɪpɪ] n. 处方
sloth [sləʊθ] n. 怠惰，懒惰
subtile=subtle ['sʌt(ə)l] adj. 准确的，精细的

译文

论读书

读书足以怡情，足以傅彩，足以长才。其怡情也，最见于独处幽居之时；其傅彩也，最见于高谈阔论之中；其长才也，最见于处世判事之际。练达之士虽能分别处理细事或一一判别枝节，然纵观统筹，全局策划，则舍好学深思者莫属。读书费时过多

易惰，文采藻饰太盛则矫，全凭条文断事乃学究故态。读书补天然之不足，经验又补读书之不足，盖天生才干犹如自然花草，读书然后知如何修剪移接；而书中所示，如不以经验范之，则又大而无当。

狡黠者鄙读书，无知者羡读书，唯明智之士用读书，然书并不以用处告人，用书之智不在书中，而在书外，全凭观察得之。读书时不可存心诘难作者，不可尽信书上所言，亦不可只为寻章摘句，而应推敲细思。书有可浅尝者，有可吞食者，少数则须咀嚼消化。换言之，有只须读其部分者，有只须大体涉猎者，少数则须全读，读时须全神贯注，孜孜不倦。书亦可请人代读，取其所作摘要，但只限题材较次或价值不高者，否则书经提炼犹如水经蒸馏，味同嚼蜡矣。读书使人充实，讨论使人机智，作文使人准确。因此不常作文者须记忆特强，不常讨论者须天生聪颖，不常读书者须欺世有术，始能无知而显有知。读史使人明智，读诗使人灵秀，数学使人周密，科学使人深刻，伦理学使人庄重，逻辑修辞之学使人善辩：凡有所学，皆成性格。人之才智但有滞碍，无不可读适当之书使之顺畅，一如身体百病，皆可借相宜之运动除之。滚球利睾肾，射箭利胸肺，慢步利肠胃，骑术利头脑，诸如此类。如智力不集中，可令读数学，盖演题须全神贯注，稍有分散即须重演；如不能辨异，可令读经院哲学，盖是辈皆吹毛求疵之人；如不善求同，不善以一物阐证另一物，可令读律师之案卷。如此头脑中凡有缺陷，皆有特药可医。

（王佐良　译）

第四单元

鲁滨逊漂流记

词汇

affright [ə'fraɪt] vt. 惊吓 n. 恐怖

ammunition [æmjʊ'nɪʃ(ə)n] n. 军火，弹药

ay [ei] int. 唉！呜呼！ Ay me！哀哉！

barley ['bɑːlɪ] n. 大麦

beckon ['bekən] v. 招手，召唤

breeches ['brɪtʃɪz] n. 马裤，〈口〉裤子

cabin ['kæbɪn] n. 小屋，船舱

chest [tʃest] n. 箱，柜

cleaver ['kliːvə(r)] n. 切肉刀，切割者，突出的悬崖

club [klʌb] n. 棍棒 vt. 棍打

comely ['kʌmlɪ] adj. 清秀的，标致的

contrive [kən'traɪv] v. 发明，设计，图谋

cordial ['kɔːdɪəl; (*US*) 'kɔːrdʒəl] n. 兴奋剂，兴奋性饮料

destitute ['destɪtjuːt] adj. 缺乏的

dispose [dɪ'spəʊz] v. 处理 vt. 布置

disposed [dɪ'spəʊzd] adj. 有……倾向的

dram [dræm] n. 打兰，一杯

draught [drɑːft] n. 拖，拉，a draught of 一份

dun [dʌn] n. 催促者，讨债者，催债 v. 催讨 adj. 暗褐色的，微暗的

ebb [eb] n. 退潮，衰落 vi. 潮退

expedition [ekspɪ'dɪʃ(ə)n] n. 迅速

forecastle ['fəʊksl] n. 船头的船楼，前甲板下面的水手舱

forsaw=foresaw, foresee [fɔː'siː] vt. 预见，预知

fowling ['faʊlɪθ] n. 捕鸟，打鸟

freight [freɪt] n. 船货 vt. 运送

grief [grɪːf] n. 悲痛，忧伤

hallow ['hæləʊ] vt. 喊叫

indraft ['ɪndrɑːft;-dræft] n. 吸入

lay by 搁置，储蓄

linen=linnen ['lɪnɪn] n. 亚麻布

loath [ləʊθ] adj. 不情愿的，勉强的

loathe [ləʊð] vt. 厌恶，憎恶

mortification [ˌmɔːtɪfɪˈkeɪʃən] n. 羞辱，禁欲
necessitate [nɪˈsesɪteɪt] v. 成为必要
outstrip [aʊtˈstrɪp] v. 超过
perspective [pəˈspektɪv] n. 望远镜，观察
plump [plʌmp] adj. 圆胖的，鼓起的 vt. 使丰满 vi. 鼓起
providence [ˈprɒvɪdəns] n. 天意
provision [prəˈvɪʒ(ə)n] n. 供应，（一批）供应品
rack [ræk] n. 架
raisin [ˈreɪz(ə)n] n. 葡萄干
rudder [ˈrʌdə(r)] n. 舵，方向舵
rum [rʌm] n. 朗姆酒
rummage [ˈrʌmɪdʒ] v. 到处翻寻
setting in 开始，涨潮
skipper [ˈskɪpə(r)] n. 船长
stow [stəʊ] v. 装载
stump [stʌmp] n. 树桩
surf [sɜːf] n. 海浪，浪的拍打 vt. 在激浪上驾（船），在……冲浪
surly [ˈsɜːlɪ] adj. 粗暴的，乖戾的，阴沉的，无礼的，板面孔的
tawny [ˈtɔːnɪ] n. 茶色 adj. 茶色的
thereabouts [ˈðeərəbaʊts] adv. 在那附近，大约
thither [ˈðɪðə(r)] adv. 到那边，向那方 adj. 在那边的
vivacity [vɪˈvæsətɪ, vaɪ-] n. 活泼
viz. [vɪz]〈拉〉即，就是
whimsy [ˈwɪmzɪ] n. 怪念头，奇想，任意
wretch [retʃ] n. 不幸的人

译文

1. 克鲁索到搁浅的船上

过午以后，海面平静，潮水退得很远，我和大船之间的距离只有四分之一海里了。这时我心里不由得又难过起来，因为我想，倘若昨天我们全船的人都不下小艇，我们大家定然平安无事，定然平平安安地上了岸，我也不会像现在一样，孤孤零零，既无乐趣，又无伴侣了。想到这里，我的眼泪不禁流了下来。但现在悲伤也于事无补，于是我便决定，如果可能，还是先到船上去。这时天气热极了，于是我便脱了衣服，跳到水里。可是，当我泅到船边的时候，却没法上去，因为它搁在沙滩上，离水很高，在我两臂所能伸到的距离以内，没有什么东西可以抓住。我绕着它游了两个圈子，到了第二圈时，忽然发现了一根很短的绳子。我心里很奇怪，我为什么先前没有看见呢？那绳子从船头上挂下来，挂得很低，因此我不用费事就抓住了它，靠了它的帮助，攀上船的前舱。上去之后，我才发现船已经漏了，舱底进满了水。不过船是斜搁在一片硬沙岸上，船尾翘起来，船头几乎接近水面，所以船的后半截都没有水。不用说，我的第一步工作是要搜寻一下，看看有些什么东西已经坏了，什么东西还没有浸水。首

先，我看见船上的粮食都还干燥无恙；这时我急于想吃点东西，便走进面包房，把我的衣袋都装满了饼干，一边吃着一边做着别的事，因为我必须抓紧时间才行。我又在大舱里找到了一些甘蔗酒；我就喝了一大杯，因为在当前的情况下，我很需要喝点酒提提神。现在我什么都不想，只想有一只小艇，把我认为需要的东西，装到岸上去。

一个人只是呆呆地坐着，空想自己所得不到的东西，是没有用的；这个绝对的真理，使我重新振作起来。我们船上有几根多余的帆杠，还有两三块木板，还有一两根多余的第二接桅。我决定先从这些东西着手，只要搬得动的，都把它们从船上扔下来，每根上面都绑上绳子，防备它们被水冲走。这一步做好了，我又走到船边，把它们拉到我跟前来，把四块木头绑在一起，两头尽可能地绑紧，扎成一只木排的样子，又用两三块短木板横放在上面。我在上面走了走，倒还行，不过因为木块太轻，吃不住多少重量。于是我又动起手来，用木匠的锯把一根第二接桅锯成三段，把它们加在我的木排上。这个工作非常吃力，非常辛苦，但由于我急于想把应用的东西装到岸上去，这就鼓舞着我做出平常所做不到的事情。

我的木排这时已经比较牢固，能够吃得住相当的重量了。第二步就是考虑把什么东西装上去，并且怎样使我装上去的东西不至于被海浪打湿。但我不久便想到了办法。我首先把船上所能找到的木板都铺了上去，然后，我把自己最需要的东西考虑了一番，我把三只船员用的箱子打开，把里面的东西倒出来，把它们吊到我的木排上。在第一只箱子里，我装上了许多粮食，面包，米，三块荷兰酪干，五块干羊肉，以及一些剩下来的欧洲麦子——这点麦子本来是准备用来饲养我们带到船上的一些家禽的，但家禽现在已经死了。船上本来还有一点大麦跟小麦，后来才发现都被老鼠吃掉了或毁完了，使我非常失望。至于酒类，我也找到了几箱，都是属于船主的；里面有几瓶甜酒，还有几加仑白酒。我一概把它们放在一边，因为放进箱子里既没有必要，又没有地方。我正在做这些事情的时候，只见潮水已开始上涨，来势虽然很平和，却把我留在岸上的上衣，衬衫，和背心通通冲走了。这使我非常懊丧，因为我游泳上船的时候，身上只穿一条麻纱开膝短裤，一双袜子。这样一来，倒使我不得不来搜罗一些衣服了。我在船里找到了许多衣服，但是我只取了几件目前要用的——因为我心目中还有一些更重要的东西要找，尤其是土木工具。我找了半天，终于找到了木匠的箱子。这东西对于我非常有用，就算这时有一满船金子，也没有它值钱。我把它原封不动放在我的木排上，也没有花时间把它打开看看，因为我早已知道里面大概装的是什么了。

其次我想要弄到的是弹药和枪械。大舱里本来有两支很好的鸟枪和两支手枪；我先把它们拿到手里，又拿了几只装火药的角筒，一小包子弹和两把上了锈的旧刀剑。我知道船上有三桶火药，只是不知道我们的炮手把它们放到什么地方去了。我找了半天，终于找到了它们；有两桶还很干燥，很好，另外一桶却已经沾了水了。我把这两桶干燥的火药连同那些枪械都搬到我的木排上。这时我觉得我所装的东西已经够多了，便开始盘算，怎样才能把它们运到岸上。因为我既没有帆，又没有桨，又没有舵，只要有一点风，就会把我的木排打翻。

有三件事鼓励着我。第一，海面平静，第二，潮水正在上涨，正在向岸上冲，第三，虽然有一点风，却是向岸上吹的。同时我又找到了两三只断桨，并且除了箱子里的工具之外，又找到了两把锯，一把斧子，一只锤子；于是我便载了这些货，向岸上出发。最初一英里来路，我的木排走得倒挺好，不过它所飘去的地方，却和我昨天登陆的地点有些距离，在那一带我看到水面有回流；因此，我希望附近有一条小溪或是小河，可以用来作一个港口，起货上岸。果然不出我的意料，我不久便看到了一个小港口，并且看见潮水正往里面直涌。于是我尽可能地驾驶着我的木排，顺着急流的中心漂去。在这里，我几乎再一次碰到船只失事的灾祸。（倘若真的这样，那我就太伤心了）原来，由于我不熟悉地形，我的木排忽然一头搁在浅沙上，而另一头还在水里飘荡着，只差一点，我的全部货物就要从漂在水里的一头滑到水里去了。我拼命用我的背顶住那些箱子，不让它们滑下去。可是，使出了我的全部力气，我也没法把木排撑开；我只好用全力顶住箱子，足足站了半个钟头，直到后来，潮水上来，才使我比较平衡一点。又过了一会，潮水愈涨愈高，我的木排才又浮了起来。我用桨把它一直向海口撑去，一直撑到一条小河的入口处，这地方两边都是陆地，潮水直往里流。我向两岸望了望，打算找一个适当的地方起岸，因为我不愿意太走进小河，想尽量靠近海边，希望能看到海上的船只。

2. 脚印

有一天，大概是正午时候，我正要去看我的船，忽然在海边上发现一个人的赤脚脚印，清清楚楚地印在沙滩上。我简直吓坏了。我呆呆地站在那里，就像挨了一个晴天霹雳，又像是活见了鬼。我侧耳静听，又回头环顾，可是什么也听不见，也看不见。我跑上一个高地，向远处望去，又在海边上来回跑了几趟，可是毫无所获，除了这一个，再也找不到其他的脚印。我跑到脚印跟前，看看有没有别的脚印，看看它会不会是我个人的幻觉，可是，完全不是那么回事，因为一点儿也不错，不折不扣是一个人的脚印，脚指头，脚后跟，样样俱全。至于它是怎么来的，那我就不得而知，无从猜测了。我像一个方寸已乱、神经失常的人似的胡思乱想了一阵，拔腿就往我的防御工事跑去，就像脚不沾地一样。我心里恐慌已极，走不到两三步就要回头看一看，连远处一丛小树，一个枯树干，我都误会它是个人。至于一路上我的受惊的想象使我看到多少各种各样的幻景，我的幻觉里出现了多少荒诞不经的想法，以及我的头脑里产生了一些什么离奇古怪的妄想，那简直说也说不清。

我一跑到我的城堡（我以后就这样称呼好了），马上就像有人在后面追着似的，一下子就钻进去了。至于我是按照原来的设计，用梯子爬进去的，还是从那被我称为门的岩洞里钻进去的，我自己也不记得了，甚至到了第二天早上还想不起来，因为，我跑进这个藏身之所的时候，心里恐怖已极，就是一只受惊的兔子逃进它的草窝里去，一只狐狸逃进它的地穴里去，也没有我那么胆战心惊。

3. 鲁滨逊从食人族那里救出了星期五

我正这样望着的时候，从望远镜里，我又看见他们从小船上拖出两个倒霉的野人来，这两个野人大概是他们事先放在船上的，现在要拿出来屠杀了。我看见其中有一个被他们用一根木棍或一把木刀一阵乱打，登时倒了下来，跟着便有两三个野人跑上来，动手把他破腹开膛，准备烹调。至于另外一个受害人，则呆呆地站在一边，等候他们前来动手。这时，这个可怜虫看见自己手脚松了绑，没人照管，不由地起了逃命的希望，突然跳出他们的圈子，用一种难以相信的速度沿着海岸往我这边跑，也就是说，朝我所住的这一带跑来。

我一见他朝我这边跑来，尤其是乍一看来，全部的野人都在他后头紧紧追赶，说句老实话，我真吓坏了。我看出我的梦有一部分要实现了，我预料他一定会躲到我的小树林里来。可是，下面的事情，我却信不过我的梦——这就是说，我不相信那些野人不追到小树林里来，把他捉住。可是，我还是站在那里，动也不动。后来，我发现追他的只不过三个人，我的胆子就慢慢壮了起来。尤其使我勇气百倍的是，我看出他跑得比他们快得多，而且把他们愈甩愈远，只要他能维持半小时，就不难完全逃出他们的掌握。

在他们和我的城堡之间，有一条小河。这条小河，我在本书的开头部分，已经提到过了，我把船上的东西运下来的时候，就是在那里起岸的。我看得很清楚，他必须游过这条小河，否则就一定会被他们在河边捉住。不料那逃走的野人跑到河边上，尽管潮水已经涨了，他还是不把它当回事，一下子就跳了下去，只划了三十来下，便游过河面，爬到岸上，非常迅速而有力地向前跑。那三个人到了小河边，只有两个会游水，第三个却不会，只好站在河那边，看着其余的两个过河；又过了一会，就一个人悄悄回去了——这对于他实在是一件好事。

我注意到，那两个会游水的野人游过小河，比那逃走的野人费了一倍以上的时间。这时候，我脑子里忽然产生了一个强烈的、不可抗拒的念头：我要想找到一个仆人，现在正是时候，说不定我还会找到一个伴侣，一个帮手哩，这明明是上天号召我救这个可怜虫的命哩。我登时急忙跑下了梯子，拿起我的两支枪来（前面已经讲过，这两支枪都摆在梯子脚下），又同样迅速爬上去，翻过山顶，向海边跑去。我抄了一个小路，跑下山去，插身在追者和被追者的中间。我向那逃跑的野人大声呼唤。他回头望了望，起初仿佛对我也很害怕，但是我用手招他回来，同时慢慢地向后面追赶的两个野人迎上去。等我走近他们时，我一下子就冲到最前面一个野人跟前，用枪杆子把他打倒了。我不愿意开枪，因为我不想叫其余的野人听见。其实离这么远，枪声是很难听到的；就是隐隐约约听到了，他们看不见硝烟，也弄不清是怎么回事。我把第一个野人打倒之后，和他一起追来的那个野人也停住脚步，仿佛吓住了，于是我急急地向他迎上去。但当我走近他时，一眼就瞧见他手里拿着一副弓箭，正在那里拉弓向我放箭。因此我不得不先向他开枪，头一枪就把他打死了。那逃跑的野人这时也停住脚步，虽然亲眼看见他的两个敌人都已经倒在地下，而且多半是死了，却给我的枪声和火光吓坏了，呆呆地站在那里，既不进又不退，看起来逃跑的意思比过来的意思要多些。我向他大声招呼，做手势叫他过来。他明白了我的意思，向前走了几步，可是又站住了；接着又走了几步，又站住了。这时候，我才看出他站在那里，浑身发抖，仿佛已经成了我的俘虏，要像他的两个仇人一样地被杀了。我又向他招手，叫他过来，并且尽量做出各种的姿势来鼓励他。他这才慢慢地往前走，每走十步二十步，便下一个跪，仿佛对我搭救他的性命表示感谢。我对他微笑着，作出和蔼的样子，又用手招他，叫他再走近一点。末了，他走到我的跟前，再跪下去，吻着地面，把头贴在地上，把我的一只脚放在他的头上，看样子仿佛在宣誓终身作我的奴隶。我把他扶了起来，和善地对待他，并且尽可能地鼓励他。可是事情还没有完，因为我看见我用枪杆打倒的那个野人并没有死，只是给我打昏了，现在又开始苏醒过来。于是我把那野人指给他看，表示他没有死。他看见之后，就叽里咕噜地向我说了几句话。我虽然不明白他的话，可是听起来却非常悦耳，因为除了我自己的声音以外，这是二十五年以来我第一次听见人的声音。可是现在已经没有时间来想这些事情了。那被打倒的野人现在已经完全清醒过来，居然坐了起来。我见我那野人这时又有点害怕起来，便举起我另外一杆枪，对准那个人，准备开枪。这时候，我那野人（我现在这样叫他了）向我做了一个动作，要求我把腰间挂的那把没有鞘的刀借给他。于是我就把刀借给他。他接过我的刀，登时跑到他的仇人前面，手举刀落，一下子就把他的头砍了下来，就是一个德国刽子手，也不见得比他砍得更快，更好。这使我大为惊奇，因为我有充分的理由相信，这个人除了他们自己的木刀以外，一生没有见过一把刀。后来我才知道，他们的刀都制造得又锋利又沉重，而且是用很硬的木头做成的，拿来砍人头，砍手膀，都没有问题，而且可以一刀就砍下来。他砍完了头，带着胜利的笑声回到我跟前，同时也把刀带了回来，又做了许多使我莫名其妙的姿势，把刀和他砍下来的野人头，一齐放在我的脚下。

最使他感到惊异的，是我怎么从这么远的距离把另外一个野人打死。于是他指着那野人，向我做手势，要我放他到那野人身边去。我也尽可能地向他做手势，叫他尽管过去。他走到那死人身边，仿佛很吃惊地站在那里，两眼直直地望着死人，一会把他翻过去，一会把他翻过来，查看那子弹打成的伤痕。原来那子弹正打在腌口上，在那里穿了一个小洞，但是没有流多少血，因为人已经死了，血流到内脏里去了。他把那野人的弓箭取了下来，走了回来，于是我就离开那地方，并且叫他跟我走，同时用手势告诉他，后面说不定还有别的人来哩。

他懂了我的意思，就向我打手势，表示要把他们用沙土埋起来，免得给后面来的野人看见。我作手势叫他照办，他马上很起劲地干起来，不到一会的工夫，就用双手在沙土上刨了一个坑，刚刚容得下那第一个野人，把尸首拖了进去，用沙土掩盖好。接着他又把第二个如法埋了起来。我相信，他只用了一刻钟的工夫，就把两个人都埋上了。然后，我叫他跟着我走。我没有把他带到我的城堡里去，却把他带到更远一点，带到岛那头的石洞里去。我这样做，是因为我有意不让自己的梦应验不爽，因为在梦里，他是跑到我城堡外边的小树林里来藏身的。

到了洞里，我给了他一些面包和一串葡萄干吃，又给了他一点水喝，因为我看他跑了半天，已经饥渴不堪了。我等他吃喝已毕，又指给他一个地方（我在那里铺了一堆干草，上面还有一条毯子，我自己有时也在上面睡觉），做着手势，叫他躺下来睡觉。于是这可怜虫便倒了下来，呼呼睡去。

他是一个眉目清秀、修短合度的汉子，四肢长得又直又结实，但并不粗大；个子很高，处处长得都很匀称；年纪看来大约有二十六岁。他的五官生得很端正，没有那种狰狞可憎的样子；脸上带着一种男子汉的英勇气概，可是又具有欧洲人的和蔼可亲，尤其当他微笑的时候。他的头发是长而且黑，并不像羊毛似的卷着；他的前额又高又大，两眼活泼而有光。他的皮色不很黑，略带褐色，然而又不像巴西人、弗吉尼亚人和其他美洲土人那样，褐黄得那样难看，却是一种爽朗的橄榄色，叫人看起来舒服，却不容易形容。他的脸是圆圆的，胖胖的；鼻子很小，但又不像黑人那样扁；一张嘴的样子也很好，嘴唇很薄，牙齿生得很整齐，白得同象牙一样。他打了半小时的盹就醒了，一醒来就到洞外来找我。这时我正在挤羊奶，因为我的羊圈就在附近。他一瞧见我，就向我跑来，趴在地上，用各种各样的手势和许多古怪的姿势，表示他的恭顺感激的心情。最后，他又把头放在地上，靠近我的脚边，像上回那样，把我的一只脚放在他的头上，然后又对我做出各种归顺诚服的姿势，让我知道他将一生一世为我效力。我明白他的意思，就向他表示，我对他很满意。不久，我就开始和他说话，并且教他和我说话。首先，我让他知道，他的名字应该叫“星期五”，因为我在星期五救了他的命，而我这样叫他，是为了纪念这个日子。我教给他说“主人”，然后让他知道，这就算作我的名字。我又教他说“是”和“不是”，并且使他知道它们的意义。我拿了一个瓦罐，盛了一些羊奶给他，让他当面看着我喝，看着我把面包浸在羊奶里。然后又给了他一块面包，叫他照着我的样子吃。他马上照办了，并且向我做手势，表示很好吃。

（徐霞村　译）

第五单元

弃儿汤姆·琼斯史

词汇

alacrity [ə'lækrɪtɪ] n. 敏捷，活泼，爽快
Alban ['ɔːlbən,'æl-] n. 奥尔本
alight [ə'laɪt] vi. 落下 adj. 点着的，发亮的
allege [ə'ledʒ] vt. 宣称，断言 = alledge
antagonist [æn'tægənɪst] n. 敌手，对手
applaud [ə'plɔːd] v. 拍手喝彩，称赞，赞同
argue v. 表明；显示出
assert [ə'sɜːt] v. 断言，声称 asserted adj. 宣称的（尚待证实的）的
bestow [bi'stəu] vt. 给与（on，upon），赠予；安置，安顿（住宿）
bluntness ['blʌntnəs] n. 率直，迟钝
burthen ['bɜːðən] n. 负荷，重荷，负担 v. 使负重担，累
caper ['keɪpə(r)] n. 跳跃 vi. 雀跃
compassion [kəm'pæʃ(ə)n] n. 同情，怜悯
comply [kəm'plaɪ] vi. 顺从，答应，遵守 comply with
construe [kən'struː] v. 解释，分析，直译
countenance ['kaʊntɪnəns] n. 面容，脸色 vt. 支持，赞助
digression [daɪ'greʃən] n. 离题，脱轨，扯到枝节上
fall to 开始，开始吃
firearms ['faɪr,ɑrmz] n. 火器，轻武器
forbear [fɔː'beə(r)] v. 忍耐，克制，避免 n. 祖先
fortitude ['fɔːtɪtjuːd; (*US*) -tuːd] n. 坚韧
foundling ['faʊndlɪŋ] n. 弃儿，育婴堂
gallant [gæ'lənt] adj. 英勇的，豪侠的，对妇女献殷勤的
genteel [ədʒen'tiːl] adj. 上流社会的
Guinea ['gɪnɪ] n. 几内亚，几尼（英国的旧金币，值一镑一先令）
highwayman ['haɪweɪmən] n. 路劫，拦路强盗
hypocrisy [hɪ'pɔkrɪsɪ] n. 伪善

hypocrite ['hɪpəkrɪt] n. 伪君子，伪善者
hypocritical [hɪpə'krɪtɪk(ə)l] adj. 伪善的，伪善者的
imminent ['ɪmɪnənt] adj. 即将来临的，逼近的
impetuosity [ɪmˌpetjʊ'ɔsətɪ] n. 激烈，冲动，性急
impetuous [ɪm'petjʊəs] adj. 冲动的，猛烈的
impetuously [ɪmˌpetjʊ'ɔsəlɪ] adv. 激烈地，性急地
impute [ɪm'pjuːt] vt. 归罪于，归咎于，归因于
inducement [ɪn'djuːsmənt] n. 诱导，诱因，动机，刺激物
masculine ['mæskjʊlɪn] adj. 男性的，男子气概的
matrimonial [mætrɪ'məʊnɪəl] adj. 与婚姻有关的
mettle ['met(ə)l] n. 勇气
mettlesome ['met(ə)lsəm] adj. 精神饱满的，勇敢的
mischief ['mɪstʃɪf] n. 伤害，恶作剧
mishap ['mɪshæp] n. 灾祸
modesty ['mɔdɪstɪ] n. 谦逊，虚心
muzzle ['mʌz(ə)l] n. 动物之鼻口，（动物的）口套 vt. 戴口络于，上口罩
novice ['nɔvɪs] n. 新手，初学者
oath [əʊθ] n. 誓言，宣誓，诅咒
oblige [ə'blaɪdʒ] vt. 迫使
panoramic [ˌpænə'ræmɪk,-'rɑː-] adj. 全景的
partiality [pɑːʃɪ'ælɪtɪ] n. 偏爱
partridge ['pɑːtrɪdʒ] n. [鸟] 山鹑，鹧鸪
peril ['perɪl] n. 危险
pert [pɜːt] adj. 无礼的，鲁莽的，辛辣的，活跃的
prance [prɑːns] n.（马）后足立地腾跃，昂首阔步 vi. 腾跃 vt. 使腾跃
prevail on 说服，诱使
prevail [prɪ'veɪl] vi. 流行，盛行，获胜，成功
rogue [rəʊg] n. 流氓，无赖 vt. 欺诈 vi. 流浪，耍无赖，游手好闲
sentiment ['sentɪmənt] n. 情操，情感，情绪，观点，多愁善感，感情
solicitous [sə'lɪsɪtəs] adj. 热切期望的
Sophia [sə'faɪə] 索菲娅（女子名）
squire ['skwaɪə(r)] n. 乡绅
timidity [tɪ'mɪdətɪ] n. 胆怯
transgression [træns'greʃən] n. 违反，犯罪，[地] 海侵，海进
trifle ['traɪf(ə)l] n. 琐事，少量，蛋糕，小事 v. 开玩笑，玩弄，虚度，浪费，嘲弄
unruly [ʌn'ruːlɪ] adj. 不受拘束的，不守规矩的，蛮横的，难驾驭的
valor ['vælə(r)] n. 英勇，勇猛 = valour
vehement ['viːəmənt] adj. 激烈的，猛烈的
veracity [və'ræsətɪ] n. 说真实话，老实，精确性
victorious [vɪk'tɔːrɪəs] adj. 获胜的，胜利的
villainy ['vɪlənɪ] n. 邪恶，恶行，罪恶
whence [wens] n. 来处，根源 adv. 从何处，从哪里 = from where
wrest [rest] n. 扭，拧 vt. 夺取，猛扭，费力取得

译文

第四卷 第十三章

一件非常可怕的意外发生在苏菲娅身上，琼斯的义勇行动，和那番行动给那位年轻小姐带来非常可怕的后果；附带加几句对女性说的好话。

威斯屯先生对于他女儿的疼爱，真是一天一天地与日俱增，到后来，连他最喜好的猎狗，在他心里几乎都得让位给他对女儿之爱。但是让他自觉放弃猎狗，还是办不到的，因此他想了一个很巧妙的办法，既能让自己享到和猎狗在一块儿的快乐，同时又能使他女儿不离开他的身边，这种办法就是，叫他女儿和他一块儿骑马逐猎。

苏菲娅是把她父亲的话当作圣旨一样看待的，所以一下就俯首帖耳，言听计从，以顺应她父亲的意愿；虽然她对于逐猎这种游戏，丝毫不感兴趣；因为这种游戏太猛烈，太男性化了，不适于她这种人的性格。不过，她除了要服从她父亲以外，要和老人家一块儿逐猎，还有另一种动机；因为，有她在眼前，她希望多少能把他那种鲁莽的劲头加以节制，同时免得使他时常有折颈断脰之虞。

她现在对这件事反对最力的方面，正是这件事以前对她最具吸引力的，那就是：和年轻的琼斯时常见面儿。而如今她决心避而不再见他。现在逐猎结束的季节就近在眼前，她希望，逐猎结束之后，她和她姑姑短短地待一个时期，她就可以用理智完全战这番不幸的热烈感情而胜之，同时还一点儿都不怀疑，在下一季的猎场上和他相遇的时候，重新坠入情网的危险就一点儿也没有了。

她第二天参加了逐猎；逐猎已毕，在归途中，正走到离威斯屯先生的家没有多远的地方，她骑的那匹马，本来性子就暴躁，得有善骑的人才能驾驭，忽然开始又举后腿，又蹦高儿，那种样子，把她弄得大有立刻就摔下马来的危险。汤姆·琼斯那时正在她后面离她不远，看到这种情况，就打马飞奔，前去援救。他刚一来到她跟前，就从自己的马上跳下来，抓住了她那匹马的缰绳。那匹野性难驯的畜生，立刻把后腿完全举起，把那个可爱的骑马人，从马背上掀了下来，琼斯急忙双手把她托住。

她当时突然一惊，丢魂失魄，所以琼斯战战兢兢，万分担心，问她是否受了伤，她竟没能立刻回答。但是，过了一会儿，她心神稍微安定下来了，才对他说，她平安无事，同时对他的救护，表示感谢。琼斯回答说，“小姐，我既然使您安全无恙，那就足够偿还我的所失了，因为我可以对您实说，我能豁出去受比这次更大得多的不幸，好叫您免于即便最小的伤害。”

“什么不幸？”苏菲娅急煎煎地问道，“我只希望，你可别受到什么伤害。”

“您不必挂怀，小姐，”琼斯回答说。“看您刚才这种险情，您能毫无损伤就逃出危境，真得谢天谢地。虽然我的胳膊折了，但是我一想到我替您担的惊怕，那我的胳膊只能算是小事一桩。”

苏菲娅于是尖声喊道，“胳膊折了！哎哟，我的天，可别真出这种事儿！”

“我恐怕我的胳膊是折了，”琼斯说，“不过我求您先允许我照顾您。我还有右手，可以服侍您，能把您扶到前面那块地里。从那儿再往您父亲的家里去，就没有几步路了。”

苏菲娅看到他的左手耷拉下来了，他只用右手带着她前进，就对于事实丝毫没有疑问了。她现在脸上的灰白，比刚才为自己害怕时更厉害。她全身连胳膊带腿，都不由自主地哆嗦起来，因此琼斯都几乎扶不住她了。同时，她心里既然也同样骚动扰乱，所以不由得带着满怀温柔之情，看了琼斯一眼，这一眼所表示的，假设只有感激和怜悯，联合一起，从最温柔的女性胸怀里发出，而没有第三种更强烈的感情掺入其中，决不会那样富于柔情。

在这件意外发生的时候，威斯屯先生正走到前面相当远的地方，他现在勒马转回，其余骑马的人也都勒马转回。苏菲娅马上告诉了他们，说琼斯怎样受伤，请他们照顾他。威斯屯先生原先看到他女儿的马空无人骑，吓了一跳，现在看到女儿安然无恙，就不胜欣慰，听她这样一说，马上喊道，“没比这个再坏，就好极了。汤姆要是把胳膊折了，那咱们找个接骨匠，给他把骨头接起来。”

乡绅下了马，和他女儿，还有汤姆，一块儿步行回到家里。那时候，要是一个胸无成见的人，在路上遇到他们，而留神看他们各自脸上的神色，一定会认为，只有苏菲娅自己是怜悯的对象，因为说到琼斯，他只认为，他这是十有八九只伤了一只胳膊，而就把那个年轻女士的命救了，心里正不胜欢喜，威斯屯先生呢，他虽然对琼斯所遭的意外，并非漠不关心，但是却因为女儿侥幸脱险免难，他的快乐，远远超过他对琼斯的关切。

苏菲娅的性格里那种高远超逸，把琼斯这番行动解释为大义大勇，所以他这次的行动，在她心里印上了很深的印象，因为，毫无疑问，没有任何品质，能像现在这一种这样，普遍地使男子受到女子的欢心青眼的了。其所以如此，如果我们相信一般人的意见，只是由于妇女鸡心小胆，出于天性。奥兹本说过，“妇女性最胆小，在上帝所创造的人和物里，没有比女人更怯懦的了。”——这种意见里，直率的成分，多于真实的成分。亚里士多德在他的《政治学》里对于妇女更公正一些。他说，“男子之谦虚退让与坚忍不拔和女子在这两方面有所不同，因为适合于女子的坚忍不拔，在男子身上，就变成了怯懦畏葸。适合于男子的谦虚退让，在女子身上，则变成了冒失鲁莽。”有的人，把妇女易于对勇敢的男人特别垂爱这一点，归之于妇女之特别胆小心怯，这种意见也同样不错。培尔先生，我想，在他记载《海伦》那一条里，把这种情况归之于妇女强烈地喜欢光荣，这也是更合事理之常。这种解释，我们有一个最有权威的人，他在一切人中最能深远地了解人性。他把他那部《奥德赛》里的女主角，作为夫妻之爱，守贞不渝的代表人物写在书里，他就把她丈夫的荣耀作为是她所以爱他的唯一根源。

反正不管怎么样，这件事却一点儿也不错，在苏菲娅心里起了强烈的作用。并且，实在说起来，我把这件事经过大力考查了以后，极为相信，就在同时，那位迷人的苏菲娅也同样在汤姆心里留下了深刻的印象。要据实以书，那就得说，他早就已经对她那种迷人之处不可抵抗的力量心领神会了。

第十二卷　第十四章

琼斯先生从圣奥勒贲出发后，路上所遇。

他们现在出了巴奈特以外有二英里地左右，就暮色苍茫了，这时候，一个样子很文雅的人，却骑着一匹瘦弱不堪的劣马，走到琼斯跟前，开口问他，是不是要往伦敦去。对这个问题，琼斯答了个是字。那位绅士于是说，“先生，您要是肯让我跟您搭个伴儿，那我可就太感激您了。因为天色已经很晚了，我又是这条路上的稀客。”琼斯慨允所请，于是他们就一同前行，所谈的话无非是在这种场合里普通常谈的那一类。

当然，他们所谈，还是以强盗路劫为主：对这方面，那个新来的旅伴深表忧惧，但是琼斯却当众宣称，他几乎无所可失，因此自然也同样就无所可畏了。说到这儿，派崔济却忍不住掺上他要所说的一言半语。“先生您，”他说，“当然可以认为，那几乎如同无物，但是我自己可一定知道，要是我兜儿里有一百镑钱的钞票，像先生您兜儿里那样，那我要是把它丢了，一定要觉得难过，但是，说到我自己，我一生中，没有比现在更胆子大的了，因为我们一共有四个人，如果我们互相帮助，那即便英国顶强悍的大盗也抢不了我们。假设他有手枪，那他也只能打死一个人，而人总归都未免要死一回。——这就是我可以聊以自慰的，一个人都要死一回。”

除了人多势众（就凭这种优势，近代诸国中的某一国得到高度荣誉），派崔济还表现了另一种使他们勇气勃勃的原因，因为他现在刚喝过大量的酒，而酒力给他的胆量，正如酒量之大。

我们这一伙旅客现在来到离亥盖特不足一英里的地方了，这时候，那个生人突然转身朝着琼斯，掏出一支手枪来，对准了琼斯，跟他要刚才派崔济提到的那张小小的钞票。

琼斯冷不防听到这个人索取钞票，刚一开始未免有些吃了一惊。但是，他马上就镇定下来，对那个马上的强盗说，他口袋儿里所有的钱，全都归他随便花用，他一面这样说，一面把三个还多的几尼掏了出来，想要交到路劫手里；但是那个路劫骂了一句，说那可不成。琼斯冷静地答道，那他可就对不起了，把钱又装回口袋儿里。

马贼于是威吓说，要是他不把钞票马上就交出来，那他可要开枪了，同时把枪很近地对准了琼斯的胸膛。琼斯一下把那个家伙的手抓住了（只见那只手哆嗦得很厉害，几乎连手枪都拿不住的样子），把枪口拨到离开他那一面儿。于是跟着来了一场争夺战，在这场争夺战里，琼斯从敌人手里把手枪扭取过去，两个一齐落到马下，强盗仰卧地上，取得胜利的琼斯就俯临强盗身上。

那个可怜的人现在哀告起胜利者来，叫他大发慈悲，因为，要说实在的，他的气力远非琼斯的对手。“我说实话，先生，我绝没有拿枪打您的意思；因为您可以看出来，枪里并没装子弹。我想劫人，这还是初出茅庐，我实在是为穷所逼，没有法子，才出此下策。”

在这会儿了，离得有一百五十码左右的地方，另一个人躺在地上，大呼饶命，其吼声之高远远过于那个强盗。这不是别人，正是派崔济自己，他刚才看到两人交起手来，尽力临阵脱逃，因而翻身落马，来了个嘴啃泥，一点儿也不敢抬头看，只等每一分钟都挨枪子儿。

他就在这样的姿势里，趴在地上，一直等到向导，一心不想别的，只顾马有个好歹，他把打前失的马用手带起来以后，才来到派崔济跟前，告诉他说，他的主人已经占了强盗的上风了。派崔济一听这个消息，一跃而起，跑到琼斯身边，那时琼斯正拔剑在手，挺身看着那个可怜的战败者。派崔济一见这样，马上就大声喊道，“把这个浑蛋宰了，先生，把他捅个透明，马上就把他报销了！”

但是，对于这个可怜的苦人，总得说运气好，正落到一个心地慈悲的人手里；因为琼斯，在派崔济还没来到他跟前的时候早已把手枪检查了一下，只见枪膛里确实没装子弹，就开始相信这个人对他所说的一切来，那也就是说，这个干这种事的人还是个雏儿，他所以干这种事，实在是为他说的那种困苦所逼，而这个困苦，还真正是人所想得到的困苦中最大的困苦，因为他有五个嗷嗷待哺的孩子，他老婆又生了第六个，正坐月子，都是贫穷困苦得不能再贫穷困苦了。这个强盗指天誓日地坚决声称，说他说的都是实话，并且请琼斯多多受累，亲自到他家里去看一看，以证明他所说的无一虚假，他的家离那儿只二英里多点儿。

他说，他不敢求他施恩加惠，只是要证实一下，他所说的一切，是否可靠。

琼斯一开始的时候，假装着要以实为实，听这个人的话，和他一同到他家里去；他当众宣称，这个人的命运完全决定于他说的话真实不真实。这个可怜的人，一听这话，马上表示急于让他快快去看一看，这样一来，琼斯就完全认为，他的话确实不假，同时还对那个人生出一番恻隐之心，怜悯之情。他把那支空手枪还了那个人，教他想一种规规矩矩的谋生之道，以解决他的困苦，给了他两个几尼，以解他太太和孩子的燃眉之急，又找补了一句说，他倒恨不得能多给他点儿，可是刚才说的那一百镑并不是他自己的。

对于这个行动，我们的读者大有可能分营对垒，意见不同。有一些也许要把这件事看作是异常仁慈而大加赞赏，另外那些性情较阴郁黏糊的就要认为，这种办法，是不顾人人对国家应尽的那种重视法律的职责。派崔济毫无疑问，就是用这种眼光看待这番举动的；因为他由于这件事，展现了好多不满的情绪，引了一句古老谚语，并且说，如果这个坏蛋，在他们到伦敦以前，再打劫他们一番，他丝毫不觉得奇怪。

这个强盗是满口感恩戴德之言，满怀感恩戴德之情。他还当真流起泪来，或者也许是假装着流起泪来。他起咒赌誓地说，他要一直回家，从此以后永远也不再干这种犯法的勾当了，至于他是否言而有信，我们也许以后可以看到。

我们的旅人又上了马，没再遇到任何别的不幸，就到了伦敦。一路之上，琼斯和派崔济之间，对于他们刚碰到的这件奇事，交谈了好些颇为可乐的话，在这番交谈里，琼斯只对那些强盗表示大大的怜悯，因为他们都是由于无法逃避的困苦，才铤而走险，以身试法，这般人一般都落到死于非命的可耻下场。“我的意思，”他说，“只指着那般做的坏事最大也不超过抢劫的人而言，那也就是，除了抢劫，永远没犯残酷或者侮辱罪行的人而言，这种情况，我得说，是我们这个国家可以引为自豪的，是使英国的盗匪有异于所有其他各国的盗匪的，因为在其他各国里，杀人的事件几乎和抢劫是分不开的。”

“毫无疑问，”派崔济答道，“只把人的钱夺去，比把人的命夺去，要好得多，然而忠厚老实人，因为出门办事，在路上可不免遭到这种恶人的危险，这对他们来说，日子也太不好过了。一点儿不错，所有的坏蛋都绞死，以免妨害别人，总要比一个老实人遭殃受祸要好。说到我自己，我确实不愿意我的手沾上他们之中任何人的血，但是按法把他们个个都绞死，可是恰当不易的。要是我自己不是出于情愿，那什么人有权力能把我的六便士拿走？这样的人难道还懂得什么是羞恶之心吗？”

“当然没有，这是不错的，”琼斯喊道，“这也跟从别人的马棚里把马拉走，或者把他捡到的钱，明知道是谁的，而可昧起心来，留着自己用的人，同样地不知道什么叫羞恶之心。”

这样的暗讽明嘲，把派崔济的嘴一下封住；他没再开口，一直等到琼斯用几句笑话，挖苦他胆小如鼠，才张嘴为自己解脱说，火器哪能和肉身等量齐观？他说，“一千个赤手空拳的人对付一支手枪，完全无济于事，因为固然不错，一支枪放一次只能打死一个人，但是有谁敢担保，说枪子有眼，打死的那个不会是自己呢？”

（张谷若　译）

第六单元

十八世纪的诗歌

词汇

ablution [əˈbluːʃ(ə)n] n. 清洗

adieu [əˈdjuː] int. n. 再见，再会

aloft [əˈlɔft] adv. 在高处，在上

anthem [ˈænθəm] n. 圣歌，赞美诗

Arcady [ˈɑːkədɪ] n.〈诗〉=Arcadia，Arcadia n. 阿卡狄亚，世外桃源

aristo [əˈrɪstəʊ] n.〈英口〉（一个）贵族

attic [ˈætɪk] n. 阁楼，顶楼，adj.（古希腊）雅典（Athens）的

aurelian [ɔːˈriːljən] adj. 蛹的，水母的，n. 蝶蛾研究家，昆虫采集家

Bacchus [ˈbækəs] n. 巴克斯，酒神

balboa [bælˈbəʊə] n. 巴拿马的银币

bard [bɑːd] n. 吟游诗人

beechen [ˈbiːtʃən] adj. 山毛榉制的

bleat [bliːt] n. 叫声 v. 低声诉说

bourn [bʊən] n. 小溪，目的地，界限，境界

bower [ˈbaʊə(r)] n. 凉亭

breaker [ˈbreɪkə(r)] n. 断路器

brede [briːd] n. 编带，刺绣

chaff [tʃɑːf; (*US*) tʃæf] n. 谷壳，糠，愚弄 v. 戏弄，开玩笑

chapman [ˈtʃæpmən] n. 商人，小贩，叫卖者

choir [ˈkwaɪə(r)] n. 唱诗班，唱诗班的席位

citadel [ˈsɪtəd(ə)l] n. 根据地，大本营

clammy [ˈklæmɪ] adj. 湿粘的，湿冷的

cloy [klɔɪ] vt. 过饱，使厌腻 vi. 吃饱

colossal [kəˈlɔs(ə)l] adj. 巨大的，庞大的

consumption [kənˈsʌmpʃ(ə)n] n. 消费，消费量，肺病

croft [krɔft] n. 小田地

crux [krʌks] n. 症结

dale [deɪl] n. 宽谷，溪谷

darkling [ˈdɑːklɪŋ] adv. 在暗中 adj. 令人可怕的，黑暗的

dawning ['dɔːnɪŋ] n. 拂晓，黎明

deity ['diːɪtɪ] n. 神，神性

delve [delv] v. 钻研

demesne [dɪ'miːn, dɪ'meɪn] n. 土地之所有，领地，私有地

Dionysian [daɪə'nɪzɪən] adj. 酒神节的，狂饮的

drowse [draʊz] n. 困，瞌睡 vi. 打瞌睡 vt. 使瞌睡

dryad ['draɪæd] n. [希神] 森林女神

ecstasy ['ekstəsɪ] n. 入迷

eglantine ['egləntaɪn] n. [植] 野蔷薇的一种

elf [elf] n. 小精灵，矮人，淘气鬼，恶作剧的人，恶人

embalm [ɪm'bɑːm] vt. 涂香油于（尸体），施以防腐剂，铭记于心，使不朽

endear [ɪn'dɪə(r)] vt. 使亲密，使受钟爱

Endymion [en'dɪmɪən] n. [希神] 恩底弥翁（月神）

enigmatic [enɪg'mætɪk] adj. 谜一般的，高深莫测的

eremite ['erɪmɑɪt] n. 遁世修行的人，隐士

exordium [ek'sɔːdɪəm] n.（讲话论文等）开端，绪言，绪论

faery ['feɪərɪ] n. 仙子，仙境 adj. 幻想的，仙女的

famed [feɪmd] adj. 著名的，闻名的

fealty ['fiːəltɪ] n.（对封建主义的）效忠，孝顺，忠诚，忠贞，忠实

flank [flæŋk] n. 侧面 vi. 侧面与……相接

foliage ['fəʊlɪɪdʒ] n. 树叶，植物

forlorn [fɔː'lɔːn] adj. 被遗弃的

fret [fret] v.（使）烦恼，（使）焦急，（使）腐蚀，（使）磨损

fringe [frɪndʒ] n. 边缘

gnat [næt] n. 小昆虫，小烦扰

gourd [gʊəd] n. 葫芦

granary ['grænərɪ] n. 壳仓，粮仓

Grecian ['griːʃ(ə)n] adj. 希腊的，希腊式的 n. 希腊学家

haply ['hæplɪ] adv.〈古〉偶然地，大致上，或许

hast [hæst] vbl.have 的第二人称单数现在式

hawthorn ['hɔːθɔːn] n. 山楂

hazel ['heɪz(ə)l] n. 榛子，淡褐色 adj. 榛树的，淡褐色的

heath [əhiːθ] n. 荒地；石南丛生的荒地

hedge [hedʒ] n. 树篱，障碍物 v. 用树篱围住，避免作正面答复

heifer ['hefə(r)] n. 小母牛

hemlock ['hemlɔk] n. [植] 芹叶钩吻，用芹叶钩吻制取的毒药

Hippocrene [ˌhɪpəʊ'kriːniː,'hɪpəʊkriːn] n. 山之灵泉，诗的灵感

immature [ɪmə'tjʊə(r)] adj. 不成熟的，未完全发展的

incense [ɪn'sens] n. 熏香，熏香的烟 vt. 激怒

indenture [ɪn'dentʃə(r)] n. 契约

instinctive [ɪn'stɪŋktɪv] adj. 本能的

knell [nel] n. 丧钟 v. 敲丧钟

lamia ['leɪmɪə] n. 女怪，妖妇

Leigh [liː] n. 利（Lee 的异体）（m.）

Lethe ['liːθiː] n. [希神] 遗忘河，忘却，

遗忘

livery stable 马车行，马房

loth [lɔθ]（=loath）adj. 憎恶的，勉强的

lustrous ['lʌstrəs] adj. 有光泽的，光辉的

marble ['mɑːb(ə)l] n. 大理石，adj. 无情的，坚硬的

mellow ['meləʊ] adj.（因熟透而）醇香的

mellow ['meləʊ] adj.（因熟透而）醇香的、甘美的

morn [mɔːn] n.〈诗〉早晨，〈苏格兰〉明天

mortal ['mɔːt(ə)l] n. 凡人，人类 adj. 必死的

moss [mɔs; (*US*) mɔːs] n. 苔，藓

musk [mʌsk] n. 麝香鹿，能发出麝香的各种各样的植物

myriad ['mɪrɪəd] n. 无数，〈诗〉一万 adj. 无数的，一万的，种种的

opiate ['əʊpɪət,-eɪt] n. 鸦片剂 adj. 安眠的 v. 缓和

over-brimmed, brim [brɪm] n.（杯，碗等）边，边缘，（河）边 vt. 注满

palsy ['pɔːlzɪ] n. 瘫痪

pard [pɑːd] n. 豹，伙伴

pedestal ['pedɪst(ə)l] n. 基架，底座，基础 vt. 加座，搁在台上，支持

perplex [pə'pleks] v. 困惑

pious ['paɪəs] adj. 虔诚的，尽责的

poesy ['pəʊɪsɪ] n. 作诗法，诗歌

poppy ['pɔpɪ] n. [植] 罂粟，深红色

Provencal [prɔvɔn'sɑːl] adj. 普罗旺斯的 n. 普罗旺斯人

ravish ['rævɪʃ] v. 强夺

reap [riːp] v. 收割，收获 half-reaped

requiem ['rekwɪəm,'reɪ-,'riː-] n. [天主教] 安灵弥撒，安灵曲，挽歌，悲歌

robust [rəʊ'bʌst] adj. 精力充沛的

rue [ruː] n.〈古〉懊悔，后悔，[植] 芸香 v. 后悔，悲伤，懊悔

sallow ['sæləʊ] adj. 菜色 v. 变成菜色

seasonable ['siːzənəb(ə)l] adj. 合时的

serene [sɪ'riːn] adj. 平静的

sever ['sevə(r)] v. 切断

sod [sɔd] n. 草地 v. 铺草皮于

spectre-thin adj. 瘦骨嶙峋的

stedfast ['stedfəst] adj. 笃定的，踏实的

steep [stiːp] adj. 陡峭的，不合理的 n. 悬崖，浸渍，沉浸

stout [staʊt] adj. 结实的，勇敢坚定的，激烈的

stubble ['stʌb(ə)l] n. 断株，茬，短发

surmise [sə'maɪz] v. 猜测 n. 猜度

tease [tiːz] n. 戏弄 vt. 取笑，嘲弄，强求，梳理

thatch [θætʃ] n. 茅草屋顶，浓密的头发 vt. 用茅草覆盖屋顶

thicket ['θɪkɪt] n. 灌木丛

timbrel ['tɪmbr(ə)l] n. 小手鼓

treble ['treb(ə)l] adj. 三倍的，最高音部的 v. 成三倍

trunkless ['trʌŋklɪs] adj. 无躯干的，与躯干分离的

twitter ['twɪtə(r)] n. 鸟鸣声，喋喋不休，vi. 鸟鸣，摆动

urn [ɜːn] n. 瓮，缸

verdurous ['vɜːdʒərəs] adj. 碧绿的，草

木青翠的

vintage ['vɪntɪdʒ] n. 制造年期，葡萄收获期 adj. 洒的 v. 收葡萄

visage ['vɪzɪdʒ] n.〈书〉面貌，容貌

wailful ['weɪlfʊl] adj. 悲叹的，哀悼的

watcher ['wɔtʃə(r), 'wɔː-] n. 看守人，岗哨，观察者，注视者

wherewith [weə'wɪθ,-'wɪð] adv. 用什么，用那个，以其

winnow ['wɪnəʊ] vt. 簸，扬（谷），精选 vi. 扬谷

woe [wəʊ] n. 悲哀

writ [rɪt] n. 文书，正式文件，书面命令

wrought [rɔːt] vbl. work 的过去式和过去分词 adj. 做成的，形成的，精炼的

译文

1. 扫烟囱的小男孩

布莱克

风雪里一个满身乌黑的小东西，
“号啊，号”在那里哭哭啼啼！
“你的爹娘上哪去了，你讲讲？”
“他们呀都去祷告了，上了教堂。

“因为我原先在野地里欢欢喜喜，
我在冬天的雪地里也总是笑嘻嘻，
他们就把我拿晦气的黑衣裳一罩，
他们还叫我唱起了悲伤的曲调。

“因为我显得快活，还唱歌，还跳舞，
就以为并没有把我害苦，
就跑去赞美上帝，教士和国王，
夸他们拿我们的苦难造成了天堂。”

（卞之琳　译）

2. 一朵红红的玫瑰花

彭斯

呵，我的爱人像朵红红的玫瑰，
六月里迎风初开；
呵，我的爱人像支甜甜的曲子，
奏得合拍又和谐。

我的好姑娘，你有多么美，

我的情也有多么深。
我将永远爱你，亲爱的，
直到大海干枯水流尽。

直到大海干枯水流尽，
太阳把岩石烧作灰尘，
我也永远爱你，亲爱的，
只要我一息犹存。

珍重吧，我唯一的爱人，
珍重吧，让我们暂时别离，
我准定回来，亲爱的，
哪怕跋涉千万里！

（王佐良　译）

3. 我曾在海外异乡漫游

华兹华斯

我曾在海外异乡漫游，
接触的全都是陌生人；
英格兰啊！那时我才知，
我对你的眷恋多么深！

那忧郁的梦已成往事！
你的海岸我不愿离开，
再也不愿；因为，看起来，
我对你越来越更热爱！

在你那起伏的山峦中，
我感受过满足的欢乐；
我心爱的她踏着纺车，
在英国式壁炉边工作。

露西留连忘返的亭榭，
在你夜色、晨曦中隐现；
你那碧绿田野，也是她
最后凝视过的美好景象。

（田乃钊　译）

4. 在威斯敏斯特桥上

华兹华斯

世界上没别的能比这更加美丽，
要是谁竟能忽略这动人的美景，
那么，这人真有个迟钝的性灵：
现在，美丽的清晓像一袭晨衣

罩着这都会，静谧而一览无遗——
船舶塔楼，剧场教堂和圆屋顶，
从野外和高处望去，一一分明，
在无烟无雾的清朗晴空里闪熠；
太阳从没有用它那华美的初照
把山，谷和岩石染得更加艳丽，
这宁静我真从未见到或感觉到。
泰晤士河自由自在轻快流去：
上帝啊，那些房看来都睡着；
那颗强大的心脏正躺着歇息！

（黄杲炘　译）

5. 当我俩分手时

拜伦

我俩当初分手时
默默无言，泪流满面，
我们的心儿已半碎，
一别将是多少年，
你的脸苍白冰冷，
你的吻更加冰凉；
就是那个时光，
预示着今天的凄凉。
那天黎明的露水
将寒气渗透我的额眉；
像是一种警告，
预示我此刻的伤悲。
你的誓言早已破碎，
名声也不再珍贵；
听人提到你的名字，
我只有感到羞愧。
他们对我提到你的名字，
像丧钟敲进我耳里；
我感到浑身颤栗——
当初为什么那么亲密？
他们不知我认识你，
不知我对你太熟悉；
我会久久为你痛苦，
太深太深言语无法表述。
我们曾幽期密约，
如今我默默哀伤，
你的心竟能忘却，
你的灵魂竟会欺诳。
多少年以后
你我如再次相见，
我该怎样迎接你？——
唯有泪水，默默无言。

（马海波　译　何功杰　校译）

6. 奥西曼提斯

雪莱

客自海外归，曾见沙漠古国
有石像半毁，唯余巨腿
蹲立沙砾间。像头旁落，
半遭沙埋，但人面依然可畏，
那冷笑，那发号施令的高傲，
足见雕匠看透了主人的心，
才把那石头刻得神情唯肖，
而刻像的手和像主的心
早成灰烬。像座上大字在目：
“吾乃万王之王是也，
盖世功业，敢叫天公折服。”
此外无一物，但见废墟周围，
寂寞平沙空莽莽，
伸向荒凉的四方。

（王佐良　译）

7. 夜莺颂

济慈

一
我的心疼痛啊，似有一种昏昏欲睡
感官麻木的痛苦，仿佛饮了毒芹，
或吞服了大量鸦片使全身麻醉，
顷刻之间就向列斯忘川下沉。
这并非是我羡慕你的幸福命运，
而是你的欢乐使我太欢欣，
你呀，森林之仙，羽翼轻盈，
在长满山毛榉的
欢悦之地，在无数的树影里，
你放声自由歌唱夏季。

二
哦！我多么想饮一杯葡萄佳酿，
在深掘的地窖里冷藏的年代很久，
它有乡村的花香和绿野的风光，
普鲁旺斯的阳光、舞蹈和歌声悠悠。
哦！要是能饮上一杯真正的灵泉，
来自南国，充溢着殷红和温暖，
珍珠般的泡沫在杯沿眨眼，
染成紫色的嘴唇闪灿，
一杯过肠就悄然离开这个世界，
和你一道遁隐到那幽暗的林间。

三
远远地退隐，消融，完全忘却
你在枝叶间从不知道的事情，
那劳累，那烧热，和那烦忧；

这儿，人们坐听着彼此的呻吟；
瘫痪老人最后几根悲哀白发在摇晃，
年轻人变得苍白，消瘦，最后死亡；
这儿，你只要想一想就满腹悲伤，
双眼沉重，完全失望；
这儿，美难以保持她的双眸发亮，
新欢在憔悴，待不到明天。

四
去吧！去吧！因为我将要飞向你，
不乘酒神之车，不要群豹驾辕，
只乘那无形的诗神羽翼，
虽然迟钝的大脑使我困惑，迟缓：
我早已和你在一起！夜如此温柔，
后也正好登上了她的宝座，
四周有璀璨的星仙侍候：
但这儿没有亮光，
除了从天上吹来的微风，
穿过葱绿的幽暗和苔藓曲径。

五
我看不清脚下是什么花草，
也辨不清枝头上飘溢的是什么清香，
但是，在芬芳的黑暗里我可以猜到
五月时节赋予的是什么芬芳
给野果树，丛林，和绿草；
田园里的野蔷薇、白山楂；
叶丛下那些易谢的紫罗兰；
五月中旬最先开放的宠花，
以及露珠晶莹即将开放的麝香玫瑰，
夏夜蚊蝇，嗡嗡造访的地方。

六
我在黑暗中倾听；曾有多少次
我几乎爱上了安逸的“死亡”，
多少次在诗中轻轻呼唤你的名字，
请你把我的气息带到空中。
此刻死去似更富情味，
半夜里停止呼吸，没有痛苦，
而你仍在倾吐你的心声，
如此神醉，如此狂喜！
你将一直歌唱，我有耳也听不见——
你的安魂曲，如草泥一片。

七
永生的鸟儿啊，你天生不会死去！
没有任何饥饿的一代能把你蹂躏；
我在这消逝的夜晚听到的歌声
古代的帝王和村民也曾聆听；
或许就是这同样的一首歌曲
曾使露丝心碎，当她思念家乡，
在异乡的麦地里泪水汪汪；
这同样的歌曲
常把魔窗深深吸引，开着窗扉，
在凄凉的仙境，把汹涌的大海眺望。

八
凄凉啊！这个词的本身犹如钟鸣
把我从你处唤回，回到孤独的自己！
再见！幻想虽有欺骗的名声，但决不能
欺骗得如此巧妙竟能欺骗她自己。
再见！再见！你那哀怨的圣歌
飞过附近草地，飘过静谧小溪，
爬上了山坡，此刻它已深藏
在下个山谷的林间空地：

这是幻觉，抑或是醒着做梦？
那乐曲消失了：我是醒着还是在睡乡？

（何功杰　译）

8. 希腊古瓮颂

济慈

一

你委身“寂静”的、完美的处子，
受过了“沉默”和“悠久”的抚育，
呵，田园的史家，你竟能铺叙
一个如花的故事，比诗还瑰丽：
在你的形体上，岂非缭绕着
古老的传说，以绿叶为其边缘；
讲着人，或神，敦陂或阿卡狄？
呵，是怎样的人，或神！在舞乐前
多热烈的追求！少女怎样地逃躲！
怎样的风笛和鼓谣！怎样的狂喜！

二

听见的乐声虽好，但若听不见
却更美；所以，吹吧，柔情的风笛；
不是奏给耳朵听，而是更甜，
它给灵魂奏出无声的乐曲；
树下的美少年呵，你无法中断
你的歌，那树木也落不了叶子；
卤莽的恋人，你永远、永远吻不上，
虽然够接近了——但不必心酸；
她不会老，虽然你不能如愿以偿，
你将永远爱下去，她也永远秀丽！

三

呵，幸福的树木！你的枝叶
不会剥落，从不曾离开春天；
幸福的吹笛人也不会停歇，
他的歌曲永远是那么新鲜；
呵，更为幸福的、幸福的爱！
永远热烈，正等待情人宴飨，
永远热情地心跳，永远年轻；
幸福的是这一切超凡的情态：
它不会使心灵餍足和悲伤，
没有炽热的头脑，焦渴的嘴唇。

四

这些人是谁呵，都去赶祭祀？
这作牺牲的小牛，对天鸣叫，
你要牵它到哪儿，神秘的祭司？
花环缀满着它光滑的身腰。
是从哪个傍河傍海的小镇，
或哪个静静的堡寨山村，
来了这些人，在这敬神的清早？
呵，小镇，你的街道永远恬静；
再也不可能回来一个灵魂
告诉人你何以是这么寂寥。

五

哦，希腊的形状！唯美的观照！
上面缀有石雕的男人和女人，
还有林木，和践踏过的青草；
沉默的形体呵，你像是“永恒”
使人超越思想：呵，冰冷的牧歌！
等暮年使这一世代都凋落，
只有你如旧；在另外的一些
忧伤中，你会抚慰后人说：
“美即是真，真即是美”，这就包括
你们所知道，和该知道的一切。

（查良铮　译）

第七单元

傲慢与偏见

词汇

amend [ə'mend] n.（对毁坏、损坏的）赔偿，赔礼

assembly [ə'semblɪ] n. 集合，装配，集会，集结，汇编

caprice [kə'pri:s] n. 反复无常，任性，怪想

chuse [tʃu:z] v.〈古〉=choose

circumspection ['sə:kəm'spekʃn] n. 细心，慎重

condescension [kɔndɪ'senʃ(ə)n] n. 谦虚，硬要人家领情的态度

conjecture [kən'dʒektʃə(r)] n.v. 推测，臆说，猜想

decline [dɪ'klaɪn] vi. 下倾，v. 拒绝，衰落 n. 下倾，衰落

deign [deɪn] vi. 屈尊 vt. 赐予

discretion [dɪ'skreʃ(ə)n] n. 判断力

elope [ɪ'ləʊp] vi. 私奔，潜逃，出走

emphatic [ɪm'fætɪk] adj. 语势强的，用力的，显著的，断然的

engage for v. 保证

entail [ɪn'teɪl] vt. 限定继承权

fastidious [fæ'stɪdɪəs] adj. 难取悦的，挑剔的

fastidiousness [fæ'stɪdɪəsnəs] an. 严格，一丝不苟

fatigue [fə'ti:g] n. 疲乏

fret [fret] v.（使）烦恼，（使）焦急，fretfully adv. 焦躁地

insolent ['ɪnsələnt] n. 侮慢无礼的人 adj. 傲慢的，无礼的，侮慢的

justify ['dʒʌstɪfaɪ] v. 证明……是正当的

Michaelmas ['mɪkəlməs] n. 米迦勒节

patroness ['peɪtrənɪs, 'pæ-] n. 女资助人，女赞助者，女主顾

rapture ['ræptʃə(r)] n. 全神贯注，兴高采烈，欢天喜地 vt. 使狂喜

resentfully [rɪ'zentfəli] adv. 充满愤恨地

resolutely ['rezəluːtli] adv. 毅然地，坚决地
scandal ['skænd(ə)l] n. 丑行，丑闻，诽谤，耻辱，流言蜚语
scrupulous ['skruːpjʊləs] adj. 小心谨慎的，细心的
snobbishness ['snɔbɪʃnəs] n. 势利
solace ['sɔləs] n. 安慰 v. 安慰
stout [staʊt] adj. 结实的，矮胖的
tumult ['tjuːmʌlt] n. 吵闹，骚动，拥挤，混乱
vex [veks] vt. 使烦恼，恼怒
vulgar ['vʌlgə(r)] adj. 粗俗的，普通的，通俗的，本土的 n. 平民，百姓

译文

第一章

凡是有钱的单身汉，总想娶位太太，这已经成了一条举世公认的真理。这样的单身汉，每逢新搬到一个地方，四邻八舍虽然完全不了解他的性情如何，见解如何，可是，既然这样的一条真理早已在人们心目中根深蒂固，因此人们总是把他看作自己某一个女儿理所应得的一笔财产。

有一天班纳特太太对她的丈夫说："我的好老爷，尼日斐花园终于租出去了，你听说过没有？"

班纳特先生回答道，他没有听说过。

"的确租出去了，"她说，"朗格太太刚刚上这儿来过，她把这件事的底细，一五一十地告诉了我。"

班纳特先生没有理睬她。

"你难道不想知道是谁租去的吗？"太太不耐烦地嚷起来了。

"既是你要说给我听，我听听也无妨。"

这句话足够鼓励她讲下去了。

"哦！亲爱的，你得知道，郎格太太说，租尼日斐花园的是个阔少爷，他是英格兰北部的人；听说他星期一那天，乘着一辆驷马大轿车来看房子，看得非常中意，当场就和莫理斯先生谈妥了；他要在'米迦勒节'以前搬进来，打算下个周末先叫几个用人来住。"

"这个人叫什么名字？"

"彬格莱。"

"有太太的呢，还是单身汉？"

"噢！是个单身汉，亲爱的，确确实实是个单身汉！一个有钱的单身汉；每年有

四五千磅的收入。真是女儿们的福气！”

“这怎么说？关女儿们什么事？”

“我的好老爷，”太太回答道，“你怎么这样叫人讨厌！告诉你吧，我正在盘算，他要是挑中我们一个女儿做老婆，可多好！”

“他住到这儿来，就是为了这个打算吗？”

“打算！胡扯，这是哪儿的话！不过，他倒作兴看中我们的某一个女儿呢。他一搬来，你就得去拜访拜访他。”

“我不用去。你带着女儿们去就得啦，要不你干脆打发她们自己去，那或许倒更好些，因为你跟女儿们比起来，她们哪一个都不能胜过你的美貌，你去了，彬格莱先生倒可能挑中你呢？”

“我的好老爷，你太捧我啦。从前也的确有人赞赏过我的美貌，现在我可不敢说有什么出众的地方了。一个女人家有了五个成年的女儿，就不该对自己的美貌再转什么念头。”

“这样看来，一个女人家对自己的美貌也转不了多少念头喽。”

“不过，我的好老爷，彬格莱一搬到我们的邻近来，你的确应该去看看他。”

“老实跟你说吧，这不是我分内的事。”

“看女儿的分上吧。只请你想一想，她们不论哪一个，要是攀上了这样一个人家，该多么好。威廉爵士夫妇已经决定去拜望他，他们也无非是这个用意。你知道，他们通常是不会拜望新搬来的邻居的。你的确应该去一次，要是你不去，叫我们怎么去。”

“你实在过分心思啦。彬格莱先生一定高兴看到你的；我可以写封信给你带去，就说随便他挑中我哪一个女儿，我都心甘情愿地答应他把她娶过去；不过，我在信上得特别替小丽萃吹嘘几句。”

“我希望你别这么做。丽萃没有一点儿地方胜过别的几个女儿；我敢说，论漂亮，她抵不上吉英一半；论性子，她抵不上丽迪雅一半。可你老是偏爱她。”“她们没有哪一个值得夸奖的，”他回答道，“她们跟人家的姑娘一样，又傻，又无知；倒是丽萃要比她的几个姐妹伶俐些。”

“我的好老爷，你怎么舍得这样糟蹋自己的亲生女儿？你是在故意叫我气恼，好让你自己得意吧。你半点儿也不体谅我的神经衰弱。”

“你真错怪了我，我的好太太。我非常尊重你的神经。它们是我的老朋友。至少在最近二十年以来，我一直听到你慎重其事地提到它们。”

“啊！你不知道我怎样受苦呢！”

“不过我希望你这毛病会好起来，那么，像这种每年有四千镑收入的阔少爷，你就可以眼看着他们一个个搬来做你的邻居了。”

“你既然不愿意去拜访他们，即使有二十个搬了来，对我们又有什么好处！”

“放心吧，我的好太太，等到有了二十个，我一定去一个个拜望到。”

班纳特先生真是个古怪人，他一方面喜欢插科打诨，爱挖苦人，同时又不苟言笑，变幻莫测，真使他那位太太积二十三年之经验，还摸不透他的性格。太太的脑子是很容易加以分析的。她是个智力贫乏、不学无术、喜怒无常的女人，只要碰到不称心的事，她就以为神经衰弱。她生平的大事就是嫁女儿；她生平的安慰就是访友拜客和打听新闻。

第二章

班纳特先生尽管在自己太太面前自始至终都说是不想去拜访彬格莱先生，事实上一直都打算去拜访他，而且还是跟第一批人一起去拜访他的。等到他去拜访过以后，当天晚上太太才知道实情。这消息透露出来的经过是这样的——他看到第二个女儿在装饰帽子，就突然对她说：

“我希望彬格莱先生会喜欢你这顶帽子，丽萃。”

她母亲气愤愤地说：“我们既然不预备去看彬格莱先生，当然就无从知道他喜欢什么。”

“可是你忘啦，妈妈，”伊丽莎白说，“我们将来可以在跳舞会上碰到他的，郎格太太不是答应过把他介绍给我们吗？”

“我不相信郎格太太肯这么做。她自己有两个亲侄女。她是个自私自利、假仁假义的女人，我瞧不起她。”

“我也瞧不起她，”班纳特先生说，“你倒不指望她来替你效劳，这叫我听到高兴。”

班纳特太太没有理睬他，可是忍不住气，便骂起女儿来。

“别那么咳个不停，吉蒂，看老天爷分上吧！稍许体谅一下我的神经吧。你简直叫我的神经要胀裂啦。”

“吉蒂真不知趣，”她的父亲说，“咳嗽也不知道拣个时候。”

“我又不是故意咳着玩儿。”吉蒂气恼地回答道。

“你们的跳舞会定在哪一天开，丽萃？”

“从明天算起，还得再过两个星期。”

“唔，原来如此，”她的母亲嚷道，“郎格太太可要挨到开跳舞会的前一天才能赶回来；那么，她可来不及把他介绍给你们啦，她自己也还不认识他呢。”

“那么，好太太，你正可以占你朋友的上风，反过来替她介绍这位贵人啦。”

“办不到，我的好老爷，办不到，我自己还不认识他呢；你怎么可以这样嘲笑人？”

“我真佩服你想得这般周到。两个星期的认识当然谈不上什么。跟一个人相处了两个星期，不可能就此了解他究竟是怎样一个人。不过，要是我们不去尝试尝试，别人可少不了要尝试的。话说到底，郎格太太和她的侄女一定不肯错过这个良机。因此，要是你不愿意办这件事，我自己来办好了，反正她会觉得这是我们对她的一片好意。”

女儿们都对父亲瞪着眼。班纳特太太只随口说了声：“毫无意思！”

“你怎么这样大惊小怪！”他嚷道。“你以为替人家效点儿劳介绍是毫无意思的事吗？你这样的说法我可不大同意。你说呢，曼丽？我知道你是个有独到见解的少女，读的书都是皇皇巨著，而且还要做札记。”

曼丽想说几句有见识的话可又不知道怎么说才好。

于是班纳特先生接下去说：“让曼丽仔细想一想再发表意见吧，我们还是重新来谈谈彬格莱先生。”

“我就讨厌谈彬格莱先生。”他的太太嚷起来了。

“遗憾得很，你竟会跟我说这种话；你怎么不早说呢？要是今天上午听到你这样说，那我当然不会去拜访他啦。这真叫不凑巧。现在既然拜访也拜访过了，我们今后就少不了要结交这个朋友。“

果然不出他所料，娘儿们一听此说，一个个都大为惊异，尤其是班纳特太太，比谁都惊异得厉害；不过，这样欢天喜地地喧嚷了一阵以后，她便当众宣布，说这件事她早就料到的。

“你真是个好心肠的人，我的好老爷！我早就知道你终究会给我说服的。你既然疼爱自己的女儿，当然就不会把这样一个朋友不放在心上。我真太高兴了！你这个玩笑开得真太有意思，谁想到你竟会今天上午去拜访他，而且到现在一字不提。”

“吉蒂，现在你可以放心大胆地咳嗽啦。”班纳特先生一面说，一面走出房间，原来他看到太太那样得意忘形，不免觉得有些厌恶。门一关上，班纳特太太便对她的几个女儿说：“孩子们，你们的爸爸真太好了，我不知道你们怎样才能报答他的恩典；再说，你们还应该好好报答我一番呢。老实跟你们说吧，我们老夫妻活到这么一把年纪了，哪儿有兴致天天去交朋结友；可是为了你们，我们随便什么事都乐意去做。丽迪雅，乖宝贝，虽然你年纪最小，开起跳舞会来，彬格莱先生或许就偏偏要跟你跳呢。”

“噢！”丽迪雅满不在乎地说。

“我才不当它一回事。年纪虽然是我最小，个儿算我顶高。”

于是她们一方面猜测那位贵人什么时候会来回拜班纳特先生，一方面盘算着什么时候请他来吃饭，就这样把一个晚上的工夫在闲谈中度过去了。

（王科一　译）

第八单元

大卫·科波菲尔

词汇

a rash of 同时大量出现的事件

affable ['æfəb(ə)l] adj. 和蔼可亲的

affectionately [ə'fekʃənəth] adv. 亲切地

afore [ə'fɔː(r)] adv. prep. 在前

akimbo [ə'kɪmbəʊ] adj. adv. 两手叉腰的（地）

breeches ['brɪtʃɪz] n. 马裤,〈口〉裤子

ale [eɪl] n. 淡色啤酒

allude [ə'luːd] vi. 暗指，影射，间接提到

ascertain [æsə'teɪn] vt. 确定，探知

assent [ə'sent] n. 赞成 vi. 同意

bashfully adv. 羞怯地，内向地

batter ['bætə] n. 糊状物

boa ['bəʊə] n. 蟒蛇，女用毛皮，围巾

castor ['kɑːstə(r)] n. 调味瓶，车辘，小脚轮

child wife n. 年轻的妻子

choker ['tʃəʊkə(r)] n. 噎住的人，使人窒息之物，宽领带

comic ['kɔmɪk] n. 滑稽演员 adj. 滑稽的

conscience ['kɔnʃəns] n. 良心，道德心

dexterity [dek'sterɪtɪ] n. 灵巧，机敏

diffidence ['dɪfɪdəns] n. 缺乏自信

disconcert [dɪskən'sɜːt] vt. 使惊惶，

diversion [daɪ'vɜːʃ(ə)n] n. 转移，牵制，解闷，娱乐

entreat [ɪn'triːt] v. 恳求，乞求，对付

expediency [ɪk'spiːdɪənsɪ] n. 方便，私利，权宜

farthing ['fɑːðɪŋ] n.〈英〉1/4 旧便士，极少量，一点儿

fluctuation [ˌflʌktʃu'eɪʃ(ə)n] n. 波动，起伏

for good 永久地，一劳永逸地

gaiter ['geɪtə(r)] n. 长筒橡胶靴，绑腿

gravy ['greɪvɪ] n. 肉汁，不法利润，肉汤

guileless ['gaɪllɪs] adj. 不狡诈的，正直的

gulp [gʌlp] vt. 吞，一口吞（下），忍住，抑制 vi. 吞咽 n. 吞咽

hedge [hedʒ] n. 树篱，障碍物 v. 用树篱围住，避免作正面答复
husky ['hʌskɪ] adj. 谷的，像谷的，沙哑的
constrictor [kən'strɪktə(r)] n. 使压缩之物，大蟒
idiosyncrasy [ɪdɪə'sɪŋkrəsɪ] n. 特质，特性
idiosyncratic [ˌidiəsɪŋ'krætɪk] adj. 特殊物质的，异质的
joint [dʒɔɪnt] n. 关节，（牛、羊等的腿）大块肉
keepsake ['ki:pseɪk] n. 纪念品
lamented [lə'mentɪd] adj. 被哀悼的，令人遗憾的
look over v. 从……上面看，察看，检查，原谅，调查，从上面看过去
lunatic ['lu:nətɪk] adj. 精神错乱的 n. 疯子
matrimony ['mætrɪmənɪ] n. 结婚
muster ['mʌstə(r)] n. 集合，清单，一群 v. 集合，召集
negligible ['neglɪdʒɪb(ə)l] adj. 可以忽略的，不予重视的
phlegmatic [fleg'mætɪk] adj. 冷静的，冷淡的
pimple ['pɪmp(ə)l] n. [医] 丘疹，面泡，疙瘩
pock [pɔk] n. 痘痕，麻子 vt. 使有麻点
prematurely [ˌpremə'tʃʊəli] adv. 过早地，早熟地
procure [prə'kjʊə(r)] v. 获得，取得
prospective [prə'spektɪv] adj. 预期的
rapacity [rə'pæsətɪ] n. 贪婪，掠夺
refreshment [rɪ'freʃmənt] n.（常 pl.）点心，饮料，精力恢复，爽快
rejoin [rɪ'dʒɔɪn] vt. 再加入，再回答
repudiate [rɪ'pju:dɪeɪt] v. 批判
relapse [rɪ'læps] n. 复发，恢复原状
latent ['leɪtənt] adj. 潜在的，隐藏的
retain [rɪ'teɪn] vt. 保持，保留
rouse [rauz] v. 唤醒，激起，使振奋，惊起 n. 觉醒，奋起
ruminate ['ru:mɪneɪt] v. 反刍，沉思
sanctity ['sæŋktɪtɪ] n. 圣洁
seasonable ['si:zənəb(ə)l] adj. 合时的
seduce [sɪ'dju:s; (*US*) sɪ'du:s] v. 诱使
simulacrum [ˌsɪmjʊ'leɪkrəm] n. 像，幻影
six-foot 六尺来高的人
slouching ['slautʃɪŋ] adj. 没精打采的
pastry ['peɪstrɪ] n. 面粉糕饼，馅饼皮
sophisticated [sə'fɪstɪkeɪtɪd] adj. 诡辩的，久经世故的
stage-cutch 长途脚车
tenderness n. 嫩，亲切，柔和，敏感，棘手
tumbler ['tʌmblə(r)] n. 大玻璃杯，一杯的容量
uncharacteristic [ˌʌnˌkærəktə'rɪstɪk] adj. 不典型的
disregard [dɪsrɪ'gɑ:d] v. 不理，漠视 n. 忽视
veneration [ˌvenə'reɪʃən] n. 尊敬，崇拜
vindictive [vɪn'dɪktɪv] adj. 报复性的
wattle ['wɔt(ə)l] n. 编条，枝条
whop [wɔp] v. 打，抽出，打败 n. 重击

译文

第五章（片段）

我被从家中打发开

我们走了大约有半英里路，我的小手巾完全湿透了，这时脚夫突然停下来。

我向外张望，想明白停车的缘故，使我惊奇的是，我看见辟果提从一道围篱中突然出现，爬到车上来。她把我抱起来，搂向她的胸围，把我的鼻子压得非常疼，不过我在当时完全不曾想到疼，直到后来我才觉得我的鼻子很不舒服。辟果提并不说一句话。她松开一只胳臂，伸进胳臂肘下的衣袋中，掏出几纸袋的点心，塞进我的衣袋，又把一个钱包放在我的手中，但是她不说一句话。又用双臂做了最后一挤之后，她下了车，跑走了；我现在相信，也从来相信，她的长衫上没有一只纽扣了。我从滚来滚去的几个纽扣中捡起了一个，把它作为纪念物宝藏了很久。

脚夫瞪着眼看我，仿佛探问她是否回来。我摇了摇头，并且说我想不会了。“那么前进吧。”脚夫对那匹懒马说道，马就遵命前进了。

这时我已经哭到不能再哭，我开始想，再哭也没有用了，况且洛德里克·兰顿和大英皇家海军中的那个舰长，我记得，在困难情形下都不曾哭过。脚夫见我有了这决心，于是提议把我的小手巾铺在马背上晾干。我谢过他，也同意了；在那种情形下，那条小手巾显得格外小了。

我现在有空闲来看那个钱包了。那是一个硬皮钱包，有一个弹簧，里边有三个光亮的先令，显然为了使我更加喜欢的缘故，辟果提用漂白粉打磨过。但是其中最贵重的内容是用一片纸包在一起的两个半克朗，纸上我母亲亲笔写着：“给卫儿。附致我的爱心。”我被这个感动得又恳求那个脚夫拿回我的小手巾了；但是他说，他认为我最好不用它；我也认为真是最好不用；于是我用袖子揩了揩眼，自动停止了。

再也不哭了；不过，由于我先前的感情，我有时依然陷入剧烈的呜咽中。我们挨过不多的时候以后，我问脚夫他是否一直走到底。

“走到哪里？”脚夫问道。

“那里。”我说道。

“那里是哪里？”脚夫问道。

“挨近伦敦吧？”我说道。

"呵，那匹马，"脚夫抖着缰绳指着那匹马说道，"它走不到一半路，就要变得比猪肉更没有活气了。"

"那么说，你只到雅茅斯吗？"我问道。

"大致不错，"脚夫说道，"在那里我把你送到长途脚车上。长途脚车再把你送到——不拘什么地方。"

这些话在脚夫（他的名字是巴吉斯先生）说来是很多了——如我在前一章所说，他是一个沉默的人，一点也不喜欢谈话——我给他一块点心，作为酬劳的表示，他一口就吃下去了，完全像一头象，那块点心在他那大脸上，比在一头象的脸上，引不起更多的表情。

"这是她做的吗？"巴吉斯先生说道，他总是无精打采地在车踏板上向前弯着腰，每一只膝盖上放着一只胳臂。

"你说的是辟果提吗，你老？"

"啊！"巴吉斯先生说道，"她。"

"是的。我们的点心都是她做的，我们的饭也都是她做的呢。"

"真的？"巴吉斯先生说道。

他噘起嘴来，仿佛要吹口哨，但是他并未吹口哨。他坐在那里，看马的耳朵，仿佛他看见那里有一点新奇的东西；像那样坐了不少时候，慢慢地，他说道：

"没有情人吧？我相信。"

"你是说杏仁糖吗，巴吉斯先生？"因为我想他要吃一点别的，于是明白指出那一类点心。

"情，"巴吉斯先生说道，"情人，没有人跟她相好吧！"

"跟辟果提？"

"啊！"他说道，"她。"

" 没有。她从来不曾有过情人。"

"真的没有吗？"

他又噘起嘴来要吹口哨，但是他又不曾吹，不过坐在那里，看他的马耳朵。

"那么她做，"巴吉斯先生想了好半天以后说道，"各种苹果糕，煮各种饭菜，是吧？"

我回答说，事实是那样。

"喂。我要告诉你，"巴吉斯先生说道，"或许你可以写信给她吧？"

"我当然要写信给她啦。"我回答道。

"啊！"他慢慢地把眼睛转向我说道，"喂！假如你写信给她，或许你记得说，巴吉斯愿意；可以吗？"

“巴吉斯愿意，”我天真地重复道，“就是一句话吗？”

“是——的，”他考虑着说道，“是——的。巴吉斯愿意。”

“不过你明天又要到布兰德斯通了，巴吉斯先生，”想到那时我已经离那里很远了，我支支吾吾地说道，“你大可以当面去讲呵。”

他一面摇头反对那意见，一面又一次郑重其事地说着“巴吉斯愿意，就是这一句”，来重申先前的请求，因此我就答应替他传达。（就在那一下午，当我在雅茅斯旅店等车时，我要了一张纸和一瓶墨水，写了一封短信给辟果提，内容如下：“我的亲爱的辟果提。我已平安抵此。巴吉斯愿意。问妈妈好。你的亲爱的。再者，他说，他特别要你知道——巴吉斯愿意。”）

我既已预先负起这一项委托，巴吉斯先生又陷入完全的沉默中了；近来的一切遭遇使我觉得十分疲乏，我躺在车里一条口袋上睡着了。我一直沉睡到我们到达雅茅斯的时候；我们的车子赶进一家旅店的院子，我觉得那地方是那么新奇和生疏，立即放弃了跟辟果提先生家的一些人在那里相遇的潜藏的希望，或许连跟小爱弥丽相遇的希望也放弃了。

长途脚车已经停在院子里，通体非常光洁，但是还没有马套在上面；看它那时的样子，一点也不像它就要去伦敦。我正在想这个，也想知道巴吉斯先生放在边道上柱子旁边的我的箱子（他把车子赶进院子去转身）最后怎样处置，还有我自己最后怎样处置，这时有一个女人从一个挂有一些家禽和大块肉的弓形窗子里望出来，并且说道：

“那就是从布兰德斯通来的小先生吗？”

“是的，你老。”我说道。

“姓什么呀？”那女人问道。

“科波菲尔，你老。”我说道。

“那不成，”那女人口答道，“这里不曾收过用那个姓预付的饭钱。”

“是摩德斯通吧，你老？”我说道。

“假如你是摩德斯通少爷，”那女人说道，“你为什么先说另一个姓呢？”

我对那女人解释其中的缘故，她于是一面摇铃，一面叫，“威廉！领进餐厅去！”这时一个茶房从院子对面的厨房里跑出来领我，当他发现他所领的不过是我时，似乎大为惊奇了。

那是一个悬有一些地图的大而长的房间。假如这些地图是真的外国，我被抛在它们中间，我怀疑我会不会更觉得生疏。我手里拿着帽子坐在离门最近的一把椅子角上，觉得这是失礼的；当茶房为我铺下一块布，把一套调味瓶放在上面时，我想我一定羞得满面通红了。

他拿给我一些排骨和青菜，用了那样粗暴的态度掀开盖子，我害怕我一定得罪过他了。但是他后来的举动使我大为安心，他为我在桌旁放下一张椅子，并且很殷勤地说道:“喂，六英尺来高的！来呀！”

我谢过他，坐在桌旁。但是他站在对面那么目不转睛地瞪着眼看我，每次我碰到他的眼光，我就脸红得一塌糊涂，这时我觉得要想灵活地运用我的刀叉，或不把肉汁溅在我身上，乃是极端困难的。他看见我吃到第二块排骨的时候，就说道:

“还有为你预备的半品特麦酒呢。你现在要喝吗？”

我谢过他，然后说“要”。他于是把麦酒从一把壶里斟进一只大杯里，把杯子对着光举起来，使它看起来很美丽。

“哎呀！”他说道，“似乎很多呢，是不是？”

“真的似乎很多呢。”我微笑着回答道。因为见他那么高兴，我觉得十分开心了。他是一个眨眼的、满脸疙瘩的人，他的头发直竖在整个头上；他站在那里，一只手叉着腰，另一只手对着光拿着杯子，这时他的样子是十分友好了。

“昨天这里有一位先生，”他说道，“一个很强壮的人，名叫陶普骚耶——或许你认识他吧！”

“不，”我说道，“我想我不——”

“戴着宽边帽子，穿着短裤和裹腿，灰外衣，花围脖。”茶房说道。

“不，”我羞怯地说道，“我没有缘分——”

“他来到这里，”那茶房看着透过杯子的光说道，“点了一杯这样的麦酒——我教他不要点——他一定要点——喝下去，就倒下去死了。这酒对于他是太陈了。这酒不应当取出来了；事实就是这样。”

听了这个可悲的故事，我非常吃惊，于是说，我想我还是喝一点水好。

“哼，你知道，”那茶房依然看着透过杯子的光，闭着一只眼睛说道，“我们这里的人不喜欢点过的东西剩下来。剩下来的东西使他们生气。不过，假如你喜欢，我可以喝掉它。我喝惯这东西，习惯是一切。假如我仰起头来，一气喝下去，我不相信它会对我有害。我可以喝吗？”

我回答说，假如他以为他喝下去安全，我很欢迎他喝，但是绝对不可以冒险。当他果真仰起头来一气喝下去时，我承认，我非常怕看他会遭遇到可悲的陶普骚耶先生的命运，无声无气地倒在地毯上。但是那东西并不于他有害。正相反，我觉得他喝过之后似乎更加精神了。

“我们这儿是什么呀？”他一面说，一面把一把叉子伸进我的碟子。“不是排骨吧？”

“排骨。”我说道。

“哎呀！”他大叫道，“我不知道这是排骨。嘿，排骨正是解除那种麦酒的毒的东西。这不运气吗？”

于是他一手拿起一块排骨，一手拿起一个马铃薯，津津有味地吃下去，使我极端满意。他随后拿起另一块排骨，另一个马铃薯；随后，又一块排骨，又一个马铃薯。当我们吃完时，他拿给我一个布丁，既经放在我前面，他有一会儿似乎想什么，又似乎心神不定。

“饼好吗？”他振作起来说道。

“这是布丁。”我回答道。

“布丁呵！”他大叫道，“哼，哈，真的！什么！”走近一点来看。“你的意思不是说，这是一个巴特—布丁吧！”

“是的，不错。”

“喂，巴特—布丁，”他拿起一个羹匙来说道，“是我爱吃的布丁！这不运气吗？来，小朋友，让我们看，谁吃得最多。”

那个茶房当然吃得最多了。他不只一次地要我来比赛，但是因为他的羹匙对我的茶匙，他的速度对我的速度，他的饭量对我的饭量，从第一口起我就被远远地抛在后头，没有机会追上他了。我想，我从来未见过像这样爱吃布丁的人；当完全吃光时，他大笑起来，仿佛他对于那东西的嗜好依然不变。

见他是那么友善，那么好相与，于是我就向他要笔、墨水和纸，写信给辟果提了。他不仅立刻拿来，并且在我写信时，承他的好意来监督我。当我写完时，他问我去哪里入学校。

我说：“伦敦附近。”我所知道的不过如此。

“哎呀！”他露着很丧气的样子说道，“我为这件事发愁。”

“为什么？”我问他道。

“天哪！”他摇着头说道，“那是他们弄断一个孩子的肋骨的学校——两根肋骨——那是一个小孩子呦。我可以说他——让我看——你几岁了，大概？”

我告诉他在八岁和九岁之间。

“这正是他的年纪，”他说道，“他们弄断他的第一条肋骨的时候，他是八岁零六个月；八岁零八个月时，他们弄断他的第二条，于是要了他的命。”

我无法对自己掩饰，也无法对那个茶房掩饰，这是一种不舒服的类比，于是问这是怎样弄断的。他的回答并不使我高兴，因为他的回答只有三个可怕的字：“打断的。”

院子里长途脚车的号角声打了一个合时的岔，我于是站起来，为了有一个钱包（我从衣袋中取出来），心里夹杂着骄傲和羞怯，吞吞吐吐地问，有没有要付钱的东西。

“有一张信纸，”他回答道，“你买过信纸吗？”

我记不起我买过。

"信纸是贵的，"他说道，"因为纳税的关系。三个便士。在本地我们就是这样被抽税的。除了茶房，没有别的了。墨水不必提了。由我赔上吧。"

"你应当——我应当——我应当给多少——请问你，应当给茶房多少呢？"我红着脸结结巴巴地说道。

"假如我没有一个孩子，假如那个孩子不生疹子，"那个茶房说道，"我不会要六便士。假如我不供养年老的父母，还有一个可爱的妹妹，"——说到这里那个茶房很激动了——"我不会要一个法寻。假如我有一个好位置，假如这里待我好，我不但不要你的钱，还要送你一点什么。不过我是靠残羹冷饭生活——睡在煤堆上。"——说到这里那个茶房哭起来了。

我非常同情他的不幸，觉得任何少于九便士的报酬简直是虐待和狠心了。因此我把三个亮先令中的一个给了他，他很谦卑、很有礼地受下来，随后立刻用他的拇指搓拈，试验真假。

当我被人从车后扶上去时，发现大家以为我独自吃下所有的午餐，我觉得有一点难堪。我听见弓形窗内那个女人对管车人说道："当心那个孩子呀，乔治，恐怕他会胀破了的！"又看见附近那些女用人出来看我，笑我，把我当作一个小怪物，我就由这两点发现那道理。我那不幸的朋友，那个茶房，已经完全恢复常态，看样子并不为这个难过，反而一点也不难为情地参加一致的惊奇。假如我过去对他有一点怀疑，我相信一半是由这个引起的；但是我不禁怀着一个孩子的单纯信任和一个孩子对年长者的自然信赖（任何儿童先期用尘世的智慧代替这种天性，都使我很惋惜），直到那时，我总相信，我大致并未认真地猜疑他。

我应该承认，我无端成为车夫和管车人嘲笑的题目，觉得很难堪，他们说车子后边重是因为我坐在那里，又说我搭四轮马车旅行比较方便。我的饭量的故事流传到外边搭客中间，他们同样觉得开心，问我在学校是否要当作两三个兄弟付钱，我是否被人承包下来，或履行一定的条件；以及其他开心的问题。不过最坏的是，我知道当机会到来时我将羞于吃东西，吃过一顿便餐以后，我就要整夜挨饿了——因为我在匆忙中把我的点心忘在后面旅店里了。我的顾虑证实了。当我们停下来用晚饭时，虽然我非常想吃，但是我提不起勇气来吃，只好坐在火炉旁边说，我什么也不要吃。这也不能使我免除更多的嘲笑，一个声音沙哑、脸色粗暴的男人，除了从瓶子里喝水的时候，几乎一路从箱子里拿东西吃，他说，我像一条蟒蛇，吃一顿饭可以支持很久的时间；说过之后，他真就又吞下一份炖牛肉。

（董秋斯　译）

第九单元

呼啸山庄

词汇

abominable [əˈbɔmɪnəb(ə)l] adj. 讨厌的，令人憎恶的

aggravate [ˈægrəveɪt] vt. 使恶化，加重

ajar [əˈdʒɑː(r)] adj.（门窗等）微开的

aloof [əˈluːf] adv. 避开，远离

annihilate [əˈnaɪəleɪt] vt. 消灭

antipathy [ænˈtɪpəθɪ] n. 憎恶，反感

ass [æs] n. 驴，笨人

asunder [əˈsʌndə(r)] adv. 张开

bairny [beən] n. 小孩

banister [ˈbænɪstə(r)] n. 栏杆的支柱，楼梯的扶栏

beseech [bɪˈsiːtʃ] v. 恳求，哀求

blaspheme [blæsˈfiːm] v. 亵渎，咒骂，辱骂

brat [bræt] n. 乳臭未干的小孩，小子

caprice [kəˈpriːs] n. 反复无常，任性，怪想

catechism [ˈkætɪkɪz(ə)m] n. 问答法，问答

chafing [ˈtʃeɪfɪŋ] n. 摩擦

chink [tʃɪŋk] n. 裂口，裂缝

confounded [kənˈfaʊndɪd] adj. 糊涂的，讨厌的

convalescent [kɔnvəˈles(ə)nt] adj. 渐愈的

crop [krɔp] v. 剪短头发

cub [kʌb] n. 幼兽，不懂规矩的年轻人

delirium [dɪˈlɪrɪəm] n.（暂时的）精神狂乱，狂语

delude [dɪˈluːd] vt. 迷惑，欺骗，蒙蔽

doze [dəʊz] n. 瞌睡

drench [drentʃ] v. 湿透

eavesdropper [ˈiːvzˌdrɔpə(r)] n. 偷听者

ere [eə(r)] prep. 前于…… conj. 在……以前

expostulation [ɪkˌspɔstjʊˈleɪʃən] n. 劝告，谏言

ferret [ˈferɪt] n. 追赶，搜出，驱出

fit [fɪt] n. 痉挛

flay [fleɪ] vt. 剥皮，去皮

flurry ['flʌrɪ] vt. 使恐慌，使狼狈
grat [græt] v. 哭
haggard ['hægəd] adj. 憔悴的
hark [hɑːk] vi. 听！（用于命令句）
hearken ['hɑːkən] vi. 倾听
heath [hiːθ] n. 荒地
heathen ['hiːð(ə)n] n. 异教徒，野蛮人
heedless ['hiːdlɪs] adj. 不注意的
hoary ['hɔːrɪ] adj. 头发灰白的，古代的，久远的
hubbub ['hʌbʌb] n. 吵闹声，呐喊声，叫嚷声
indignation [ɪndɪg'neɪʃ(ə)n] n. 愤慨，义愤
jest [dʒest] n. 笑话
lattice ['lætɪs] n. 格子窗
lurking ['lɜːkɪŋ] n. 潜伏
mither ['mɪðə(r)] n.〈苏格兰〉=mother
obstinacy [ˌɔbstɪnəsɪ] n. 固执
peevish ['piːviʃ] adj. 易怒的，暴躁的，倔强的
perdition [pə'dɪʃ(ə)n] n. 毁灭
pliable ['plaɪəb(ə)l] adj. 圆滑的，柔韧的
red herring 提出不相干的事实或论点以分散对主题的注意力
repent [rɪ'pent] v. 后悔
Satan ['seɪt(ə)n] n. 撒旦，魔鬼
saucy ['sɔːsɪ] adj. 漂亮的
saunter ['sɔːntə(r)] n.vi. 闲逛，漫步
scowl [skaʊl] vi. 皱眉头，板着脸
simpleton ['sɪmp(ə)lt(ə)n] n. 笨蛋，傻子
smite [smaɪt] v. 重击
stow [stəʊ] v. 隐藏
sulkily ['sʌlkɪli] adv. 不高兴地
sup [sʌp] n.vi. 吃晚饭
thwart [θwɔːt] vt. 反对，阻碍
timepiece ['taɪmpiːs] n. 时钟，座钟
ungodly [ʌn'gɔdlɪ] adj. 不虔诚的
vagary ['veɪgərɪ] n. 奇特行为，反复无常的行为
vexed [vekst] adj. 焦急的，为难的，恼怒的
vociferate [və'sɪfəreɪt] v. 大声叫，大叫，喊叫
wager ['weɪdʒə(r)] vt. 下赌注
whist [wɪst] int. 嘘！肃静！
winsome ['wɪnsəm] adj. 迷人的

译文

第九章

他进来了，叫喊着不堪入耳的咒骂的话，刚好看见我正把他的儿子往厨房碗橱里藏。哈里顿对于碰上他那野兽般的喜爱或疯人般的狂怒，都有一种恐怖之感，这是因为在前一种情况下他有被挤死或吻死的机会，而在另一种情况下他又有被丢在火里或撞在墙上的机会。他的惊恐倒使我可以随意地把他放在任何地方，这可怜的东西总是不声不响。

"呐，我到底发现啦！"辛德雷大叫，抓着我脖子上的皮，像拖只狗似的往后拖。"天地良心，你们一定发了誓要谋害那个孩子！现在我知道他怎么总不在我的跟前了。可是，魔鬼帮助我，我要让你吞下这把切肉刀，耐莉！你不用笑，因为我刚刚把肯尼兹头朝下闷到黑马沼地里，两个一个都一样——我要杀掉你们几个，我不杀就不安心！"

"可我不喜欢切肉刀，辛德雷先生，"我回答，"这刀刚切过熏青鱼。要是你愿意的话，我情愿被枪杀。"

"你还是遭天杀吧，"他说，"而且你将来也非遭不可。在英格兰没有一条法律能禁止一个人把他的家弄得像样，可我的家却乱七八糟！——张开你的嘴！"

他握住刀子，把刀尖向我的牙齿缝里戳。而我可从来不太怕他的奇想。我唾一下，肯定说味道很讨厌——我无论如何不要吞下去。

"啊！"他放开了我，说道："我看出那个可恶的小流氓不是哈里顿——我请你原谅，耐儿——要是他的话，他就应该活剥皮，因为他不跑来欢迎我，而且还尖声大叫，倒好像我是个妖怪。不孝的崽子，过来！你欺骗一个好心肠的、上当的父亲，我要教训教训你。现在，你不觉得这孩子头发剪短点还可以漂亮些吗？狗的毛剪短可以显得凶些，我爱凶的东西——给我一把剪刀——凶而整洁的东西！而且，那是地狱里才有的风气——珍爱我们的耳朵是魔鬼式的狂妄，——我们没有耳朵，也够像驴子的啦。嘘，孩子，嘘！好啦，我的乖宝贝！别哭啦，揩干你的眼睛——这才是个宝贝啦。亲亲我。什么！他不肯？亲亲我，哈里顿！该死的，亲亲我！上帝呀，好像我愿意养这么个怪物似的！我非把这臭孩子的脖子摔断不可。"

可怜的哈里顿在他父亲怀里拼命又喊又踢，当他把哈里顿抱上楼，而且把他举到栏杆外面的时候，他更加倍地喊叫。我一边嚷着他会把孩子吓疯的，一边跑去救他。我刚走到他们那儿，辛德雷在栏杆上探身向前倾听楼下有个声音，几乎忘记他手里有什么了。"是谁？"他听到有人走近楼梯跟前，便问道。我也探身向前，为的是想作手势给希刺克厉夫，我已经听出他的脚步声了，叫他不要再走过来。就在我的眼睛刚刚离开哈里顿这一瞬间，他猛然一窜，便从那不当心的怀抱中挣脱出来，掉下去了。

我们只顾看这个小东西是否安全，简直没有时间来体验那尖锐的恐怖感觉了。希刺克厉夫正在紧要关头走到了楼下，他下意识地把他接住了，并且扶他站好，抬头看是谁惹下的祸。即使是一个守财奴为了五分钱舍弃一张幸运的彩票，而第二天发现他在这交易上损失了五千镑，也不能表现出当希刺克厉夫看见楼上的人是恩萧先生时那副茫然若失的神气。那副神气比言语还更能明白地表达出那种极其深沉的苦痛，因为他竟成了阻挠他自己报仇的工具。若是天黑，我敢说，他会在楼梯上打碎哈里顿的头颅来补救这错误，但是我们亲眼看见孩子得救了，我立刻下楼把我的宝贝孩子抱过来，紧贴在心上。辛德雷从容不迫地下来，酒醒了，也觉得羞愧了。

“这是你的错，艾伦，”他说，“你该把他藏起来不让我看见。你该把他从我手里抢过去。他跌伤了什么地方没有？”

“跌伤！”我生气地喊着，“他要是没死，也会变成个白痴！啊！我奇怪他母亲怎么不从她的坟里站起来瞧瞧你怎样对待他。你比一个异教徒还坏——这样对待你的亲骨肉！”

他想要摸摸孩子。这孩子一发觉他是跟着我，就马上发泄出他的恐怖，放声哭出来。但是他父亲的手指头刚碰到他，他就又尖叫起来，叫得比刚才更高，而且挣扎着像要惊风似的。

“你不要管他啦！”我接着说。“他恨你——他们都恨你——这是实话！你有一个快乐的家庭，却给你弄到这样一个糟糕的地步！”

“我还要弄得更糟哩，耐莉，”这陷入迷途的人大笑，恢复了他的顽强，“现在，你把他抱走吧。而且，你听着，希刺克厉夫！你也走开，越远越好。我今晚不会杀你，除非，也许，我放火烧房子：那只是我这么想想而已。”

说着，他从橱里拿出一小瓶白兰地，倒一些在杯子里。

“不，别！”我请求，“辛德雷先生，请接受我的警告吧。如果你不爱惜你自己，就可怜可怜这不幸的孩子吧！”

“任何人都会比我待他更好些。”他回答。

“可怜可怜你自己的灵魂吧！”我说，竭力想从他手里夺过杯子。

“我可不。相反，我宁愿叫它沉沦来惩罚它的造物主，”这亵渎神明的人喊叫着，“为灵魂的甘心永堕地狱而干杯！”

他喝掉了酒，不耐烦地叫我们走开。用一连串的可怕的，不堪重述也不能记住的咒骂，来结束他的命令。

“可惜他不能醉死。”希刺克厉夫说。在门关上时，也回报了一阵咒骂，“他是在拼命，可是他的体质顶得住，肯尼兹先生说拿自己的马打赌，在吉默吞这一带，他要比任何人都活得长，而且将像个白发罪人似的走向坟墓，除非他碰巧遇上什么越出常情的机会。”

我走进厨房，坐下来哄我的小羔羊入睡。我以为希刺克厉夫走到谷仓去了。后来才知道他只走到高背长靠椅的那边，倒在墙边的一条凳子上，离火挺远，而且一直不吭声。

我正把哈里顿放在膝上摇着，而且哼着一支曲子，那曲子是这样开始的——

“夜深了，孩子睡着了。坟堆里的母亲听见了——”

这时凯蒂小姐，已经在她屋里听见了这场骚扰，伸进头来，小声说：

“你一个人吗，耐莉？”

“是啊，小姐。”我回答。

她走进来，走近壁炉。我猜想她要说什么话，就抬头望着。她脸上的表情看来又烦又忧虑不安。她的嘴半张着，好像有话要说。她吸了一口气，但是这口气化为一声叹息而不是一句话。我继续哼我的歌，还没有忘记她刚才的态度。

“希刺克厉夫呢？”她打断了我的歌声，问我。

“在马厩里干他的活哩。”这是我的回答。

他也没有纠正我，也许他在瞌睡。接着又是一阵长长的停顿。这时我看见有一两滴水从凯瑟琳的脸上滴落到石板地上。她是不是为了她那可羞的行为而难过呢？我自忖着，那倒要成件新鲜事哩。可是她也许愿意这样——反正我不去帮助她！不，她对于任何事情都不大操心，除非是跟她自己有关的事。

“啊，天呀！”她终于喊出来，“我非常不快乐！”

“可惜，”我说，“要你高兴真不容易，这么多朋友和这么少牵挂，还不能使你自己知足！”

“耐莉，你肯为我保密吗？”她纠缠着，跪在我旁边，抬起她那迷人的眼睛望着我的脸，那种神气足以赶掉人的怒气，甚至在一个人极有理由发怒的时候也可以。

“值得保守吗？”我问，不太别扭了。

“是的，而且它使我很烦，我非说出来不可！我要想知道我该怎么办。今天，埃德加·林惇要求我嫁给他，我也已经给他回答了。现在，在我告诉你这回答是接受还是拒绝之前，你告诉我应该是什么。”

“真是的，凯瑟琳小姐，我怎么知道呢？”我回答。“当然，想想今天下午你当着他的面出了那么大的丑，我可以说拒绝他是聪明的。既然他在那件事之后请求你，他一定要么是个没希望的笨蛋，要么就是一个好冒险的傻瓜。”

“要是你这么说，我就不再告诉你更多的了，”她抱怨地回答，站起来了。“我接受了，耐莉。快点，说我是不是错了！”

“你接受了？那么讨论这件事又有什么好处呢？你已经说定，就不能收回啦。”

“可是，说说我该不该这样做——说吧！”她用激怒的声调叫着，绞着她的双手，皱着眉。

“在正确地回答那个问题之前，有许多事要考虑的，”我说教似的讲着，“首先，最重要的是你爱不爱埃德加先生？”

“谁能不爱呢？当然我爱。”她回答。

然后我就跟她一问一答：对于一个二十二岁的姑娘说来，这些问话倒不能算是没有见识。

“你为什么爱他，凯蒂小姐？”

“问得无聊，我爱——那就够了。”

“不行，你一定要说为什么。”

“好吧，因为他漂亮，而且在一起很愉快。”

“糟。”这是我的评语。

“而且因为他又年轻又活泼。”

“还是糟。”

“而且因为他爱我。”

“那一点无关紧要。”

“而且他将要有钱，我愿意做附近最了不起的女人，而我有这么一个丈夫就会觉得骄傲。”

“太糟了！现在，说说你怎么爱他吧。”

“跟每一个人恋爱一样。你真糊涂，耐莉。”

“一点也不，回答吧。”

“我爱他脚下的地，他头上的天，他所碰过的每一样东西，以及他说出的每一个字。我爱他所有的表情和所有的动作，还有整个的完完全全的他。好了吧！”

“为什么呢？”

“不，你是在开玩笑，这可太恶毒了！对我可不是开玩笑的事！”小姐说，并且皱起眉，掉过脸向着炉火。

“我绝不是开玩笑，凯瑟琳小姐！”我回答。“你爱埃德加先生是因为他漂亮、年轻、活泼、有钱，而且爱你。最后这一点，不管怎么样，没什么作用，没有这一条，你也许还是爱他；而有了这条，你倒不一定，除非他具备四个优点。”

“是啊，当然，如果他生得丑，而且是个粗人，也许我只能可怜他——恨他。”

“可是世界上还有好多漂亮的、富裕的年轻人呀——可能比他还漂亮，还有钱。你怎么不去爱他们呢？”

“如果有的话，他们也不在我的道路上！我还没有看见过像埃德加这样的人。”

“你还可以看见一些，而且他不会总是漂亮、年轻，也不会总是有钱的。”

“他现在是，而我只要顾眼前，我希望你说点合乎情理的话。”

“好啦，那就解决了，如果你只顾眼前，就嫁林惇先生好啦。”

“这件事我并不要得到你的允许——我要嫁他。可是你还没有告诉我，我到底对不对。”

“如果人们结婚只顾眼前是对的话，那就完全正确。现在让我们听听你为什么不高兴。你的哥哥会高兴的，那位老太太和老先生也不会反对。我想，你将从一个乱糟糟的、不舒服的家庭逃脱，走进一个富裕的体面人家。而且你爱埃德加，埃德加也爱你。一切看来顺心如意——障碍又在哪儿呢？”

“在这里，在这里！”凯瑟琳回答，一只手捶她的前额，一只手捶胸：“在凡是灵魂存在的地方——在我的灵魂里，而且在我的心里，我感到我是错了！”

“那是非常奇怪的！我可不懂。”

“那是我的秘密。可要是你不嘲笑我，我就要解释一下了。

我不能说得很清楚——可是我要让你感觉到我是怎样感觉的。”

她又在我旁边坐下来，她的神气变得更忧伤、更严肃，她紧攥着的手在颤抖。

“耐莉，你从来没有做过稀奇古怪的梦吗？”她想了几分钟后，忽然说。

“有时候做。”我回答。

“我也是的。我这辈子做过的梦有些会在梦过以后永远留下来跟我在一起，而且还会改变我的心意。这些梦在我心里穿过来穿过去，好像酒流在水里一样，改变了我心上的颜色。这是一个——我要讲了——可是你可别对随便什么话都笑。”

“啊，别说啦，凯瑟琳小姐！”我叫着，“用不着招神现鬼来缠我们，我们已够惨的啦。来，来，高兴起来，像你本来的样子！看看小哈里顿——他梦中想不到什么伤心事。他在睡眠中笑得多甜啊！”

“是的，他父亲在寂寞无聊时也诅咒得多甜！我敢说，你还记得他和那个小胖东西一样的时候——差不多一样的小而天真。可是，耐莉，我要请你听着——并不长；而我今天晚上也高兴不起来。”

“我不要听，我不要听！”我赶紧反复说着。

那时候我很迷信梦，现在也还是。凯瑟琳脸上又有一种异常的愁容，这使我害怕她的梦会使我感到什么预兆，使我预见一件可怕的灾祸。她很困恼，可是她没有接着讲下去。停一会她又开始说了，显然是另拣一个题目。

“如果我在天堂，耐莉，我一定会非常凄惨。”

“因为你不配到那儿去，”我回答，“所有的罪人在天堂里都会凄惨的。”

“可不是为了那个。我有一次梦见我在那儿了。”

“我告诉你我不要听你的梦，凯瑟琳小姐！我要上床睡觉啦。”我又打断了她。她笑了，按着我坐下来，因为我要离开椅子走了。

“这并没有什么呀，”她叫着，“我只是要说天堂并不是像我的家。我就哭得很伤心，要回到尘世上来。而天使们大为愤怒，就把我扔到呼啸山庄的草原中间了。我就在那儿醒过来，高兴得直哭。这就可以解释我的秘密了，别的也是一样。讲到嫁给埃德加·林惇，我并不比到天堂去更热心些。如果那边那个恶毒的人不把希刺克厉夫贬得这么低，我还不会想到这个。现在，嫁给希刺克厉夫就会降低我的身份，所以他永远也不会知道我多么爱他；那并不是因为他漂亮，耐莉，而是因为他比我更像我自己。不论我们的灵魂是什么做成的，他的和我的是一模一样的；而林惇的灵魂就如月光和闪电，或者霜和火，完全不同。”

这段话还没有讲完，我发觉希刺克厉夫就在这儿。我注意到一个轻微的动作，我回过头，看见他从凳子上站起来，不声不响地悄悄出去了。他一直听到凯瑟琳说嫁给他就会降低她的身份，就没再听下去。我的同伴，坐在地上，正被高背长靠椅的椅背挡住，看不见他在这儿，也没看见他离开。可是我吃了一惊，叫她别出声。

“干吗？”她问，神经过敏地向四周望着。

“约瑟夫来了，”我回答，碰巧听见他的车轮在路上隆隆的声音，“希刺克厉夫会跟他进来的。我不能担保他这会儿在不在门口哩。”

“啊，他不可能在门口偷听我的！”她说。“把哈里顿交给我，你去准备晚饭，弄好了叫我去跟你一块吃吧。我愿意欺骗我这不好受的良心，而且也深信希刺克厉夫没想到这些事。

“他没有，是吧？他不知道什么叫作爱吧？”

“我看不出有什么理由说他不能跟你一样地了解。”我回答，“如果你是他所选定的人，他就要成为天下最不幸的人了。你一旦变成林惇夫人，他就失去了朋友、爱情以及一切！你考虑过没有？你将怎样忍受这场分离，而他又将怎么忍受完全被人遗弃在世上，因为，凯瑟琳小姐——”

“他完全被人遗弃！我们分开！”她喊，带着愤怒的语气。

“请问，谁把我们分开？他们要遭到米罗的命运！只要我还活着，艾伦——谁也不敢这么办。世上每一个林惇都可以化为乌有，我绝不能够答应放弃希刺克厉夫。啊，那可不是我打算的——那不是我的意思！要付这么一个代价，我可不作林惇夫人！将来他这一辈子，对于我，就和他现在对于我一样地珍贵。埃德加一定得消除对希刺克厉夫的反感，而且，至少要容忍他。当他知道了我对他的真实感情，他就会的。耐莉，现在我懂了，你以为我是个自私的贱人。可是，你难道从来没想到，如果希刺克厉夫和我结婚了，我们就得作乞丐吗？

“而如果我嫁给林惇，我就能帮助希刺克厉夫高升，并且把他安置在我哥哥无权过问的地位。”

“用你丈夫的钱吗，凯瑟琳小姐？”我问，“你要发觉他可不是你估计的这么顺从。而且，虽然我不便下断言，我却认为那是你要作小林惇的妻子的最坏的动机。”

“不是，”她反驳，“那是最好的！其他的动机都是为了满足我的狂想；而且也是为了埃德加的缘故——因为在他的身上，我能感到，既包含着我对埃德加的还包含着他对我自己的那种感情。我不能说清楚，可是你和别人当然都了解，除了你之外，还有，或是应该有，另一个你的存在。如果我是完完全全都在这儿，那么创造我又有什么用处呢？在这个世界上，我的最大的悲痛就是希刺克厉夫的悲痛，而且我从一开始就注意并且互相感受到了。在我的生活中，他是我最强的思念。如果别的一切都毁灭了，而他还留下来，我就能继续活下去；如果别的一切都留下来，而他却给消灭了，这个世界对于我就将成为一个极陌生的地方。我不会像是它的一部分。我对林惇的爱像是树林中的叶子：我完全晓得，在冬天变化树木的时候，时光便会变化叶子。我对希刺克厉夫的爱恰似下面的恒久不变的岩石：虽然看起来它给你的愉快并不多，可是这点愉快却是必需的。耐莉，我就是希刺克厉夫！他永远永远地在我心里。他并不是作为一种乐趣，并不见得比我对我自己还更有趣些，却是作为我自己本身而存在。所以别再谈我们的分离了——那是做不到的；而且——”

她停住了，把脸藏到我的裙褶子里；可是我用力把她推开。对她的荒唐，我再也没有耐心了！

“如果我能够从你的胡扯中找出一点意义来，小姐，”我说，“那只是使我相信你完全忽略了你在婚姻中所要承担的责任；不然，你就是一个恶毒的、没有品德的姑娘。可不要再讲什么秘密的话来烦我。我不能答应保守这些秘密。”

“这点秘密你肯保守吧？”她焦急地问。

“不，我不答应。”我重复说。

她正要坚持，约瑟夫进来了，我们的谈话就此结束。凯瑟琳把她的椅子搬到角落里，照管着哈里顿，我就做饭。饭做好后，我的伙伴就跟我开始争执谁该给辛德雷送饭菜去，我们没能解决，直到饭菜都快冷了。然后我们达成协议说，我们就等他来要吧，如果他想吃的话。因为当他暂时单独一个人的时候，我们都特别怕走到他面前。

“到这时候了，那个没出息的东西怎么还不从地里回来？他干嘛去啦？又闲荡去啦？”这老头子问着，四下里望着，想找希刺克厉夫。

“我去喊他，”我回答，“他在谷仓里，我想没问题。”

我去喊了，可是没有答应。回来时，我低声对凯瑟琳说，我料到他已经听到她所说的大部分话，并且告诉她正当她抱怨她哥哥对他的行为的时候，我是怎样看见他离开厨房的。她吃惊地跳起来——把哈里顿扔到高背椅子上，就自己跑出去找她的朋友了，也没有好好想想她为什么这么激动，或是她的谈话会怎样影响他。她去了很久，因此约瑟夫建议我们不必再等了。他多心地猜测他们在外面逗留为的是避免听他那拖得很长的祷告。他们是“坏得只会做坏事了”，他断定说。而且，为了他们的行为，那天晚上他在饭前通常做一刻钟的祈祷外，又加上一个特别祈祷，本来还要在祈祷之后再来一段，要不是他的小女主人这时冲进来，匆忙地命令他必须跑到马路上去，不管希刺克厉夫游荡到哪儿，也得找到他，要他马上再进来！

“我要跟他说话，在我上楼以前，我非跟他说话不可，”她说。“大门是开着的，他跑到一个听不见喊叫的地方去啦。因为我在农场的最高处尽量使劲大声喊叫，他也不搭理。”

约瑟夫起初不肯，但是她太着急了，不容他反对。终于他把帽子往头上一戴，嘟哝着走出去了。

这时，凯瑟琳在地板上来回走着，嚷着，“我奇怪他在哪儿——我奇怪他能跑到哪儿去了！我说了什么啦，耐莉？我都忘啦，他是怪我今天下午发脾气吗？亲爱的，告诉我，我说了什么使他难过的话啦？我真想他来。真想他会来呀！”

“无缘无故嚷嚷什么！”我喊，虽然我自己也有点不定心。

“这一丁点儿小事就把你吓着啦！当然是没有值得大惊小怪的大事，希刺克厉夫没准在旷野上来一个月下散步，或者就躺在稻草的厩楼里，别扭得不想跟我们说话。我敢说他是躲在那儿呢。瞧，我要不把他搜出来才怪！”

我去重新找一遍，结果是失望，而约瑟夫找的结果也是一样。

“这孩子越来越糟！”他一进来就说。“他把大门敞开了，小姐的小马都踏倒了两排小麦，还直冲到草地里去了！反正，主人明天早上一定要闹一场，闹个好看。他对这样不小心的，可怕的家伙可没有什么耐心——他可没有那份耐心！可他不能老是这样——你瞧着吧，你们大家！你们不应该让他无缘无故地发一阵疯！”

“你找到希刺克厉夫没有？你这个蠢驴。”凯瑟琳打断他。

“你有没有照我吩咐的找他？”

“我倒情愿去找马，”他回答。“那还有意义些。可是在这样的夜晚，人马都没法找——黑得像烟囱似的！而且希刺克厉夫也不是听我一叫就来的人——没准你叫他还听得入耳些呢！”

正当夏天，那倒真是一个非常黑的晚上。阴云密布，很像要有雷雨，我说我们最好还是坐下来吧：即将到来的大雨一定会把他带回家的，用不着再费事。但是没法把凯瑟琳劝得平静下来。她一直从大门到屋门来回徘徊，激动得一刻也不肯休息，终于在靠近路上一面墙边站住不动。在那儿，不顾我的忠告，不顾那隆隆的雷声和开始在她四周哗啦哗啦落下的大雨点，她就待在那儿，时不时喊叫一下，又听听，跟着放声大哭。这一场放声号啕大哭是哈里顿，或任何孩子都比不过的。

大约午夜时分，我们都还坐着的当儿，暴风雨来势汹汹地在山庄顶上隆隆作响。起了一阵狂风，打了一阵霹雷，不知是风还是雷把屋角的一棵树劈倒了。一根粗大的树干掉下来压到房顶上，把东边烟囱也打下来一块，给厨房的炉火里送来一大堆石头和煤灰。我们还以为闪电落在我们中间了呢，约瑟夫跪下来，祈求主不要忘记诺亚和罗得。而且，更像从前一样，虽然他要打击不敬神的人，却要赦免无辜的人。我也有点感到这一定也是对我们的裁判。在我的心里，约拿就是恩萧先生。我就摇摇伲小屋的门柄，想弄明白他是不是还活着。他回答得有气无力，使我的同伴比刚才喊得更热闹，好像要把像他自己这样的圣人和像他主人这样的罪人划清界限似的。但是二十分钟后这场骚扰过去了，留下我们全都安全无恙。只是凯蒂，由于她固执地拒绝避雨而淋得浑身湿透，不戴帽子，不披肩巾地站在那儿，任凭她的头发和衣服渗透了雨水。她进来了，躺在高背椅上，浑身水淋淋的，把脸对着椅背，手放在脸前。

“好啦，小姐！”我叫着，抚着她的肩。“你不是下决心找死吧，是吗？你知道这是几点钟啦？十二点半啦。来吧！睡觉去。用不着再等那个傻孩子啦，他一定去吉默吞了，而且现在他一定住在那儿了。他猜想这么晚我们不会醒着等他，至少他猜到只有辛德雷先生会起来，他是宁可避免让主人给他开门的。”

“不，不，他不会在吉默吞，”约瑟夫说。“我看他一定是掉在泥塘底下去啦。这场天降之祸不是无所谓的。我希望你们瞧瞧，小姐——下一回该是你了。为了一切感谢上帝！一切配合起来都是为了他们好，仿佛从垃圾堆里挑选出来的！你们知道《圣经》上说什么——”

他开始引了好几段经文，给我们指明章节，叫我们去查。

我求这执拗的姑娘站起来换掉她的湿衣服，却是白费劲，只好走开，任她祈祷，任她发抖，我自己就带着哈里顿睡觉去了。小哈里顿睡得这么香，好像是他四周的每一个人都睡着了似的。以后我还听见约瑟夫读了一会经。然后，我还听得出他上梯子时慢腾腾的脚步，后来我就睡着了。

我比平时下楼迟些，靠着百叶窗缝中透进来的阳光，看见凯瑟琳小姐还坐在壁炉旁。大厅的门也还是半开，从那没有关上的窗户那儿进来了光亮。辛德雷已经出来了，站在厨房炉边，憔悴而懒塌塌的。

“什么事让你难过呀，凯蒂？”我进来时他正在说。“看你像个淹死的小狗那样惨凄凄的。孩子，你怎么这么湿，这么苍白？”

“我淋湿了，”她勉强回答，“而且我冷，就这么回事。”

“啊，她太不乖啦！”我大声说，看出来主人还相当清醒。

“她昨天晚上在大雨里泡，而且她又坐了个通宵，我也没法劝得她动一动。”

恩萧先生惊奇地瞅瞅我们。“通宵，”他重复着，“什么事使她不睡？当然，不会是怕雷吧？几个钟头以前就不打雷了。”

我们都不愿意提希刺克厉夫失踪的事，我们能瞒多久就瞒多久，所以我回答，我不知道她怎么想起来坐着不睡，她也没说什么。早上的空气是新鲜凉快的，我把窗户拉开，屋里立刻充满了从花园里来的甜甜的香气。可是凯瑟琳暴躁地叫唤我，“艾伦，关上窗户。我都要冻死了！”她向那几乎灭了的灰烬那边移近些，缩成一团，牙齿直打颤。

“她病了，”辛德雷说，拿起她的手腕，“我想这是她不肯上床去的缘故。倒霉！我可不愿这儿再有人生病添麻烦，你干吗到雨里去呢？”

“和平时一样，追男孩子呀！”约瑟夫嗄声说，趁我们在犹豫时，就抓住机会进谗言。

“如果我是你，主人，我就不论他们是贵是贱都给他们一顿耳光！只要有一天你不在家，那个贪嘴的猫林惇可就偷着来啦。还有耐莉小姐呀，她也是个不赖的小姐！她就坐在厨房守着你，你一进这个门，她就出了那个门。还有，我们那个贵妇人就走到她跟前巴结去！这可是好事，夜里十二点钟过了，跟那个吉卜赛人生的野鬼，希刺克厉夫，躲在地里！他们以为我是瞎子，我才不是：一点也不瞎！我瞧见小林惇来，也瞧见他走，我还瞅见你（指着我说），你这没出息的，破破烂烂的巫婆！你一听见主人的马蹄在路上响，你就跳起来窜到大厅里去。”

“住嘴，偷听话的！”凯瑟琳嚷着，“在我面前不容你放肆！辛德雷，埃德加·林惇昨天是碰巧来的，是我叫他走的，因为我知道你一直不喜欢遇见他。”

“你撒谎，凯蒂，毫无疑问，”她哥哥回答，“你是一个讨厌的呆子！可是目前先别管林惇吧。——告诉我，你昨天夜里没跟希刺克厉夫在一起么？现在，说实话。你用不着怕我害他，虽然我一直这么恨他，不久以前他却为我做了件好事，使我的良心没法让我掐断他的脖子了。为了防止这种事，我今天早上就要赶他走。等他走后，我劝你们都小心点，我可要对你们不客气哪！”

“我昨天夜里根本没有看见希刺克厉夫，”凯瑟琳回答，开始痛哭起来：“你要是把他撵出大门，我就一定要跟他走。可是，也许，你永远不会有机会啦！也许他已经走啦。”说到这儿，她忍不住放声哀哭，她下面的话就听不清了。

辛德雷向她冷嘲热讽，大骂一场，叫她立刻回她屋里去，要不然的话，就不该无缘无故地大哭！我请求她服从。当我们到了她的卧房时，我永远不会忘记她演了怎样的一场戏，真的把我吓坏了——我以为她要疯了，我就求约瑟夫快跑去请大夫。这证实是热病的开始，肯尼兹先生一看见她，就宣布她病势危险，她在发烧。他给她放血，又告诉我只给她乳浆和稀饭吃；而且要小心别让她跳楼，或是跳窗，然后他就走了。因为他在这教区里是够忙的，而在这一带，这个村和那个村，中间相隔两三英里远是常有的事。

虽然我不能说我是一个温柔的看护，可是约瑟夫和主人总不见得比我好。而且虽然我们的病人是病人中最麻烦、最任性的——可是她总算起死回生了。当然啦，老林惇夫人来拜访了好几次，而且百般挑剔，把我们都骂了一阵，吩咐了一阵，当凯瑟琳病快复原的时候，她坚持要把她送到画眉田庄去。这真是皇恩大赦，我们非常感谢。

但是这可怜的太太很有理由后悔她的善心，她和她丈夫都被传染了热病，在几天之内，两人便相继逝世了。

我们的小姐回到我们这儿来，比以前更拗，更暴躁，也更傲慢了。希刺克厉夫自从雷雨之夜后就毫无音讯。有一天她惹得我气极啦，我自认倒霉竟把他的失踪归罪于她身上了。的确这责任是该她负，她自己也明白。从那个时期起，有好几个月，她不理我，仅仅保持主仆关系。约瑟夫也受到冷遇：尽管他只顾说他自己的想法，还拿她当个小姑娘似的教训她，她却把自己当作成年女子，是我们的女主人。并且以为她最近这场病使她有权要求别人体谅她。还有，大夫也说过她不能再受很多打击了，她得由着她自己的性子才行。在她眼里，任何人若敢于站起来反对她，就跟谋杀差不多。她对恩萧先生和他的同伴们都躲得远远的，她哥哥受了肯尼兹的教导，又想到她的狂怒常常会引起一阵癫痫的严重威胁，也就对她百依百顺，尽量不去惹恼她。讲到容忍她的反复无常，他实在是太迁就了，这并不是出于感情，而是出于妄自尊大，他真心盼望能看到她和林惇家联姻以便门第增光，并且只要她不去打扰他，她就尽可以把我们当奴隶一样践踏，他才不管呢！埃德加·林惇，像在他以前和以后的多数人一样，是给迷住了。他父亲逝世三年后，他把她领到吉默吞教堂那天，他自信是世上最幸福的人。

我很勉强地被劝说离开了呼啸山庄，陪她到这儿来了。小哈里顿差不多五岁了，我才开始教他认字，我们分别得很惨。可是凯瑟琳的眼泪比我们的更有力量——当我拒绝去，而她发觉她的请求不能感动我的时候，她就到她丈夫和她哥哥跟前去恸哭。她丈夫要给我很多工钱，她哥哥命令我打铺盖——他说，现在没有女主人啦，他屋里不需要女佣人了。至于哈里顿，不久就有副牧师来照管了。因此我只有一条路可以选择，叫我做什么就照办吧。我告诉主人说，他把所有的正派人都打发走了，那只会让他毁灭得更快些。我亲亲哈里顿作为告别。从此以后他和我是陌生人啦，想起来可非常古怪，可是我敢说他已把丁艾伦一股脑儿全忘了，也忘了他曾经是她在世上最宝贵的，而她也曾是他最宝贵的！

管家把故事讲到这里，偶然向烟囱上的时钟瞅了一眼：出乎她的意料，时针已指到一点半。她就再也不肯多待一秒钟。老实说，我自己也有意让她的故事的续篇搁一搁。现在她已经不见踪影，睡觉去了，我又沉思了一两个钟头，虽然我的头和四肢痛得不想动，可是我也得鼓起勇气去睡觉了。

（杨苡　译）

第十单元

德伯家的苔丝

词汇

advocate ['ædvəkit] n. 提倡，鼓吹

Agape ['ægəpi] n. 神对世人的爱，教友间的友情

ancestry ['ænsistri] n. 祖先（集合称），家系，血统

antagonism [æn'tægənizəm] n. 对抗（状态），对抗性

apathetically [ˌæpə'θetɪkli] adv. 冷淡地，无动于衷地

aromatic [ˌærəu'mætik] adj. 芬芳的

assertion [ə'səːʃən] n. 主张，断言，声明

auricular [ɔː'rikjulə] n. 耳的，耳状的

chromatic [krə'mætik] adj. 彩色的

circuitous [sə(ː)'kju(ː)itəs] adj. 迂回线路的

Cistercian [sis'təːʃən] n. [宗] 西多会的修士 [修女]

contrivance [kən'traivəns] n. 发明，想出的办法

decrepit [di'krepit] adj. 衰老的

demoniacally [ˌdiːməu'naiəkəli] adv. 魔鬼似地

dimity ['dimiti] n. 凸花条纹布

discordant [dis'kɔːdənt] adj. 不调和的，不和的，不和谐的

effete [e'fiːt] adj. 衰老的，衰微的

ember ['embə] n. 灰烬，余烬

erroneous [i'rəunjəs] adj. 错误的，不正确的

evocation [ˌevəu'keiʃən] n. 唤出，招魂

exculpatory [ɪk'skʌlpətərɪ] adj. 辩解的，辩明无罪的

expulsion [iks'pʌlʃən] n. 逐出，开除

fitfully ['ʃɪtfəli] adv. 断断续续地

flaccid ['flæksid] adj. 软弱的，没气力的

foreboding [fɔː'bəudɪŋ] n. 预感，先兆，预兆

freakish ['friːkiʃ] adj. 异想天开的，奇

特的，畸形的
grate［greit］n. 壁炉，炉
grotesque［grəu'tesk］n. 奇异的怪事
hussif［'hʌzif］n.=house wife 家庭主妇
illicit［i'lisit］adj. 违法的
impish［'impiʃ］adj. 顽童似的，似顽童的，顽皮的
impostor［im'pɔstə］n. 冒名顶替者
inimical［i'nimikl］adj. 敌意的
inopportune［in'ɔpətju:n］adj. 不合适的
irradiation［iˌreidi'eiʃən］n. 放射，照射
listless［'listlis］adj. 倦怠的，冷漠的，情绪低落的
lurk［lə:k］n. 潜伏，埋伏 vi. 潜藏，潜伏，埋伏
mead［mi:d］n. 草地
mien［mi:n］n. 风度
mistletoe［'mɪs(ə)ltəu］n〈植〉槲寄生
monastic［mə'næstik］n. 僧侣，修道士 adj. 庙宇的
nostalgic［nɔ'stældʒɪk, nə-］adj. 乡愁的，怀旧的
ostensible［ɔs'tensəbl, -sibl］adj. 可公开的，表面的，虚假的
pedigree［'pedigri:］n. 血统，家谱
perennial［pə'renjəl］adj. 四季不断的，长期的，多年生的
perfunctory［pə'fʌŋktəri］adj. 马马虎虎的
prestidigitation［'prestiˌdidʒi'teiʃən］n. 变戏法
purblind［'pə:blaind］adj. 半盲的，惺忪眼的，迟钝的
repentant［ri'pentənt］adj. 后悔的，悔改的，有悔改表现的
sarcasm［'sɑ:kæzəm］n. 挖苦，讽刺
smother［'smʌðə］vt. 使窒息，阻断
strait［streit］adj. 艰难的，苦恼的，窘迫的
stupor［'stju:pə］n. 昏迷
supposition［ˌsʌpə'ziʃən］n. 假定，想象，推测，推想
transmutation［ˌtrænzmju:'teiʃən］n. 变形，变化
warrant［'wɔrənt］n. 正当理由，根据

译文

第 35 章

“吃亏的总是女人”

苔丝把事情讲述完了；甚至连反复的申明和次要的解释也作完了。她讲话的声调，自始至终都同她开始讲述时的声调一样，几乎没有升高；她没有说一句辩解的话，也没有掉眼泪。

但是随着她的讲述，甚至连外界事物的面貌也似乎发生了变化。炉桥里的残人露出恶作剧的样子，变得凶恶可怖，仿佛一点儿也不关心苔丝的不幸。壁炉的栅栏懒洋洋的，也似乎对一切视而不见。从水瓶里发出来的亮光，只是一心在研究颜色的问题。周围一切物质的东西，都在可怕地反复申明，它们不负责任。但是自从他吻她的时候以来，什么也没有发生变化；或者不如说，一切事物在本质上都没有发生变化。但是一切事物在本质上又发生了变化。

她讲完过去的事情以后，他们从前卿卿我我的耳边印象，好像一起挤到了他们脑子中的一个角落里去了，那些印象的重现似乎只是他们盲目和愚蠢时期的余音。

克莱尔做一些毫不相干的事，拨了拨炉火；他听说的事甚至还没有完全进入到他的内心里去。他在拨了拨炉火的余烬以后，就站了起来；她自白的力量此刻发作了。他的脸显得憔悴苍老了。他想努力把心思集中起来，就在地板上胡乱地来回走着。无论他怎样努力，他也不能够认真地思考了；所以这正是他盲目地来回走着的意思。当他说话的时候，苔丝听出来，他的最富于变化的声音变成了最不适当和最平常的声音。

"苔丝！"

"哎，最亲爱的。"

"难道要我相信这些话吗？看你的态度，我又不能不把你的话当成真的。啊，你可不像发了疯呀！你说的话应该是一番疯话才对呀！可是你实在正常得很……我的妻子，我的苔丝——你就不能证明你说的那些话是发了疯吗？"

"我并没有发疯！"她说。

"可是——"他茫然地看着她，又心神迷乱地接着说："你为什么以前不告诉我？啊，不错，你本来是想告诉我的——不过让我阻止了，我记起来了。"

他说的这一番话，还有其他的一些话，只不过是表面上应付故事罢了，而他内心里却像是瘫痪了一样。他转过身去，伏在椅子上。苔丝跟在后面，来到房间的中间，用那双没有泪水的眼睛呆呆地看着他。接着她就软倒在地上，跪在他的脚边，就这样缩成了一团。

"看在我们爱情的份上，宽恕我吧！"她口干舌燥地低声说。"我已经同样地宽恕你了呀！"

但是他没有回答，她又接着说——

"就像我宽恕你一样宽恕我吧！我宽恕你，安琪尔。"

"你——不错，你宽恕我了。"

"可是你也应该宽恕我呀。"

"啊，苔丝，宽恕是不能用在这种情形上的呀！你过去是一个人，现在你是另一个人呀。我的上帝——宽恕怎能同这种荒唐事用在一起呢——怎能像变戏法一样呢！"

他停住了口，考虑着宽恕的定义；接着，他突然发出一阵可怕的哈哈大笑——这是一种不自然的骇人的笑声，就像是从地狱里发出来的笑声一样。

“不要笑了——不要笑了！这笑声会要了我的命的！”她尖叫着。“可怜我吧——可怜我吧！”

他没有回答；她跳起来，脸色像生了病一样苍白。

“安琪尔，安琪尔！你那样笑是什么意思呀？”她叫喊说。“你这一笑对我意味着什么，你知道吗？”

他摇摇头。

“为了让你幸福，我一直在期盼，渴望，祈祷！我想，只要你幸福，那我该多高兴呀，要是我不能让你幸福，我还能算什么妻子呢！这些都是我内心的感情呀，安琪尔！”

“这我都知道。”

“我想，安琪尔，你是爱我的——爱的是我这个人！如果你爱的的确是我，啊，你怎能那样看我，那样对我说话呢？这会把我吓坏的！自从我爱上你以来，我就会永远爱你——不管你发生了什么变化，受到什么羞辱，因为你还是你自己。我不再多问了。那么你怎能，啊，我自己的丈夫，不再爱我呢？”

“我再重复一遍，我以前一直爱的那个女人不是你。”

“那是谁呢？”

“是和你一模一样的另外一个女人。”

她从他的说话中看出，她过去害怕和预感到的事出现了。他把她看成了一个骗子，一个伪装纯洁的荡妇。她意识到这一点，苍白的脸上露出了恐惧；她的脸颊的肌肉松弛下来，她的嘴巴差不多变成了一个小圆洞的样子。他对她的看法竟是如此的可怕，她呆住了，身子摇晃起来；安琪尔走上前去，认为她就要跌倒了。

“坐下来，坐下来，”他温和地说。“你病了，自然你会感到不舒服的。”

她坐了下来，却不知道她坐在什么地方。她的脸仍然是紧张的神情，她的眼神让安琪尔看了直感到毛骨悚然。

“那么我再也不属于你了，是不是，安琪尔？”她绝望地问。“他说他爱的不是我，他爱的是另外一个和我一模一样的女人。”

出现的这个女人的形象引起了她对自己的同情，觉得自己是受了委屈的那个女人。她进一步想到了自己的情形，眼睛里充满了泪水；她转过身去，于是自怜的泪水就像决堤的江水一样流了出来。

看见她大哭起来，克莱尔心里倒感到轻松了，因为刚才发生的事对苔丝的影响开始让他担心起来，其程度仅仅次于那番自白本身引起的痛苦。他耐心地、冷漠地等着，等到后来，苔丝把满腹的悲伤发泄完了，泪如泉涌的痛哭减弱了，变成了一阵阵抽泣。

“安琪尔，”她突然说，这时候她说话的音调自然了，那种狂乱的、干哑的恐怖声音消失了。“安琪尔，我太坏了，你是不能和我住在一起了是不是？”

“我还没有想过我们该怎么办。”

“我不会要求你和我住在一起的，安琪尔，因为我没有权利这样要求！本来我要写信给我的母亲和妹妹，告诉她们我结婚了，现在我也不给她们写信了；我裁剪了一个针线袋子，打算在这儿住的时候缝好的，现在我也不缝了。”

“你不缝了？”

“不缝了，除非你吩咐我做什么，我是什么也不做了；即使你要离开我，我也不会跟着你的；即使你永远不理我，我也不问为什么，除非你告诉我，我才问你。”

“如果我真的吩咐你做什么事呢？”

“我会听你的，就像你的一个可怜的奴隶一样，甚至你要我去死我也会听你的。”

“你很好。但是这让我感到，你现在自我牺牲的态度和过去自我保护的态度少了一些协调。”

这些是他们发生冲突后第一次说的话。把这些巧妙的讽刺用到苔丝身上，就完全像把它们用到猫和狗的身上一样。她领会不到话里微妙的辛辣意味，她只是把它们当作敌意的声音加以接受，知道那表示他在忍受着愤怒。她保持着沉默，不知道他也正在抑制着对她的感情。她也没有看见一滴泪水慢慢地从他的脸上流下来，那是一滴很大的泪水，好像是一架放大镜的目镜，把它流过去的皮肤上的毛孔都放大了。与此同时，他又重新明白过来，她的自白已经完全把他的生活、他的宇宙全都改变了，他想在他新处的环境里前进，但是他绝望了。必须做点儿什么；做什么呢？

“苔丝，”他说，尽量把话说得轻松些，“我不能住在——这个房间里了——就是现在。我要到外面走一走。”

他悄悄地离开了房间，他先前倒出来两杯葡萄酒准备吃晚饭，一杯是倒给她的，一杯是倒给自己的，那两杯酒现在还放在桌子上，动也没有动。这就是他们一场婚宴的下场。在两三个小时以前，他们吃茶点时还相亲相爱，用一个杯子喝酒。

房门在他的身后关上了，就像门被轻轻地拉开一样，但把苔丝从昏沉中惊醒了。他已经走了；她也待不住了。她急忙把大衣披在身上，打开门跟着走了出去，出去时她把蜡烛吹灭了，仿佛再也不回来似的。雨已经停了，夜晚也清朗了。

不久她就走到了他的身后，因为克莱尔漫无目的，走得很慢。在她淡白色的身影旁边，他的身影是黑色的，阴沉而叫人害怕，她脖子上戴的珠宝，她曾一时为之感到骄傲，现在却叫她感到是一种讽刺了。克莱尔听见了她的脚步声，转过身来，不过他虽然认出是她来了，但是却似乎没有改变态度，又继续往前走，走过屋前那座有五个拱洞的大桥。

路上奶牛和马的脚印都积满了水，天上下的雨水虽然把它们淹没了，但是却没有把它们冲刷掉。小水坑映出天上的星星，她从水坑旁边走过的时候，天上的星星也就一闪而过；她要是没有看见水坑里的星星，她就不会知道星星正在她的头顶上闪烁——宇宙中最大的物体竟反映在如此卑微的东西中。

他们今天到的这个地方，还是在泰波塞斯的同一个山谷里，不过在下游几英里的地方；四周是空旷的平地，她很容易就能看见他。有一条路从屋子那儿伸展开去，蜿蜒着穿过草地，她就沿着这条道路跟在克莱尔的后面，不过她并不想追上他，也不想吸引他，而只是默不作声、漫无目的地跟在后面。

她没精打采地走着，后来终于走到了克莱尔的身边，不过他仍然没有说话。诚实如果遭到愚弄，一旦明白过来，常常就会感到巨大的残酷；克莱尔现在的感受就是这样的。户外的空气显然已经消除了他全凭冲动行事的所有倾向；她知道他现在看见她，是觉得她毫无光彩了——她的一切都是平淡无奇了；这时候，时光老人正在吟诵讽刺他的诗句——

看吧，你的脸一暴露出来，爱你的他就要恨你；
在你倒霉的时候，你的脸也不再美丽。
你的生活就像秋叶飘零，像天上的落雨；
你头上的面纱就是悲伤，花冠就成了痛苦。[1]

他仍然在聚精会神地想着，她的陪伴现在已经没有足够的力量打断或改变他的思想之流。现在她对于他已经变得无足轻重了！她禁不住对克莱尔说开了。

“我做了什么事了——我究竟做了什么事了！我告诉你所有的事，没有一句是假的，或者是装的呀。你不要以为我是在骗你呀，你说是不是？安琪尔，你是在跟你心中想的事生气，而不是在和我生气，是不是？啊，不是在生我的气，我并不是像你认为的那样，是一个骗人的女人哪！”

“哼——好啦。我的妻子不是一个骗人的女人；但已经不是原来同一个人了。不是了，不是同一个人了。但是不要让我责备你。我已经发誓不会责备你；我会尽力不责备你的。”

但是她发狂似的恳求着；说了许多也许不如不说的话。

“安琪尔！——安琪尔！我还是个孩子啊——事情发生的时候我还是个孩子啊！男人的事我还一点也不懂啊。”

“与其说你犯了罪，不如说别人对你犯了罪，这我承认。”

1 引自史文朋的诗剧《在卡里顿的阿塔兰塔》中的合唱《并不像天崩地裂之时》。

"那么你是不会宽恕我的了？"

"我的确宽恕你了，但是这不是宽恕的问题呀。"

"你还爱我吗？"

关于这个问题，他没有回答。

"啊，安琪尔——我母亲说有时候会发生这种事的！——她就知道好几个这样的例子，比我的情形还要严重啦，但是她们的丈夫都并没有怎样在乎——至少没有成为他们之间的障碍啊。可是她们爱她们的丈夫，都不如我爱你呀！"

"不要说了，不要辩解了。社会不同，规矩就不同。你都快要让我说你是一个不懂事的乡下女人了，从来都不懂得世事人情。你都不知道你说的是什么呀。"

"从地位上看我是一个农民，但是从本质上看我并不是一个农民呀！"

她冲动地说，生起气来，但是气还没有生出来就消失了。

"这对你来说更是糟糕透顶。我倒觉得那个把你的祖先考证出来的牧师，如果他闭上嘴巴反而更好些。我忍不住要把你们家族的衰败同另外的事联系起来——同你缺少坚定联系起来。衰败的家族就意味着衰败的意志，衰败的行为。老天啊，你为什么要告诉我你的身世，给我一个把柄，让我更加瞧不起你呢？我原来以为你是一个自然的新生女儿；谁知道你竟是一个没落了的贵族家庭的后裔呢！"

"在这方面，有许多人家和我完全一样啊！莱蒂家从前是大地主，奶牛场老板毕勒特家也是一样。德比豪斯曾经是德·比叶大家族，现在不也是赶大车的了？像我这样的家族，你到处都找得到；这是我们郡的特点，让我有什么办法呢。"

"所以这个郡就更糟了。"

她只笼统地接受他的指责，但不管指责的细节；她只知道他不像从前那样爱她了，至于其他别的她都不管。

他们默默无言地朝前走。后来据说井桥有个农户，那天深夜出门去请医生，在草地上碰见了一对情人，一前一后地慢慢地走着，不说一句话，就像送葬似的，他瞧了一眼他们的脸色，感觉到他们既忧愁，又伤心。他后来回家时又在相同的地方从他们身边经过，看见他们还在像先前一样慢慢走着，也不管夜色深了，天气冷了。只是他一心想着自己的事，想着自己家里有病人，所以才没有把这件奇怪的事放在心上，是后来过了好久，他才想起来这件事。

就在那个农户从他们身边走过去和回转来的中间，她曾经对她的丈夫说——

"我不知道怎样才能让你一生中不会因为我而遭受太多的痛苦。下面就是河。我就跳河死了吧。我不怕死的。"

"我不想在我的愚蠢上又添上谋杀的罪名。"他说。

"我会给你留下证据，表明是我自杀的——是因为羞耻自杀的。那么他们就不会把罪名加在你身上了。”

“不要说这些荒唐话了——我不想听这个。在这种情形里有这种想法真是胡闹，它不是悲剧的主题，而只是讽刺嘲笑的材料。这场不幸的性质我看你是一点儿也没有明白。要是让人知道了，十个人里头有九个会感到好笑。请你听我的话，回屋睡觉去吧。”

“好吧！”她顺从地说。

他们从那条路上走过去，那条路通向磨坊后面的西斯特教团寺庙的遗迹，在过去的几百年里，那个磨坊一直是寺庙的一部分产业。磨坊还在不断地生产，因为食物是永远需要的；寺庙已经消失了，信仰也成了过眼烟云。我们不断地看到，为短暂的需要服务的东西很长久，而为永久的需要服务的东西却很短暂。他们那天是绕着圈子走的，所以始终离他们的屋子不远，她听从了他的指挥回去睡觉，只要走过那条河上的大石桥，再沿着那条路向前走几码就到了。她回到屋里的时候，炉火还在继续燃着，屋里的一切都还和她离开时一样。她在楼下没有待上一分钟，就上楼进了自己的房间，她的行李早已经拿进去了。在房间里，她坐在床沿上，茫然地看看四周，就立刻动手脱衣服。她把蜡烛拿到床头，烛光照在白布的帐子顶上，看见里面挂着什么东西，就把蜡烛举起来，想看看是什么。是一束槲寄生。那是安琪尔挂在那儿的；她立刻就心里明白了。这就是原来那个不好包装也不好携带的包裹了；那个包裹里包的是什么东西，安琪尔没有向她解释，只是说到时候她就知道了。那是在他感情热烈、心里快活的时候挂在那儿的。可是那束槲寄生现在看上去，是多么愚蠢、多么不合时宜啊。

他似乎无论如何也不会宽恕她了，既然已经没有什么可怕的了，也没有什么可盼的了，所以她就感觉迟钝地睡下了。一个人在悲伤停止的时候，睡眠就会乘虚而入。许多时候，由于心情快活而不能入睡，现在她的心情反而容易睡着。不一会儿，孤独的苔丝就进入梦乡了，房间里静悄悄的，弥漫着香气，很有可能，这个房间从前还做过她的祖先的洞房呢。那天深夜，克莱尔也沿着原路回了屋子。他轻轻地走进客厅，点上蜡烛，从他的态度上看出来，他已经打定了主意，房间里有一张旧马鬃沙发，他把几床毯子铺在上面，简单地为自己做了一个睡觉的小床。在他睡下之前，他赤着脚走到楼上，在苔丝房间的门口听了听。她均匀的呼吸表明，她已经完全睡熟了。

“感谢上帝！”克莱尔嘟哝着；可是他一想，又感到了一阵钻心的痛苦——他觉得，她现在毫无牵挂地睡着了，却把一生的重担移到了他的肩上，他这种想法虽然不是完全如此，但大致上也是差不多的。

他转身打算下楼；接着，他又犹豫不决地向她的门口转过身去。他转身的时候，一眼看见了德贝维尔家两位贵夫人画像中的一个，那幅画像正好镶在苔丝房门的上方。在蜡烛的照明下，那幅画像更加叫人感到不快。那个女人的脸上暗藏着阴险狡诈的神气，集中了向男人报仇雪恨的心思——他当时看上去的感觉就是这样的。画像女人穿着查理时代的长袍，领口开得很低，正好和苔丝穿的那件让他把领子掖进去好露出项链的衣服一样；这又使他感到苔丝和那个女人的相似之处，因而心里十分难过。

这已经足以使他止步不前了。他就退回来，下楼去了。

他的神情既镇静又冷酷，他的小嘴紧紧闭着，说明他有自我控制的能力；他的脸上仍然是一副令人感到可怕的神情，自从苔丝自我表白以来，他的脸上就有了那副神情。只要有这种神情的男人，就不再会是感情的奴隶，但是也没有从感情的解放中得到什么好处。他只是在那儿思考人类经验中的种种烦恼，思考种种事情的难以预料。直到一个小时以前，他一直崇拜苔丝，很久以来，他都认为不可能有谁比苔丝更纯洁、更甜蜜、更贞洁的了；可是——

只是那么一点点儿，竟然是这样不同！[1]

他错误地为自己辩解，心里头在说，从苔丝诚实和生动的脸上，看不透她的内心；不过当时没有人为苔丝辩护，纠正克莱尔的错误。他接着说，是不是有这种可能，她的那双眼睛，里面的神情和嘴里说的并没有什么不同，但是想的心事，和表面上是极不一致的，全然不同的？

他熄了蜡烛，在客厅里那张小床上躺下来。客厅里夜色深沉，对他们的事一点儿也不关心，毫不同情；黑夜已经吞噬掉了他的幸福，现在正在懒洋洋地加以消化；黑夜还准备同样吞噬掉其他千万人的幸福，并且一点儿也不慌乱。

（王忠祥、聂珍钊　译）

1 见勃朗宁的诗《炉边》第二十九节第二行。

第十一单元

墙上的斑点

词汇

almanack ['ɔːlmənæk] n. 历书，年鉴

annihilation [əˌnaiə'leiʃən] n. 歼灭，灭绝

antiquary ['æntikwəri] n. 古文物研究者，收集古文物者，古董商人

archbishop ['ɑːtʃ'biʃəp] n. [宗] 大教主

ascertain [ˌæsə'tein] vt. 确定，探知

asphodel ['æsfədəl] n. [植] 日光兰，常春花，水仙

asunder [ə'sʌndə(r)] adv. 分离，成碎片

attrition [ə'triʃən] n. 摩擦，磨损

awning ['ɔːniŋ] n. 遮阳篷，雨篷

bagatelle [ˌbægə'tel] n. 微不足道的东西，琐事，小事，弹子球戏的一种，（指钢琴的）小曲

bald [bɔːld] adj. 光秃的，单调的，枯燥的

blot [blɔt] n. 污渍，污点

botany ['bɔtəni] n. 植物学

canister ['kænistə] n. 小罐，筒

carnation [kɑː'neiʃən] n. 荷兰石竹，康乃馨，粉红色

cavalcade [ˌkævəl'keid] n. 队伍

chrysanthemum [kri'sænθˌəməm] n. 菊花

clod [klɔd] n. 土块 vt. 掷土块

compartment [kəm'pɑːtmənt] n. 间隔间，车厢

crimson ['krimzn] adj. 深红色的 n. 深红色

damnation [dæm'neiʃən] n. 诅咒

daresay ['dɛə'sei] v. [只用于第一人称单数和现在时] 猜想，料想

emerald ['emərəld] n. [矿] 祖母绿，翡翠，绿宝石

feverishly ['fiːvərɪʃli] adv. 兴奋地

fin [fin] n. 鳍，鱼翅

fraud [frɔːd] n. 欺骗，欺诈行为，诡计，骗子，假货

furl [fəːl] vt. 卷收，叠

gnaw [nɔː] v. 咬，啃，啮，使苦恼，消耗，折磨，侵蚀

haphazard ['hæp'hæzəd] adj. 偶然的，随便的

hoop [huːp] n. 箍，铁环，戒指，篮 v. 加箍于，环绕

idolatry [ai'dɔlətri] n. 偶像崇拜，过度崇拜，邪神崇拜

indite [in'dait] vt. 写（文章，信等），赋诗，创作

intoxicating [ɪn'tɔksɪkeɪtɪŋ] adj. 醉人的，使人兴奋的

liken ['laikən] vt. 把……比作

lodge [lɔdʒ] vi. 临时住宿 vt. 寄存，把……射入，存放

miniature ['minjətʃə] n. 缩小的模型，缩图，缩影

moorhen ['mʊəhen, 'mɔːhen] n. 雌苏格兰雷鸟

murderess ['mɜːdərɪs] n. 女杀手，女凶犯

omnibus ['ɔmnibəs] n. 公共汽车

ooze [uːz] n. 膏状物，黏液

opal ['əʊp(ə)l] n. 猫眼石，蛋白石

perceptible [pə'septəbl] adj. 可察觉的，显而易见的，感觉到的

phantom ['fæntəm] n. 幻影

precedency ['presidənsi] n. 领先，上席

quiescent [kwaɪ'esənt] adj. 静止的

scuttle ['skʌt(ə)l] vi. 仓皇奔逃，疾走

shrew [ʃruː] n. 地鼠

sown [səun] v. 播种，布满（sow 的过去分词）

stealthily ['stelθɪli] adv. 暗地里，悄悄地

swish [swiʃ] vi. 带着嗖嗖声挥动

tapestry ['tæpistri] n. 织锦，挂毯 vt. 编织锦或织画，用挂毯装饰

tassel ['tæsl] n. 穗，缨

tumbling ['tʌmbliŋ] n. 摔跤，翻跟头，翻筋斗 adj. 歪斜状的

tumulus ['tjuːmjuləs] n. 冢，坟墓，古墓，[地] 钟状火山

turf [təːf] n. 草根土，草皮，泥炭，跑马场，赛马 vt. 覆草皮于

译文

墙上的斑点

大约是在今年一月中旬，我抬起头来，第一次看见了墙上的那个斑点。为了要确定是在哪一天，就得回忆当时我看见了些什么。现在我记起了炉子里的火，一片黄色的火光一动不动地照射在我的书页上；壁炉上圆形玻璃缸里插着三朵菊花。对啦，一定是冬天，我们刚喝完茶，因为我记得当时我正在吸烟，我抬起头来，第一次看见了墙上那个斑点。我透过香烟的烟雾望过去，眼光在火红的炭块上停留了一下，过去关于在城堡塔楼上飘扬着一面鲜红的旗帜的幻觉又浮现在我脑际，我想到无数红色骑士

潮水般地骑马跃上黑色岩壁的侧坡。这个斑点打断了我这个幻觉，使我觉得松了一口气，因为这是过去的幻觉，是一种无意识的幻觉，可能是在孩童时期产生的。墙上的斑点是一块圆形的小印迹，在雪白的墙壁上呈暗黑色，在壁炉上方大约六七英寸的地方。

我们的思绪是多么容易一哄而上，簇拥着一件新鲜事物，像一群蚂蚁狂热地抬一根稻草一样，抬了一会儿，又把它扔在那里……如果这个斑点是一只钉子留下的痕迹，那一定不是为了挂一幅油画，而是为了挂一幅小肖像画——一幅卷发上扑着白粉、脸上抹着脂粉、嘴唇像红石竹花的贵妇人肖像。它当然是一件赝品，这所房子以前的房客只会选那一类的画——老房子得有老式画像来配它。他们就是这种人家——很有意思的人家，我常常想到他们，都是在一些奇怪的地方，因为谁都不会再见到他们，也不会知道他们后来的遭遇了。据他说，那家人搬出这所房子是因为他们想换一套别种式样的家具，他正在说，按他的想法，艺术品背后应该包含着思想的时候，我们两人就一下子分了手，这种情形就像坐火车一样，我们在火车里看见路旁郊外别墅里有个老太太正准备倒茶，有个年轻人正举起球拍打网球，火车一晃而过，我们就和老太太以及年轻人分了手，把他们抛在火车后面。

但是，我还是弄不清那个斑点到底是什么；我又想，它不像是钉子留下的痕迹。它太大、太圆了。我本来可以站起来，但是，即使我站起身来瞧瞧它，十之八九我也说不出它到底是什么；因为一旦一件事发生以后，就没有人能知道它是怎么发生的了。唉！天哪，生命是多么神秘；思想是多么不准确！人类是多么无知！为了证明我们对自己的私有物品是多么无法加以控制——和我们的文明相比，人的生活带有多少偶然性啊——我只要列举少数几件我们一生中遗失的物件就够了。就从三只装着订书工具的浅蓝色罐子说起吧，这永远是遗失的东西当中丢失得最神秘的几件——哪只猫会去咬它们，哪只老鼠会去啃它们呢？再数下去，还有那几个鸟笼子、铁裙箍、钢滑冰鞋、安女王时代的煤斗子、弹子戏球台、手摇风琴——全都丢失了，还有一些珠宝，也遗失了。有乳白宝石、绿宝石，它们都散失在芜菁的根部旁边。它们是花了多少心血节衣缩食积蓄起来的啊！此刻我四周全是挺有分量的家具，身上还穿着几件衣服，简直是奇迹。要是拿什么来和生活相比的话，就只能比作一个人以一小时五十英里的速度被射出地下铁道，从地道口出来的时候头发上一根发针也不剩。光着身子被射到上帝脚下！头朝下脚朝天地摔倒在开满水仙花的草原上，就像一捆捆棕色纸袋被扔进邮局的输物管道一样！头发飞扬，就像一匹赛马会上跑马的尾巴。对了，这些比拟可以表达生活的飞快速度，表达那永不休止的消耗和修理；一切都那么偶然，那么碰巧。

那么来世呢？粗大的绿色茎条慢慢地被拉得弯曲下来，杯盏形的花倾覆了，它那紫色和红色的光芒笼罩着人们。到底为什么人要投生在这里，而不投生到那里，不会行动、不会说话、无法集中目光，在青草脚下，在巨人的脚趾间摸索呢？至于什么是树，什么是男人和女人，或者是不是存在这样的东西，人们再过五十年也是无法说清楚的。别的什么都不会有，只有充塞着光亮和黑暗的空间，中间隔着一条条粗大的茎干，也许在更高处还有一些色彩不很清晰的——淡淡的粉红色或蓝色的——玫瑰花形状的斑块，随着时光的流逝，它会越来越清楚、越——我也不知道怎样……

可是墙上的斑点不是一个小孔。它很可能是什么暗黑色的圆形物体，比如说，一片夏天残留下来的玫瑰花瓣造成的，因为我不是一个警惕心很高的管家——只要瞧瞧壁炉上的尘土就知道了，据说就是这样的尘土把特洛伊城严严地埋了三层，只有一些罐子的碎片是它们没法毁灭的，这一点完全能叫人相信。

窗外树枝轻柔地敲打着玻璃……我希望能静静地、安稳地、从容不迫地思考，没有谁来打扰，一点也用不着从椅子里站起来，可以轻松地从这件事想到那件事，不感觉敌意，也不觉得有阻碍。我希望深深地、更深地沉下去，离开表面，离开表面上的生硬的个别事实。让我稳住自己，抓住第一个一瞬即逝的念头……莎士比亚……对啦，不管是他还是别人，都行。这个人稳稳地坐在扶手椅里，凝视着炉火，就这样——一阵骤雨似的念头源源不断地从某个非常高的天国倾泻而下，进入他的头脑。他把前额倚在自己的手上，于是人们站在敞开的大门外面向里张望——我们假设这个景象发生在夏天的傍晚——可是，所有这一切历史的虚构是多么沉闷啊！它丝毫引不起我的兴趣。我希望能碰上一条使人愉快的思路，同时这条思路也能间接地给我增添几分光彩，这样的想法是最令人愉快的了。连那些真诚地相信自己不爱听别人赞扬的谦虚而灰色的人们头脑里，也经常会产生这种想法。它们不是直接恭维自己，妙就妙在这里。这些想法是这样的："于是我走进屋子。他们在谈植物学。我说我曾经看见金斯威一座老房子地基上的尘土堆里开了一朵花。我说那粒花籽多半是查理一世在位的时候种下的。查理一世在位的时候人们种些什么花呢？"我问道——（但是我不记得回答是什么）也许是高大的、带着紫色花穗的花吧。于是就这样想下去。同时，我一直在头脑里把自己的形象打扮起来，是爱抚地，偷偷地，而不是公开地崇拜自己的形象。因为，我如果当真公开地这么干了，就会马上被自己抓住，我就会马上伸出手去拿过一本书来掩盖自己。说来也真奇怪，人们总是本能地保护自己的形象，不让偶像崇拜或是什么别的处理方式使它显得可笑，或者使它变得和原型太不相像以至于人们不相信它。但是，这个事实也可能并不那么奇怪？这个问题极其重要。假定镜子打碎了，形象消失了，那个浪漫的形象和周围一片绿色的茂密森林也不复存在，只有其他的人看见的那个人的外壳——世界会变得多么闷人、多么浮浅、多么光秃、多么凸出啊！在这样的世界里是不能生活的。当我们面对面坐在公共汽车和地下铁道里的时候，我们就是在照镜子；这就说明为什么我们的眼神都那么呆滞而朦胧。未来的小说家们会越来越认识到这些想法的重要性，因为这不只是一个想法，而是无限多的想法；它们探索深处，追逐幻影，越来越把现实的描绘排除在他们的故事之外，认为这类知识是天生具有的，希腊人就是这样想的，或许莎士比亚也是这样想的——但是这种概括毫无价值。只要听听概括这个词的音调就够了。它使人想起社论，想起内阁大臣——想起一整套事物，人们在儿童时期就认为这些事物是正统，是标准的、真正的事物，人人都必须遵循，否则就得冒打入十八层地狱的危险。提起概括，不知怎么使人想起伦敦的星期日，星期日午后的散步，星期日的午餐，也使人想起已经去世的人的说话方式，衣着打扮、习惯——例如大家一起坐在一间屋子里直到某一个钟点的习惯，尽管谁都不喜欢这么做。每件事都有一定的规矩。在那个特定时期，桌布的规矩就是一定要用花毯做成，上面印着黄色的小方格子，就像你在照片里看见的皇宫走廊里铺的地毯那样。另外一种花样的桌布就不能算真正的桌布。当我们发现这些真实的事物、星期天的午餐、星期天的散步、庄园宅第和桌布等并不全是真实的，确实带着些幻影的味道，而不相信它们的人所得到的处罚只不过是一种非法的自由感时，事情是多么使人惊奇，又是多么奇妙啊！我奇怪现在到底是什么代替了它们，代替了那些真正的、标准的东西？也许是男人，如果你是个女人的话；男性的观点支配着我们的生活，是它制定了标准，订出惠特克[1]的尊卑序列表；据我猜想，大战后它对于许多男人和女人已经带上幻影的味道，并且我们希望很快它就会像幻影、红木碗橱、兰西尔版画、上帝、魔鬼和地狱之类的东西一样遭到讥笑，被送进垃圾箱，给我们大家留下一种令人陶醉的非法的自由感——如果真存在自由的话……

在某种光线下面看墙上那个斑点，它竟像是凸出在墙上的。它也不完全是圆形的。我不敢肯定，不过它似乎投下一点淡淡的影子，使我觉得如果我用手指顺着墙壁摸过去，在某一点上会摸着一个起伏的小小的古冢，一个平滑的古冢，就像南部丘陵草原地带的那些古冢。据说，它们要不是坟墓，就是宿营地。在两者之中，我倒宁愿它们是坟墓，我像多数英国人一样偏爱忧伤，并且认为在散步结束时想到草地下埋着白骨是很自然的事情……一定有一部书写到过它。一定有哪位古物收藏家把这些白骨发掘出来，给它们起了名字……我想知道古物收藏家会是什么样的人，多半是些退役的上校，领着一伙上了年纪的工人爬到这儿的顶上，检查泥块和石头，和附近的牧师互相通信。牧师在早餐的时候拆开信件来看，觉得自己颇为重要。为了比较不同的箭镞，还需要作多次乡间旅行，到本州的首府去，这种旅行对于牧师和他们的老伴都是一种愉快的职责，他们的老伴正想做樱桃酱，或者正想收拾一下书房。他们完全有理由希望那个关于营地或者坟墓的重大问题长期悬而不决。而上校本人对于就这个问题的两

1 惠特克（1820—1895），英国出版商，创办过《书商》杂志，于 1868 年开始编纂惠特克年鉴。

方面能否搜集到证据则感到愉快而达观。的确，他最后终于倾向于营地说。由于受到反对，他便写了一篇文章，准备拿到当地会社的季度例会上宣读，恰好在这时他中风病倒，他的最后一个清醒的念头不是想到妻子和儿女，而是想到营地和箭镞，这个箭镞已经被收藏进当地博物馆的展柜，和一只中国女杀人犯的脚、一把伊丽莎白时代的铁钉、一大堆都铎王朝时代的土制烟斗、一件罗马时代的陶器，以及纳尔逊用来喝酒的酒杯放在一起——我真的不知道它到底证明了什么。

不，不，什么也没有证明，什么也没有发现。假如我在此时此刻站起身来，弄明白墙上的斑点果真是——我们怎么说不好呢？——一枚巨大的旧钉子的钉头，钉进墙里已经有两百年，直到现在，由于一代又一代女仆耐心的擦拭，钉子的顶端得以露出到油漆外面，正在一间墙壁雪白、炉火熊熊的房间里第一次看见现代的生活，我这样做又能得到些什么呢？知识吗？还是可供进一步思考的题材？不论是静坐着还是站起来我都一样能思考。什么是知识？我们的学者不过是那些蹲在洞穴和森林里熬药草、盘问地老鼠或记载星辰的语言的巫婆和隐士们的后代，要不，他们还能是什么呢？我们的迷信逐渐消失，我们对美和健康的思想越来越尊重，我们也就不那么崇敬他们了……是的，人们能够想象出一个十分可爱的世界。这个世界安宁而广阔，旷野里盛开着鲜红的和湛蓝的花朵。这个世界里没有教授，没有专家，没有警察面孔的管家，在这里人们可以像鱼儿用鳍翅划开水面一般，用自己的思想划开世界，轻轻地掠过荷花的梗条，在装满白色海鸟卵的鸟窠上空盘旋……在世界的中心扎下根，透过灰黯的海水和水里瞬间的闪光以及倒影向上看去，这里是多么宁静啊——假如没有惠特克年鉴——假如没有尊卑序列表！

我一定要跳起来亲眼看看墙上的斑点到底是什么——是一枚钉子？一片玫瑰花瓣？还是木块上的裂纹？

大自然又在这里玩弄她保存自己的老把戏了。她认为这条思路至多不过白白浪费一些精力，或许会和现实发生一点冲突，因为谁又能对惠特克的尊卑序列表妄加非议呢？排在坎特伯里大主教后面的是大法官，而大法官后面又是约克大主教。每一个人都必须排在某人的后面，这是惠特克的哲学。最要紧的是知道谁该排在谁的后面。惠特克是知道的。大自然忠告你说，不要为此感到恼怒，而要从中得到安慰；假如你无法得到安慰，假如你一定要破坏这一小时的平静，那就去想想墙上的斑点吧。

我懂得大自然耍的是什么把戏——她在暗中怂恿我们采取行动以便结束那些容易令人兴奋或痛苦的思想。我想，正因如此，我们对实干家总不免稍有一点轻视——我们认为这类人不爱思索。不过，我们也不妨注视墙上的斑点，来打断那些不愉快的思想。

真的，现在我越加仔细地看着它，就越发觉得好似在大海中抓住了一块木板。我体会到一种令人心满意足的现实感，把那两位大主教和那位大法官统统逐入了虚无的幻境。这里，是一件具体的东西，是一件真实的东西。我们半夜从一场噩梦中惊醒，也往往这样，急忙扭亮电灯，静静地躺一会儿，赞赏着衣柜，赞赏着实在的物体，赞赏着现实，赞赏着身外的世界，它证明除了我们自身以外还存在着其他的事物。我们想弄清楚的也就是这个问题。木头是一件值得加以思索的愉快的事物。它产生于一棵树，树木会生长，我们并不知道它们是怎样生长起来的。它们长在草地上、森林里、小河边——这些全是我们喜欢去想的事物——它们长着、长着，长了许多年，一点也没有注意到我们。炎热的午后，母牛在树下挥动着尾巴；树木把小河点染得这样翠绿一片，让你觉得那只一头扎进水里去的雌红松鸡，应该带着绿色的羽毛冒出水面来。我喜欢去想那些像被风吹得鼓起来的旗帜一样逆流而上的鱼群；我还喜欢去想那些在河床上一点点地垒起一座座圆顶土堆的水甲虫。我喜欢想象那棵树本身的情景：首先是它自身木质的细密干燥的感觉，然后想象它受到雷雨的摧残；接下去就感到树液缓慢地、舒畅地一滴滴流出来。我还喜欢去想这棵树怎样在冬天的夜晚独自屹立在空旷的田野上，树叶紧紧地合拢起来，对着月亮射出的铁弹，什么弱点也不暴露，像一根空荡荡的桅杆竖立在整夜不停地滚动着的大地上。六月里鸟儿的鸣啭听起来一定很震耳，很不习惯；小昆虫在树皮的褶皱上吃力地爬过去，或者在树叶搭成的薄薄的绿色天篷上面晒太阳，它们红宝石般的眼睛直盯着前方，这时候它们的脚会感觉到多么寒冷啊……大地的寒气凛冽逼人，压得树木的纤维一根根地断裂开来。最后的一场暴风雨袭来，树倒了下去，树梢的枝条重新深深地陷进泥土。即使到了这种地步，生命也并没有结束。这棵树还有一百万条坚毅而清醒的生命分散在世界上。有的在卧室里，有的在船上，有的在人行道上，还有的变成了房间的护壁板，男人和女人们在喝过茶以后就坐在这间屋里抽烟。这棵树勾起了许许多多平静的、幸福的联想。我很愿意挨个儿去思索它们——可是遇到了阻碍……我想到什么地方啦？是怎么样想到这里的呢？一棵树？一条河？丘陵草原地带？惠特克年鉴？盛开水仙花的原野？我什么也记不起来啦。一切在转动、在下沉、在滑开去、在消失……事物陷进了大动荡之中。有人正在俯身对我说：

“我要出去买份报纸。”

“是吗？”

“不过买报纸也没有什么意思……什么新闻都没有。该死的战争，让战争见鬼去吧！……然而不论怎么说，我认为我们也不应该让一只蜗牛趴在墙壁上。”

哦，墙上的斑点！那是一只蜗牛。

（文美惠　译）

第十二单元

阿拉比

词汇

a religious retreat 宗教静修

adoration [ædə'reɪʃ(ə)n] n. 崇拜，爱慕，受崇拜（或爱慕）的对象

amiability [ˌeɪmiə'bɪləti] n. 和蔼可亲的，亲切的，友善的

anguish ['æŋgwɪʃ] n. 痛苦，苦恼 vt. 使极苦闷

annihilate [ə'naɪəleɪt] vt. 消灭，歼灭

Araby ['ærəbɪ] n.（=Arabia）阿拉伯半岛（亚洲东南部）

bazaar [bə'zɑː(r)] n. 集市，市场，杂货店，百货店

bizarre [bɪ'zɑː(r)] adj. 奇异的（指态度、容貌、款式等）

buckled ['bʌk(ə)ld] adj. 有扣的

cafe ['kæfeɪ; (*US*) kæ'feɪ] n. 咖啡馆，小餐馆

career [kə'rɪə(r)] n.（原意：道路，轨道）事业，生涯，速度

chafe [tʃeɪf] v.（将皮肤等）擦热，擦破，使恼火

chalice ['tʃælɪs] n. 杯，圣餐杯

charitable ['tʃærɪtəb(ə)l] adj. 仁慈的，（为）慈善事业的，宽恕的

clad [klæd] vt. adj. 穿衣的

convent ['kɔnvənt; (*US*) 'kɔnvent] n. 女修道会，女修道院

converge [kən'vɜːdʒ] v. 聚合，集中于一点 vt. 会聚

curtly ['kɜːtli] adv. 简略地，草率地

deride [dɪ'raɪd] vt. 嘲弄，嘲笑

diverge [daɪ'vɜːdʒ] vi.（道路等）分叉，（意见等）分歧，脱离

drawing room n. 客厅，休息室

emerge [ɪ'mɜːdʒ] vi. 显现，形成

energetically [ˌenə'dʒetɪkli] adv. 精力充沛地，积极地

feeble ['fiːb(ə)l] adj. 虚弱的，衰弱的，

无力的，微弱的，薄弱的

fib [fɪb] n. 小谎，一击，打 vi. 撒小谎 vt. 一击，打

florin ['flɔrɪn; (*US*) 'flɔːrɪn] n. 弗罗林，一种货币

follies ['fɔliz] n. 罪恶，时事讽刺剧

fuss [fʌs] n. 忙乱，大惊小怪 v. 忙乱，大惊小怪

garrulous ['gærʊləs] adj. 饶舌的，多嘴的

gauntlet ['gɔːntlɪt] n. 交叉射击

gird [gɜːd] v. 束缚

grail [greɪl] n. 杯，圣杯，大盘

hallstand ['hɔːlstænd] n.（=hat tree）帽架

harness ['hɑːnɪs] n.（全套）马具，甲胄 vt. 披上甲胄

humanity [hjuː'mænɪtɪ] n. 人性，人类，博爱，仁慈

imperturbable [ɪmpə'tɜːbəb(ə)l] adj. 沉着的，冷静的

impinge [ɪm'pɪndʒ] v. 撞击

incessant [ɪn'sesənt] adj. 不断的，不停的

intelligible [ɪn'telɪdʒɪb(ə)l] adj. 可理解的

jostle ['dʒɔs(ə)l] v. 挤，推，争夺 n. 挤拥，推撞

latchkey ['lætʃkiː] n. 闩锁钥匙，弹簧锁钥匙

litany ['lɪtənɪ] n. 连祷，冗长枯燥的故事（或陈述）

luxuriate [lʌg'zjʊərɪeɪt] vi. 茂盛的生长，生活奢侈，沉溺

misgive [mɪs'gɪv] vi. 疑虑 vt. 使怀疑

monotonous [mə'nɔtənəs] adj. 单调无变化的

multiplicity [mʌltɪ'plɪsɪtɪ] n. 多样性

odour ['əʊdə(r)] n. 气味，香味，臭味，意味，名声

parlor ['pɑːlə(r)] n. 客厅，会客室，营业室，业务室 adj. 客厅的

pawnbroker ['pɔːnbrəʊkə(r)] n. 典当商

petticoat ['petɪkəʊt] n. 衬裙，裙子

pitiless ['pɪtɪlɪs] adj. 无情的

porcelain ['pɔːslɪn] n. 瓷器，瓷 adj. 瓷制的，精美的，脆的

portray [pɔː'treɪ] v. 描绘

portrayal [pɔː'treɪəl] n. 描画，描写

railing ['reɪlɪŋ] n. 栏杆，扶手

resigned [rɪ'zaɪnd] adj. 顺从的，听天由命的

ruinous ['ruːɪnəs] adj. 破坏性的，招致毁灭的

salver ['sælvə(r)] n. 浅盘，托盘

sash [sæʃ] n. 框格，肩带，腰带，飒饰，窗扇 vt. 装以窗框，系上腰带

sensation [sen'seɪʃ(ə)n] n. 感觉，感情，感动，耸人听闻的

sodden ['sɔd(ə)n] adj. 浸透的

sombre ['sɔmbə(r)] adj. 昏暗的，阴沉的

sordid ['sɔːdɪd] adj. 肮脏的

spike [spaɪk] n. 穗，长钉，钉鞋 v. 用大钉钉，阻止，穿刺

stature ['stætʃə] n. 身材，身长，才干

straggling ['strægli ŋ] adj. 脱离队伍的，落后的

subtle ['sʌt(ə)l] adj. 狡猾的，敏感的，微妙的，精细的，稀薄的

summon ['sʌmənz] vt. 传唤，召集 n. 传票

tenant ['tenənt] n. 承租人，房客，租客 v. 出租

turnstile ['tɜːnstaɪl] n. 十字转门

vanity ['vænɪtɪ] n. 空虚

译文

阿拉比

里士满北大街是一条死胡同，非常安静，只有在基督兄弟会学校的孩子们放学的时候才有些喧闹。在胡同的最深处有一座无人居住的二层楼，它远离周围的建筑，孤零零地坐落在一方空地当中。街上其他房子自恃住着活生生的人家，绷着一张张褐色的面孔面面相觑。

以前住在我们家的房客是一位牧师，后来死在后客厅里了。由于长期封闭，所有房间的空气中都弥漫着一股霉味，厨房后面的废物间里堆放着很久以前的旧书籍。其中我发现了一些已经卷页的很潮湿的硬皮书：沃尔特·斯各特的《修道院》《虔诚的传教士》和《威道克文集》。我最喜欢后面这本，因为它的纸张是黄色的。房子后面是荒芜的花园，中间有一棵苹果树，一些稀稀落落的树丛分散在各处。在一片树丛下面我发现了已故房客的自行车气筒，已经锈迹斑斑。这位牧师非常慈善；他留下遗嘱，把所有的钱都捐给了社会团体，把房子里的家具都送给了他的妹妹。

到了冬季，白天很短，没等吃完晚饭，天色已经薄暮蒙蒙。我们汇聚在大街上，四周的楼房更显得幽暗阴沉。我们头顶上的天空是永远变幻着的紫色，街道上的路灯向那里投射出微弱的光亮。寒风刺骨，我们就使劲玩耍嬉戏，直到身体发热。寂静的街道上回荡着我们的呼喊声。我们奔跑游戏，在房子后面昏暗泥泞的小巷里穿行，学着原始部族人的样子藏在农舍里互相射击。我们来到漆黑一片的花园里，那里的炉灰坑散发出浓重的气味。我们跑到臭气熏天的马厩，马夫在那里或是给马梳理着皮毛或是有节奏地摇晃着叮当作响的马具。等我们回到大街上，厨房窗户里射出的灯光照亮了这里的一切。如果看到我叔叔走到了拐角处，我们就藏起来，直到他走进房内。有时曼根的姐姐出来站在门口的台阶上叫她的弟弟回家吃饭，我们就躲在暗处，看着她向大街四处张望。我们等待着，看她是继续站在那里还是回去，如果她站在那里不动，我们就从隐蔽处走出来乖乖地到曼根家的台阶那去。她在那里等着我们，灯光穿过半掩的大门，清晰地勾勒出她身体的轮廓。她的弟弟总要给她找点麻烦才肯就范。我站在栏杆旁看着她。她走起路来衣裙飘荡，柔软的发辫一左一右地跳动。

每天早晨我都躺在前客厅的地板上看着她家的大门。我拉下窗帘只留一条小缝，这样就不会被她看见。她一出来站在门口台阶上我的心就猛跳。我跑到门厅，抓起书

本就跟过去。我把她棕色的身影保持在我的视线之内，等接近我们要分开的岔路时便加快脚步，从她身边掠过。一个早晨又一个早晨，天天如此。除了几句寒暄，我从来没跟她说过话，然而她的名字犹如一声召唤，总让我热血沸腾。

即使在我的境遇已经与浪漫格格不入的时候，她的身影还是陪伴着我。每个星期六的晚上，我婶婶都要去市场购物，我必须帮她大包小袋地提东西。我们穿行在花哨的街市，拥挤在醉汉和讨价还价的妇女之间，耳畔是劳工们的咒骂声，还有店铺小伙计们尖利的叫卖声，他们站在猪肉桶旁守着摊子。还有街头艺人哼唱出的歌声，他们唱那首有关欧多诺万·罗沙的《你们都来吧》，或者唱些有关我们当地人苦难的歌曲。对我来说，这些嘈杂的声音都汇聚成我生命中唯一的感觉：我觉得自己手捧圣杯，安然地穿行在一群敌人中间。在念诵那些我一无所知的祷告词和赞颂词的时候，她的名字会突然蹦出我的双唇。我的双眼常常充满泪水（我也不知道为什么），而且在这个时候我觉得有一股热血在心头迸发，涌向我的胸怀。我很少想到将来。我不知道我将向她倾诉还是不向她倾诉；如果倾诉的话，我该如何把自己的爱慕之情和如麻的心绪道出。我的身体仿佛是一架竖琴，她的话语和身姿仿佛是拨弄琴弦的翩翩玉指。

一天晚上，我来到后客厅，牧师就死在那里。那是一个漆黑的雨夜，房子里一片寂静。透过破碎的玻璃窗我听到雨点敲打着地面，连绵的雨丝像银针一样在湿透的土地上欢跳。我能看到下面远处的街灯以及各家窗户里透出的微弱光亮。视线模糊让我心存感激。我所有的感官好像都要把自己隐藏起来，让我觉得我就要逃离这些感官。我双手用力合十直到抖动起来，喃喃低语："啊，爱情！啊，爱情！"一遍又一遍。

终于，她跟我说话了。可是她突然开口弄得我不知所措，最初的几句话我竟然无言以对。她问我是不是想去阿拉比。我记不得自己回答的是想还是不想。那是一个热闹的集市，她说她非常喜欢去。

说着话，她不时地转动着手腕上的银手镯。她说她去不成了，因为那个星期正好赶上女修道会的静修。她弟弟正和另外两个男孩争抢帽子，我自己站在栏杆那里。她手扶着栏杆，面对我低着头。门里的灯光照在她白皙的弯弯的脖颈上，照在她静静的垂发上，照在她扶着栏杆的手上。她裙子的一边卷了起来，露出了里面衬裙的白边，她放松站着的时候正好可以看见。

"你去了一定会满意的。"她说。

"如果我去，"我说，"我一定给你带点东西。"

从那天晚上起，无数千奇百怪的念头弄得我日夜神思不定，心乱如麻！真希望能铲除这些多余的无聊日子。我讨厌学校里令人恼火的功课。不管是夜晚在卧室还是白天在教室，无论我怎样集中精力读书，她的身影总是浮现在我和书本之间。冥冥之中传来一声声"阿拉比"的呼唤，我的灵魂在这寂静中沉醉了，周身萦绕着一种东方式的魔幻。

我请假要在星期六晚上去阿拉比。我的婶婶很惊讶，她希望这不是共济会的活动。上课时我很少回答问题。我看到老师脸上的表情由和蔼变成了严厉；他希望我不要放任自己游手好闲。可是我无法集中已经散乱的精力，对自己生活里的正事几乎完全失去了耐心。在我和我的欲望之间，正事反倒像是小孩子的游戏，粗鄙乏味的游戏。

星期六早上，我提醒叔叔我要在当天晚上去阿拉比。他正在衣帽架那忙着找掸帽子的刷子，草草应付着说：

“好的，孩子，我知道了。”

因为他在门厅里，我不可能到前客厅趴在窗户那了。觉得家里很压抑，我就慢慢往学校走去。外面的天气凄清阴冷，心中不觉生出重重疑虑。

我回家吃晚饭的时候叔叔还没有回来。时间还早，我就坐在那盯着钟看，看了一会儿，钟的嘀嗒声让人心烦，我就离开了这个房间。我走上楼梯，来到房子的顶层。这里的房间又高又冷，空落幽暗，让我有一种放松的感觉。我从一个房间走到另一个房间，边走边唱。透过前面的窗户，我看到我的小伙伴们正在下面的街道上玩耍，隐约还能听到他们的喊叫声。我把前额顶在冰冷的窗玻璃上，向下俯视可以模模糊糊地看到她家的房子。

我又回到楼下，发现麦瑟夫人坐在炉火旁。她上了年纪，爱饶舌，是一位典当商的遗孀，出于某种念头一心一意地搜集旧邮票。我只好在茶桌旁忍受她啰唆。晚饭拖了一个多小时，我叔叔还没回来。麦瑟夫人起身走了：她很遗憾不能再等了，时间已经八点多了，她不能在外面待得太晚，夜里的寒气对她身体不利。她走后，我在房间里来回踱步，使劲握拳头。我婶婶说：“我恐怕你要把你的阿拉比之行推迟到我们的圣诞之夜了。”

九点钟我听到叔叔在门厅用钥匙开门的声音。我听到他自言自语，以及衣帽架在挂上大衣时摇晃的声音。我从声音就能判断出叔叔在干什么。他吃饭时，我向他要去集市用的钱。他已经把这件事情忘了。

“这时候那的人都已经上床睡了一觉了。”他说。

我不觉得好笑。婶婶粗声大气地说：“你就不能给他钱让他去吗？你已经让他等得这么晚了！

我叔叔说他很抱歉把这件事给忘了。他说他相信一句老话：“只用功不玩耍，聪明的孩子也变傻。”他问我要去哪里，我又告诉他一遍，这时候他又问起我是不是知道《阿拉伯人告别他的骏马》那首诗。我走出厨房时候，他要给我婶婶朗诵一下那首诗的头几行。

我手里紧紧攥着这一弗罗林钱，沿着白金汉大街赶往车站。街上挤满了买东西的人，汽灯把各处照得通明。眼前的一切提醒着我奔向自己的目的地。火车上空无一人，我在三等车厢里坐了下来。苦苦地等了好久，火车终于缓缓地驶出了车站。列车在破败的房子间穿行，跨过波光闪烁的河流。在威斯兰·罗火车站，一群人向车厢门口涌来，但都被看门的挡了回去，还告诉他们说这是直达集市的特别快车。我还是独自一个人坐在空荡荡的车上。过了几分钟，火车在一处简陋的木站台停下了。我下了车来到马路上，借着灯光看大钟上的时间，差十分不到十点。终于来到了一座大楼前面，写在上面的名称让人莫名其妙。

我没有找到便宜的入口，又担心集市就要关门，便急忙从一个十字转门走了进去，顺手把一个先令递给了一个看上去很憔悴的人。我来到一个大厅，看到墙的半腰高处横排挂满了画，成了一个画廊。大多数摊位都已经关张了，大厅里黑漆漆的。我感到一种寂静，就像教堂里人群散去以后那样的寂静。我怯生生地走到市场中央，这有几个摊位还开着，一些人聚集在那里。此处有一个门帘，门帘的上方有由彩灯构成的“音乐咖啡馆”的字样，有两个人正在门帘前面数着盘子里的钱。我能听到硬币落在盘子里的声音。

我竭力提醒自己不要忘记来这里的缘由，便走到一个摊位前仔细看那里的瓷花瓶和装饰着花朵图案的茶具。在摊位的门口，一位年轻的女子在和两位年轻的男士说笑。我注意到他们是英国口音，依稀听到他们的谈话。

“哦，我可没这么说过！”

“哎，你说过！”

“哎，我就是没说过！”

“她说过吗？”

“是的，我听到了。”

“哦，真是……骗人！”

年轻的女士看到了我，走过来问我想买什么东西。听她的口气并不希望我买什么，跟我搭话只是出于工作责任。摊位黑洞洞的入口两侧各有一个大瓮，看上去就象两个东方卫士，我猥琐地看着它们，低声咕哝道：

“不，谢谢。”

那位年轻女士挪动了一下花瓶，又回到了两个年轻男子那里。他们又继续以前的话题，有那么一两次，她转过头来向我这里扫视。

我在她的摊位前徘徊，越来越像真的对她的瓷器感兴趣，但我知道待在那里已经毫无意义。我慢慢转身走开，来到市场的中央。在衣兜里，我让手里的两便士硬币滑落在六便士的硬币上。我听到有人在画廊的一端高喊关灯了，大厅的上半部分随即一片漆黑。

望着黑暗深处，我感到自己就是一个被空虚所驱使和耍弄的傀儡，双眼燃烧起懊恼和愤怒的火焰。

（顾铁军　译）

第十三单元

快乐王子

词汇

agility [ə'dʒiliti] n. 敏捷，活泼
beryl ['beril] n. 绿玉，绿宝石
bulrush ['bulrʌʃ] n. [植] 芦苇，纸草
cataract ['kætərækt] n. 大瀑布，奔流
chirrup ['tʃirəp] n. 吱喳声 vi. 吱喳地叫
coquette [kəu'ket] n. 卖弄风情的女子
drench [drentʃ] v. 湿透
flirt [flə:t] vi. 调情
foundry ['faundri] n. 铸造厂
garret ['gærət, -rit] n. 顶楼
ghetto ['getəu] n. 犹太人区
gilded ['gildid] adj. 镀金的
granite ['grænit] n. 花岗岩
hilt [hilt] n. 柄，刀把
ibis ['aibis] n. 朱鹭
icicle ['aisikl] n. 垂冰，冰柱
lotus ['ləutəs] n. 荷（花），莲（花）
Memnon ['memnɔn] n.（古典神话）门农
ornithology [ˌɔ:ni'θɔlədʒi] n. 鸟类学
overseer ['əuvə'si:ə] n. 监督，工头
pedestal ['pedistl] n. 基架，底座，基础
pinafore ['pinəfɔ:, -fɔə] n. 围裙，（小孩）围涎
pomegranate ['pɔmgrænit] n. 石榴
pygmy ['pigmi] n. 俾格米人，矮人，侏儒
Reed [ri:d] n. 芦苇小姐
ruby ['ru:bi] n. 红宝石
sapphire ['sæfaiə] n. 蓝宝石
seamstress ['semstrɪs] n. 女裁缝，做针线工的
snap [snæp] v. 突然折断，崩裂
steeple ['sti:pl] n. 尖塔
swoop [swu:p] v. 突然下降，猛扑
thimble ['θimbl] n. 顶针
tumbler ['tʌmblə] n. 大玻璃杯
twitter ['twitə] vt. 喊喊喳喳地讲，抖动

译文

快乐王子

快乐王子的像在一根高圆柱上面，高高地耸立在城市的上空。他满身贴着薄薄的纯金叶子，一对蓝宝石做成他的眼睛，一只大的红宝石嵌在他的剑柄上，灿烂地发着红光。

他的确得到一般人的称赞。一个市参议员为了表示自己有艺术的欣赏力，说过："他像风信标那样漂亮。"不过他又害怕别人会把他看作一个不务实际的人（其实他并不是不务实际的），便加上一句："只是他不及风信标那样有用。"

"为什么你不能像快乐王子那样呢？"一位聪明的母亲对她那个哭着要月亮的孩子说，"快乐王子连做梦也没想到会哭着要东西。"

"我真高兴世界上究竟还有一个人是很快乐的。"一个失意的人望着这座非常出色的像喃喃地说。

"他很像一个天使。"孤儿院的孩子们说。他们正从大教堂出来，披着光亮夺目的猩红色斗篷，束着洁白的遮胸。

"你们怎么知道？"数学先生说，"你们从没有见过一位天使。"

"啊！可是我们在梦里见过的。"孩子们答道。数学先生皱起眉头，板着面孔，因为他不赞成小孩子做梦。

某一个夜晚一只小燕子飞过城市的上空。他的朋友们六个星期以前就到埃及去了，但是他还留在后面，因为他恋着那根最美丽的芦苇。他还是在早春遇见她的，那时他正沿着河顺流飞去，追一只黄色飞蛾，她的细腰很引起他的注意，他便站住同她谈起话来。

"我可以爱你吗？"燕子说，他素来就有马上谈到本题的脾气。芦苇对他深深地弯一下腰，他便在她的身边不停地飞来飞去，用他的翅子点水，做出许多银色的涟漪，这便是他求爱的表示，他就这样地过了一整个夏天。

"这样的恋爱太可笑了，"别的燕子呢喃地说，"她没有钱，而且亲戚太多。"的确河边长满了芦苇，到处都是。后来秋天来了，他们都飞走了。

他们走了以后，他觉得寂寞，讨厌起他的爱人来了。他说："她不讲话，我又害怕她是一个荡妇，因为她老是跟风调情。"这倒是真的，风一吹，芦苇就行着最动人的屈膝礼。他又说："我相信她是惯于家居的，可是我喜欢旅行，那么我的妻子也应该喜欢旅行才成。"

“你愿意跟我走吗？”他最后忍不住了问她道，然而芦苇摇摇头，她非常依恋家。

“原来你从前是跟我寻开心的，”他叫道，“我现在到金字塔那边去了。再会吧！”他飞走了。

他飞了一个整天，晚上他到了这个城市。“我在什么地方过夜呢？”他说，“我希望城里已经给我预备了住处。”

随后他看见了立在高圆柱上面的那座像。他说：“我就在这儿过夜吧，这倒是一个空气新鲜的好地点。”他便飞下来，恰好停在快乐王子的两只脚中间。

“我找到一个金的睡房了，”他向四周看了一下，轻轻地对自己说。他打算睡觉了，但是他刚刚把头放到他的翅子下面去的时候，忽然大大的一滴水落到他的身上来。“多么奇怪的事！”他叫起来，“天上没有一片云，星星非常明亮，可是下起雨来了。北欧的天气真可怕。芦苇素来喜欢雨，不过那只是她的自私。”

接着又落下了一滴。

“要是一座像不能够遮雨，那么它又有什么用处？”他说，“我应该找一个好的烟囱去。”他决定飞开了。

但是他还没有张开翅膀，第三滴水又落了下来，他仰起头去看，他看见——啊！他看见了什么呢？

快乐王子的眼里装满了泪水，泪珠沿着他的黄金的脸颊流下来。他的脸在月光里显得这么美，叫小燕子的心里也充满了怜悯。

“你是谁？”他问道。

“我是快乐王子。”

“那么你为什么哭呢？”燕子又问，“你看，你把我一身都打湿了。”

“从前我活着，有一颗人心的时候，”王子慢慢地答道，“我并不知道眼泪是什么东西，因为我那个时候住在无愁宫里，悲哀是不能够进去的。白天有人陪我在花园里玩，晚上我又在大厅里领头跳舞。花园的四周围着一道高墙，我就从没有想到去问人墙外是什么样的景象，我眼前的一切都是非常美的。我的臣子都称我做快乐王子，不错，如果欢娱可以算作快乐，我就的确是快乐的了。我这样地活着，我也这样地死去。我死了，他们就把我放在这儿，而且立得这么高，让我看得见我这个城市的一切丑恶和穷苦，我的心虽然是铅做的，我也忍不住哭了。”

“怎么，他并不是纯金的？”燕子轻轻地对自己说，他非常讲究礼貌，不肯高声谈论别人的私事。

“远远的，”王子用一种低微的、音乐似的声音说下去。“远远的，在一条小街上有一所穷人住的房子。一扇窗开着，我看见窗内有一个妇人坐在桌子旁边。她的脸很瘦，又带病容。她的一双手粗糙、发红，指头上满是针眼，因为她是一个裁缝。她正在一件缎子衣服上绣花，绣的是西番莲，预备给皇后的最可爱的宫女在下一次宫中舞会里穿的。在这屋子的角落里，她的小孩躺在床上生病。他发热，嚷着要橙子吃。他母亲没有别的东西给他，只有河水，所以他在哭。燕子，燕子，小燕子，你肯把我剑柄上的红宝石取下来给她送去吗？我的脚钉牢在这个像座上，我动不了。"

"朋友们在埃及等我，"燕子说。"他们正在尼罗河上飞来飞去，同大朵的莲花谈话。他们不久就要到伟大的国王的坟墓里去睡眠了。那个国王自己也就睡在那里他的彩色的棺材里。他的身子是用黄布紧紧裹着的，而且还用了香料来保存它。一串浅绿色翡翠做成的链子系在他的颈项上，他的一只手就像是干枯的落叶。"

"燕子，燕子，小燕子，"王子要求说，"你难道不肯陪我过一夜，做一回我的信差么？那个孩子渴得太厉害了，他母亲太苦恼了。"

"我并不喜欢小孩，"燕子回答道，"我还记得上一个夏天，我停在河上的时候，有两个粗野的小孩，就是磨坊主人的儿子，他们常常丢石头打我。不消说他们是打不中的；我们燕子飞得极快，不会给他们打中，而且我还是出身于一个以敏捷出名的家庭，更不用害怕。不过这究竟是一种不客气的表示。"

然而快乐王子的面容显得那样地忧愁，叫小燕子的心也软下来了。他便说："这儿冷得很，不过我愿意陪你过一夜，我高兴做你的信差。"

"小燕子，谢谢你。"王子说。

燕子便从王子的剑柄上啄下了那块大红宝石，衔着它飞起来，飞过栉比的屋顶，向远处飞去了。

他飞过大教堂的塔顶，看见那里的大理石的天使雕像。他飞过王宫，听见了跳舞的声音。一个美貌的少女同她的情人正走到露台上来。"你看，星星多么好，爱的魔力多么大！"他对她说。"我希望我的衣服早点送来，赶得上大跳舞会，"她接口道，"我叫人在上面绣了西番莲花；可是那些女裁缝太懒了。"

他飞过河面，看见挂在船桅上的无数的灯笼，他又飞过犹太村，看见一些年老的犹太人在那里做生意讲价钱，把钱放在铜天平上面称着。最后他到了那所穷人的屋子，朝里面看去，小孩正发着热在床上翻来覆去，母亲已经睡熟，因为她太疲倦了。他跳进窗里，把红宝石放在桌上，就放在妇人的顶针旁边。过后他又轻轻地绕着床飞了一阵，用翅子扇着小孩的前额。"我觉得多么凉，"孩子说，"我一定好起来了。"他便沉沉地睡去了，他睡得很甜。

燕子回到快乐王子那里，把他做过的事讲给王子听。他又说："这倒是很奇怪的事，虽然天气这么冷，我却觉得很暖和。"

"那是因为你做了一件好事。"王子说。小燕子开始想起来，过后他睡着了。他有这样的一种习惯，只要一用思想，就会打瞌睡的。

天亮以后他飞下河去洗了一个澡。一位禽学教授走过桥上，看见了，便说："真是一件少有的事，冬天里会有燕子！"他便写了一封讲这件事的长信送给本地报纸发表。每个人都引用这封信，尽管信里有那么多他们不能了解的句子。

"今晚上我要到埃及去，"燕子说，他想到前途，心里非常高兴。他把城里所有的公共纪念物都参观过了，并且还在教堂的尖顶上坐了好一阵。不管他到什么地方，麻雀们都吱吱叫着，而且互相说："这是一位多么显贵的生客！"因此他玩得非常高兴。

月亮上升的时候，他飞回到快乐王子那里。他问道："你在埃及有什么事要我办吗？我就要动身了。"

"燕子，燕子，小燕子，"王子说，"你不肯陪我再过一夜吗？"

"朋友们在埃及等我，"燕子回答道。"明天他们便要飞往尼罗河上游到第二瀑布去，在那儿河马睡在纸草中间，门农神坐在花岗石宝座上面。他整夜守着星星，到晓星发光的时候，他发出一声欢乐的叫喊，然后便沉默了。正午时分，成群的黄狮走下河边来饮水。他们有和绿柱玉一样的眼睛，他们的吼叫比瀑布的吼声还要响亮。"

"燕子，燕子，小燕子，"王子说，"远远的，在城的那一边，我看见一个年轻人住在顶楼里面。他埋着头在一张堆满稿纸的书桌上写字，手边一个大玻璃杯里放着一束枯萎的紫罗兰。他的头发是棕色的，乱蓬蓬的，他的嘴唇像石榴一样地红，他还有一对朦胧的大眼睛。他在写一个戏，预备写成给戏院经理送去，可是他太冷了，不能够再写一个字。炉子里没有火，他又饿得头昏眼花了。"

"我愿意陪你再待一夜，"燕子说，他的确有好心肠。"你要我也给他送一块红宝石去吗？"

"唉！我现在没有红宝石了，"王子说，"我就只剩下一对眼睛。它们是用珍奇的蓝宝石做成的，这对蓝宝石还是一千年前在印度出产的，请你取出一颗来给他送去。他会把它卖给珠宝商，换钱来买食物、买木柴，好写完他的戏。"

"我亲爱的王子，我不能够这样做。"燕子说着哭起来了。

"燕子，燕子，小燕子，"王子说，"你就照我吩咐你的话做罢。"

燕子便取出王子的一只眼睛，往学生的顶楼飞去了。屋顶上有一个洞，要进去是很容易的，他便从洞里飞了进去。那个年轻人两只手托着脸颊，没有听见燕子的扑翅声，等到他抬起头来，却看见那颗美丽的蓝宝石在枯萎的紫罗兰上面了。

"现在开始有人赏识我了，"他叫道。"这是某一个钦佩我的人送来的。我现在可以写完我的戏了。"他露出很快乐的样子。

第二天燕子又飞到港口去。他坐在一只大船的桅杆上，望着水手们用粗绳把大箱子拖出船舱来。每只箱子上来的时候，他们就叫着："杭唷！……""我要到埃及去了！"燕子嚷道，可是没有人注意他，等到月亮上升的时候，他又回到快乐王子那里去。

“我是来向你告别的，”他叫道。

“燕子，燕子，小燕子，”王子说，“你不肯陪我再过一夜吗？”

“这是冬天了，”燕子答道，“寒冷的雪就快要到这儿来了，这时候在埃及，太阳照在浓绿的棕榈树上，很暖和，鳄鱼躺在泥沼里，懒洋洋地朝四面看。朋友们正在巴伯克的太阳神庙里筑巢，那些淡红的和雪白的鸽子在旁边望着，一面在讲情话。亲爱的王子，我一定要离开你了，不过我决不会忘记你，来年春天我要给你带回来两粒美丽的宝石，偿还你给了别人的那两颗。我带来的红宝石会比一朵红玫瑰更红，蓝宝石会比大海更蓝。”

“就在这下面的广场上，站着一个卖火柴的女孩，”王子说。“她把她的火柴都掉在沟里了，它们全完了。要是她不带点钱回家，她的父亲会打她的，她现在正哭着。她没有鞋、没有袜，小小的头上没有一顶帽子。你把我另一只眼睛也取下来，拿去给她，那么她的父亲便不会打她了。”

“我愿意陪你再过一夜，”燕子说，“我却不能够取下你的眼睛。那个时候你就要变成瞎子了。”

“燕子，燕子，小燕子，”王子说，“你就照我吩咐你的话做罢。”

他便取下王子的另一只眼睛，带着它飞到下面去。他飞过卖火柴女孩的面前，把宝石轻轻放在她的手掌心里。“这是一块多么可爱的玻璃！”小女孩叫起来；她一面笑着跑回家去。

燕子又回到王子那儿。他说：“你现在眼睛瞎了，我要永远跟你在一块儿。”

“不，小燕子，”这个可怜的王子说，“你应该到埃及去。”

“我要永远陪伴你，”燕子说，他就在王子的脚下睡了。

第二天他整天坐在王子的肩上，给王子讲起他在那些奇怪的国土上见到的种种事情。他讲起那些红色的朱鹭，它们排成长行站在尼罗河岸上，用它们的长嘴捕捉金鱼。他讲起斯芬克斯，它活得跟世界一样久，住在沙漠里面，知道一切的事情。他讲起那些商人，他们手里捏着琥珀念珠，慢慢地跟着他们的骆驼走路。他讲起月山的王，他黑得像乌木，崇拜一块大的水晶。他讲起那条大绿蛇，它睡在棕榈树上，有二十个僧侣拿蜜糕喂它。他讲起那些侏儒，他们把扁平的大树叶当作小舟，载他们渡过大湖，又常常同蝴蝶发生战争。

“亲爱的小燕子，”王子说，“你给我讲了种种奇特的事情，可是最奇特的还是那许多男男女女的苦难。再没有比贫穷更不可思议的了。小燕子，你就在我这个城的上空飞一转罢，你告诉我你在这个城里见到些什么事情。”

燕子便在这个大城的上空飞着，他看见有钱人在他们的漂亮的住宅里作乐，乞丐们坐在大门外挨冻。他飞进阴暗的小巷里，看见那些饥饿的小孩伸出苍白的瘦脸没精打采地望着污秽的街道。在一道桥的桥洞下面躺着两个小孩，他们紧紧地搂在一起，想使身体得到一点温暖。“我们真饿啊！”他们说。“你们不要躺在这儿，”看守人吼道，他们只好站起来走进雨中去了。

他便回去把看见的景象告诉了王子。

“我满身贴着纯金，”王子说，“你给我把它一片一片地拿掉，拿去送给那些穷人，活着的人总以为金子能够使他们幸福。”

燕子把纯金一片一片地啄了下来，最后快乐王子就变成灰暗难看的了。他又把纯金一片一片地拿去送给那些穷人。小孩们的脸颊上现出了红色，他们在街上玩着，大声笑着。“我们现在有面包了，”他们这样叫道。

随后雪来了，严寒也到了。街道仿佛是用银子筑成的，它们是那么亮，那么光辉，长长的冰柱像水晶的短剑似的悬挂在檐前，每个行人都穿着皮衣，小孩们也戴上红帽子溜冰取乐。

可怜小燕子却一天比一天地更觉得冷了，可是他仍然不肯离开王子，他太爱王子了。他只有趁着面包师不注意的时候，在面包店门口啄一点面包屑吃，而且拍着翅膀来取暖。

但是最后他知道自己快要死了。他就只有一点气力，够他再飞到王子的肩上去一趟。“亲爱的王子，再见罢！”他喃喃地说，“你肯让我亲你的手吗？”

“小燕子，我很高兴你到底要到埃及去了，”王子说，“你在这儿住得太久了，不过你应该亲我的嘴唇，因为我爱你。”

“我现在不是到埃及去，”燕子说，“我是到死之家去的。听说死是睡的兄弟，不是吗？”

他吻了快乐王子的嘴唇，然后跌在王子的脚下，死了。

那个时候在这座像的内部忽然起了一个奇怪的爆裂声，好像有什么东西破碎了似的。事实是王子的那颗铅心已经裂成两半了。这的确是一个极可怕的严寒天气。

第二天大清早市参议员们陪着市长在下面广场上散步。他们走过圆柱的时候，市长仰起头看快乐王子的像。“啊，快乐王子多么难看！”他说。

“的确很难看！”市参议员们齐声叫起来，他们平日总是附和市长的意见的，这时大家便走上去细看。

“他剑柄上的红宝石掉了，眼睛也没有了，他也不再是黄金的了，”市长说，“讲句老实话，他比一个讨饭的好不了多少！”

“比一个讨饭的好不了多少。”市参议员们说。

“他脚下还有一只死鸟！”市长又说，“我们的确应该发一个布告，禁止鸟死在这个地方。”书记员立刻把这个建议记录下来。

以后他们就把快乐王子的像拆下来了。大学的美术教授说：“他既然不再是美丽的，那么不再是有用的了。”

他们把这座像放在炉里熔化，市长便召集一个会来决定金属的用途。“自然，我们应该另外铸一座像，”他说，“那么就铸我的像吧。”

“不，还是铸我的像，”每个市参议员都这样说，他们争吵起来。我后来听见人谈起他们，据说他们还在争吵。

“真是一件古怪的事，”铸造厂的监工说，“这块破裂的铅心在炉里熔化不了。我们一定得把它扔掉。”他们便把它扔在一个垃圾堆上，那只死燕子也躺在那里。

“把这个城里两件最珍贵的东西给我拿来。”上帝对他的一个天使说。天使便把铅心和死鸟带到上帝面前。

“你选得不错，”上帝说，“因为我可以让这只小鸟永远在我天堂的园子里歌唱，让快乐王子住在我的金城里赞美我。”

（巴金　译）

第十四单元

马贩子的女儿

词汇

affected [ə'fektid] adj. 受到影响的，受（疾病）侵袭的，假装的，做作的

agony ['ægəni] n. 苦恼，极大的痛苦

antagonism [æn'tægənizəm] n. 对抗（状态），对抗性

apropos ['æprəpəu] adj. adv. 适当地，恰好的 apropos of nothing 凭空地，突如其来地，没有任何联系地，顺便地

avert [ə'vəːt] v. 转移

ay [ei] int. 唉！呜呼！

bob [bɔb] v. 剪短（头发）

bobbed [bɔbd] adj. 剪短的，成束的

boisterous ['bɔistərəs] adj. 狂暴的，喧闹的

bray [brei] n. 驴叫声，喇叭声 v. 叫，嘶叫

brutally ['bruːtəli] adv. 兽性地，残酷地

callous ['kæləs] adj. 无情的，冷淡的，硬结的，起老茧的

cast about v. 放任，使乱跑

causeway ['kɔːzwei] n. 堤道，铺道

cavalcade [ˌkævəl'keid] n. 队伍

chagrin ['ʃægrin] n. 懊恼，气愤，委屈

chenille [ʃə'niːl] n. 绳绒线，绳绒织物

chrysanthemum [kri'sænθˌəməm] n. 菊花

cinder ['sində] n. 煤渣，灰烬

cinder tract 煤渣铺成的一片地

clairvoyant [klɛə'vɔiənt] adj. 透视的，有洞察力的 n. 透视者，有千里眼的人

clayey ['kleii] adj. 黏土的，黏土状的

clean-limbed [ˌkliːn'lɪmd] adj. 手足匀称的，姿势好的

collier ['kɔliə] n. 矿工，运煤船，煤船员

colliery ['kɔljəri] n. 煤矿

confiscate ['kɔnfiskeit] vt. 没收，充公，查抄，征用 adj. 被没收的

connexion [kə'nekʃən] n. 联系，联结

consultation [ˌkɔnsəl'teiʃən] n. 请教，咨

询，磋商，［医］会诊

controversial［ˌkɔntrəˈvəːʃəl］adj. 争论的，争议的

crane［kreɪn］vt. vi. 引颈，伸长脖子

craving［ˈkreiviŋ］n. 渴望

crave［kreiv］v. 恳求，渴望

croak［krəuk］n. 蛙或鸦的叫声 vi. 嘎嘎叫，发牢骚 vt. 用嘶哑的声音说

curbstone［ˈkɜːbstəʊn］n. 路边石 adj. 场外交易的，偶感而发的，非专业的

dank［dæŋk］adj. 透水的，潮湿的，阴湿寒冷的

dazed［deizd］adj. 头昏的，眼花的

deadened［ˈdedənd］adj. 使失去光泽或无感觉的，削弱的，隔音的

demean［diˈmiːn］vt. 举止，贬低身份

depression［diˈpreʃən］n. 沮丧，消沉，低气压，低压

desultory［ˈdesəltəri］adj. 散漫的，不连贯的，断断续续的

dip［dip］n. 地底，斜坡

dismal［ˈdizməl］adj. 阴沉的，凄凉的，暗的 vt. 使人消沉 n. 低落的情绪，沼泽

distasteful［disˈteistful］adj. 味道不佳的，（令人）不愉快的，讨厌的

distress［disˈtres］n. 悲痛，穷困，不幸，危难，忧伤 v. 使悲痛，使穷困，使忧伤

divest［daiˈvest］v. 剥夺

draught［drɑːft］n. 拖，拉，一网（鱼），气流

draught-horse n. 挽马，役马

droop［druːp］v. 低垂，凋萎，萎靡

drudgery［ˈdrʌdʒəri］n. 苦差事，苦工

eulogy［ˈjuːlədʒi］n. 赞词，颂词，歌功颂德的话

evade［iˈveid］v. 规避，逃避，躲避

exasperation［igˌzɑːspəˈreiʃən］n. 恼怒

expurgate［ˈekspəːgeit］v. 删除

extinct［ɪkˈstɪŋkt］adj. 已绝种的，已灭绝的，已熄灭的

an extinct volcano 死火山

extricate［ˈekstrikeit］vt. 使解脱，救出，使（气体）游离，放出

faculty［ˈfækəlti］n. 才能，本领，能力，全体教员，（大学的）系，科，（授予的）权力

falter［ˈfɔːltə］vt. 支吾地说，结巴地讲出 vi. 支吾，蹒跚跟跄，摇摆，（声音）颤抖 n. 颤抖，支吾，踌躇

faltering［ˈfɔːltəriŋ］adj. 犹豫的，支吾的，蹒跚的

fatuously［ˈfætjuəsli］adv. 愚蠢地，愚昧地；荒唐的，虚幻地

fender［ˈfendə］n. 防卫物，挡泥板

fixity［ˈfiksiti］n. 固定性，固定物，不变性

flippancy［ˈflipənsi］adj. 无礼，轻率，浮躁

flout［flaut］vt. 嘲弄，轻视，嘲笑 flout me to my face 当面嘲弄我

footing［ˈfutiŋ］n. 立足处，（社会）地位，关系

foul［faul］adj. 污秽的，邪恶的，肮脏的，淤塞的，恶劣的 vt. 弄脏，妨害，污蔑，犯规，淤塞

foul-mouthed [ˌfəʊl'məʊðd] adj. 说话下流的，满嘴脏话的

foundry ['faundri] n. 铸造，翻砂，铸工厂，玻璃厂，铸造厂

fretted ['fretɪd] adj. 焦躁的

futile ['fju:tail, -til] adj. 琐细的，无用的，无效果的，（人）没有出息的

gamekeeper ['geɪmki:pə(r)] n 猎场看守人

glaze [gleiz] v. 装玻璃，上釉，使表面光滑 n. 釉料，釉面，光滑面，上釉，上光

grate [greit] n. 壁炉，炉

gratify ['grætifai] vt. 使满足

grimace [gri'meis] n. 面部的歪扭，痛苦的表情，鬼脸 vi. 扮鬼脸，作苦相

grip [grip] v. 紧握，紧夹 n. 掌握，控制，把手

groom [grum, gru:m] n. 马夫，新郎，男仆 vt. 喂马，推荐，整饰 vi. 修饰

grumble ['grʌmbl] adj. 抱怨地表示，嘟囔地说 n. 怨言，满腹牢骚 vi. 抱怨，发牢骚，咕哝，嘟囔，隆隆响 vt. 喃喃地说出

gypsy ['dʒipsi] n. 吉卜赛人，吉卜赛语 adj. 像吉卜赛人的 vi. 流浪

hastily ['heistili] adv. 急速地，轻率地，慌忙地，草率地

haunch [hɔ:ntʃ] n. 腰，臀部，腰部

headstone ['hedstəʊn] n. 墓石，基石

hearthrug ['hɑ:θrʌg] n. 炉前的地毯

heed [hi:d] n. 注意，留意 v. 注意，留意

hellish ['heliʃ] adj. 地狱般的

hideous ['hidiəs] v. 骇人听闻的，可怕的 adj. 丑恶的

holly ['hɔli] n. 冬青树

horsy ['hɔ:si] adj. 马的，爱马的，显出爱马的样子

husky ['hʌski] adj. 谷的，像谷的；（声音）沙哑的，嘶哑的

immutable [i'mju:təbl] adj. 不可变的，不变的，不能变的，永恒的

impassive [im'pæsiv] adj. 冷漠的

inarticulate [ˌinɑ:'tikjulit] adj. 口齿不清的，说话不连贯的，不善于表达的，（动物）无关节的

indiscriminate [ˌindis'kriminit] adj. 不加区别的，不分青红皂白的，任性的，杂乱的，不受限制的

ineffectual [ˌini'fektjuəl] adj. 无效的，不灵验的，无力的，无法施展的 n. 无一技之长的人

inscrutable [in'skru:təbl] adj. 难以了解的，不能预测的

instantaneous [ˌinstən'teinjəs] adj. 瞬间的，即刻的，即时的

intent [in'tent] n. 意图，目的，意向，［律］（犯罪或侵权行为的）故意 adj. 专心的，决心的，热心的

interpolate [in'tə:pəuleit] vi. 插话，插嘴

irritable ['iritəbl] adj. 易怒的，急躁的

irritably ['ɪrɪtəbli] adv. 性急地，暴躁地

jaunty ['dʒɔ:nti] adj. 感到自信和自满的，洋洋得意的

jeer [dʒiə] n. 嘲笑，讥讽，戏弄 v. 嘲弄，戏弄

knockout ['nɔ'kaut] n. 击昏，击倒 adj.

击倒的，摧毁性的〈美俚〉引人注目，杰出的，迷人的
laconical［lə'kɔnikəl］adj.（用词）简洁的，简明的
laconically［lə'kɔnikəli］adv. 简洁地
lest［lest］conj. 唯恐，以免，免得，（用于 fear，be afraid 之后，等于 that）
loin［lɔin］n. 腰
looming［'luːmiŋ］n.［光］幽影，［纺］穿综筘
Mabel［'meɪbl］n. 梅布尔（女子名）
mahogany［mə'hɔgəni］n.［植］桃花心木，红木，红褐色
Malcolm［'mælkəm］n 马尔科姆（男子名）
mantel［'mæntl］n. 壁炉架
mesmerize［'mezməraiz］v. 施催眠术
mysticism［'mistisizəm］n. 神秘，神秘主义，谬论
negate［ni'geit］vt. 否定，打消
nomadic［nəu'mædik］adj. 游牧的
Nottinghamshire［'nɔtɪŋəmʃɪə(r)］n. 诺丁汉郡（英国英格兰郡名）
objectionable［əb'dʒekʃənəbl］adj. 引起反对的，讨厌的
obscene［ɔb'siːn］adj. 淫秽的，猥亵的
obscurity［əb'skjuəriti］n. 阴暗，朦胧，偏僻，含糊，隐匿，晦涩，身份低微
outbuilding［'autbildiŋ］n.［建］外屋，（指车库、谷仓等）
outpatient［aut'peiʃənt］n. 门诊病人
pansy［'pænzɪ］n. 三色紫罗兰，三色堇；无丈夫气的男子，女性化的男人
penury［'penjuri, -juəri］n. 贫困，贫穷
perpetual［pə'petjuəl］adj. 永久的
pitch［pɪtʃ］v. 扎（营），搭（帐篷），扔，丢弃；〈音〉定基音，为……定调（常与 by，against 连用）；倒下，坠落，（船或飞机）上下颠簸
pledge［pledʒ］n. 保证，誓言，抵押，抵押品 vt. 保证，使发誓，抵押，典当
plume［pluːm］n. 羽毛 plumed 有羽毛的，用羽毛装饰的
portentous［pɔː'tentəs］adj. 预示性的
primitivism［'primitivizəm］n.（宗教、艺术或生活方式上的）原始主义，尚古主义，原始的风格
Prussian［'prʌʃən］adj. 普鲁士的 n. 普鲁士人
pupil teacher n. 小老师
relentlessly adv. 无情地，残酷地
repel［ri'pel］vt. 击退，抵制，使厌恶，使不愉快
restlessly［'restləsli］adv. 不安地，慌张地
retrieve［ri'triːv］v. 重新得到 n. 找回
revolted［rɪ'vəʊltɪd,-'vɔː-］adj. 起来反抗的，起义的，厌恶的
rhapsodic［ræp'sɔdik］adj. 狂想的，狂想曲的
rind［raɪnd］n 外皮；果皮
cheese rind 干酪的外皮
rip［rip］v. 撕，剥，劈，锯，裂开，撕裂 n. 裂口，裂缝
ripped［rɪpt］adj. 喝醉的，受毒品麻醉的
rove［rəuv］v. 漫游，流浪，转来转去，纺成粗纱 n. 漫游，流浪，粗纱
rub-down［'rʌbdaʊn］n. 擦洗，磨平

sangfroid ['sɑːŋ'frwɑː] n. 冷静，泰然，镇静或沉着

saturate ['sætʃəreit] v. 使饱和，浸透，使充满

saturated ['sætʃəreitid] adj. 渗透的，饱和的，深颜色的

scrupulously ['skruːpjələsli] adv. 小心翼翼地，多顾虑地

scullery ['skʌləri] n. 碗碟洗涤处，碗碟储藏室

sensual ['sensjuəl] adj. 肉欲的，色情的，世俗的，感觉的，感觉论的

shire ['ʃaiə] n.（=county）郡（英国行政区），[the shires] 英国中部各郡

shrivel ['ʃrivl] v.（使）起皱纹，（使）枯萎，（使）束手无策

shuffle ['ʃʌfl] n. 拖着脚走，混乱，蒙混，洗纸牌 v. 拖曳，搅乱，慢吞吞地走，推诿，洗牌

skivvy ['skivi] n. 女仆，内衣

slumberous ['slʌmbərəs] adj. 昏昏欲睡的，催眠的

smolder ['sməuldə(r)] vi. 闷烧，冒烟

smouldering ['sməuldəriŋ] v. 燃烧，闷烧

sodden ['sɔdn] vt. 浸湿使呆头呆脑，使（头脑）麻木 vi. 被浸湿

spell-bound ['spelbaund] adj. 被迷住

spire ['spaiə] n. 尖顶

stagger ['stægə] v. 摇晃，蹒跚，交错，摇摇摆摆 adj. 交错的

stagnant ['stægnənt] adj. 停滞的，迟钝的

steward ['stjuːəd; (*US*) 'stuːərd] n.（俱乐部或大学里的）膳务员、伙食管理员，（轮船或飞机上的）服务员、乘务员，（聚会、会议和赛马等的）筹备人、组织者，（房舍、地产或农庄等的）管家、管事

stint [stint] v. 紧缩，节省

straddle ['strædl] v. 跨骑

stupor ['stjuːpə] n. 昏迷

suck [sʌk] v. 吸，吮，吸取

suffocating ['sʌfəkeɪtɪŋ] adj. 令人窒息的，憋气的

sulk [sʌlk] n. 生气，愠怒，愠怒的人 v. 生气，愠怒

sullen ['sʌlən] adj. 愠怒的，沉沉不乐的，（天气等）阴沉的

sumptuous ['sʌmptjuəs] adj. 奢侈的，华丽的

sumptuously ['sʌmptjuəsli] adv. 奢侈地，豪华地

supplication [ˌsʌplɪ'keɪʃən] n. 恳求，祈愿，哀求

taut [tɔːt] adj.（绳子）拉紧的，整洁的，紧张的

terrier ['teriə] n. [动] 狗的一种，国防自卫队，地籍册

transcendent [træn'sendənt] adj. 卓越的，出众的，[宗]（神）超然的，[哲] 先验的

transfiguration [ˌtrænsfigju'reiʃən] n. 变形；显容；变貌，改观美化；理想化

trap [træp] n.（双轮）轻便马车

trespass ['trespəs] n. 过失，罪过，侵入 v. 侵入

trespasser ['trespəsə(r)] n. 侵犯（他人

土地）者

tweed［twiːd］n. 斜纹软呢，斜纹软呢服

unfathomable［ʌn'fæðəməbl］adj. 深不可测的，无底的，难解的

unsettle［'ʌn'setl］v. 不安

unsettling［'ʌn'setliŋ］adj. 使人不安的，（消息）混乱的

unstinted［ʌn'stɪntɪd］adj. 不受限制的，不吝惜的，充裕的 vi. 腐烂，犯规，缠结 n. 犯规，缠绕 adv. 违反规则地，不正当地

void［vɔid］n. 空间，空旷，空虚，怅惘 adj. 空的，无人的，空闲的，无效的，无用的，没有的

voile［vwɑːl, vɔil］n.［纺］薄纱，纱

wade［weid］vi. 跋涉 vt. 涉水，费力行走 n. 跋涉，可涉水而过的地方

well-set［'wel'set］adj. 结构牢固的

wistful［'wistful］adj. 渴望的，思念的

译文

马贩子的女儿

“那么，马蓓娜，你打算怎么办？”乔问道，轻率而又无礼。他自己觉得没事。没等回答，他便转过身，把嘴里的一点儿烟叶弄到舌尖，吐了出来。他什么都不在乎，因为他觉得自己没事儿。三个兄弟和妹妹围坐在凄凉的早餐桌旁，想做一个非正式的磋商。早上的邮件给了这个家庭的命运最后轻轻的一击，结果一切都完了。这间沉闷的餐厅，加上笨重的红木家具，那样子就好像在等待着处理。可磋商什么结果也没有达成。三个男人伸开四肢坐在桌边，抽着烟，各自茫然地想着自己的处境，他们脸上露出了一种奇怪的软弱无能的神情。姑娘独自坐在一边，一个相当矮小，满脸郁郁不乐的年轻女子，二十七岁。她过着与三个兄弟不太一样的生活。她本来会好看一些的，要不是她脸上给人印象深刻的僵硬表情的话，她的兄弟称之为“叭喇狗”。屋外传来一阵杂乱的马蹄声。三个男人在椅子上伸展四肢张望着。墨绿的冬青灌木把草地和马路隔开，从冬青灌木的后面，他们可以看到一队重挽马从他们自己的院子摇摇摆摆地出来，是带出去遛马。这是最后一次了。这也是他们经手的最后一批了。年轻的男人们带着挑剔、冷漠的神情注视着。他们都为自己生活的倒塌感到惊恐，置身其中的灾难感使他们没有丝毫内心的自由。然而，他们确实是三个一表人才、身材坚实的小伙子。乔是最大的，三十五岁，宽肩阔背，英俊潇洒，脾气暴躁，爱红脸。他有一张红红的脸，用粗大的手指捻着黑胡子，一双浅浅的眼睛不太安分。他笑起来的时候，露出牙齿的样子给人色眯眯的感觉，而他的举止却很愚笨。这时，他目光呆痴地注视着马，眼里有一种无助的神情，算得上是衰败后的那种恍惚样子。高大的拉车马摇摇摆摆地

走了过去。马匹头尾相套，共四匹，喘息着朝马路分岔出来的一条小路走去，大蹄子旁若无人地踩在黑泥中，炫耀地摆动着它们滚圆的大腰腿，当它们在拐弯处被带上小路时，还突然快跑了几步。每一个动作都显示出一股巨大的、令人昏昏欲睡的力量，和一副使它们俯首帖耳的蠢相。走在前头的马夫回头看了一看，猛地拉了一下牵马的绳子。于是，马队便上了小路不见了，最后一匹马的尾巴，僵硬地上下摆动着，当腰腿像边走边睡似的在树篱笆后面摆动着的时候，那尾巴在摆动着的大腰腿衬托下绷得紧紧的。乔目光呆痴而又无助地注视着。马就像他自己的身体。他觉得自己现在是全完了。所幸的是，他跟一个和自己一样大的女子订了婚，因此她那在附近一个庄园做管家的父亲会给他找一份活干的。他会结婚，套上马具一般地干活。他的生活结束了，他现在就要做牛做马了。他不安地转过脸去，越走越远的马蹄声还在他耳旁回响。接着，带着一种愚蠢的躁动，他从盘子里拿了几块熏肉皮，轻轻地打了一声口哨，便把肉皮扔向躺在围栏旁边的狗。他注视着狗把肉皮吞下，一直等到畜牲望着他的眼睛。这时，他的脸上露出一丝淡淡的笑容，接着他傻乎乎地高声说："你以后吃不了多少熏肉了，对不对，你这个小畜牲？"狗轻轻地忧郁地摇了摇尾巴，然后蹲下腿腰，蜷起身子，又躺下了。餐桌上又是一阵无助的沉默。乔伸开四肢，不安地坐在座位上，不愿意走开，要等家庭集会解散。弗雷德·亨利，排行第二，身体挺直，四肢匀称，活泼敏捷。他刚才注视着马过去的时候，就要冷静得多。如果说他是一头动物，像乔，那他也是一头会控制的动物，而不是一头受控制的动物。

任何马匹，他都是驾驭的高手，并且他有一种驾轻就熟的气质神情。可他却无法驾驭种种生活的境遇。他把粗糙的棕色胡子向上推着，露出嘴唇，恼怒地瞥了他的妹妹一眼，她无动于衷而又高深莫测地坐在那儿。"你要去跟露西待上一阵子，是不是？"他问道。姑娘没有回答。"我看不出你还能有别的什么办法，"弗雷德·亨利继续说。"做女佣，"乔直截了当地插了一句。姑娘纹丝不动。"我要是她，就去参加护士培训，"马尔科姆说，他是他们中最小的。他是这个家庭的孩子，一个二十二岁的年轻人，长着一张充满青春活力、无忧无虑的脸。可马蓓娜根本没有理睬他。这么多年来，他们一直对着她讲，围着她讲，她几乎是听而不闻了。壁炉台上的大理石钟在半点钟的时候轻柔地敲响了，狗不安地从壁炉前的地毯上起来，张望着餐桌旁的这些人。可他们继续在毫无成效的家庭集会上坐着。"喔，好吧，"乔突然不知所云地说。"我得走了。"他把椅子往后一推，叉开双腿往下一蹲，放松一下，那姿势就像骑马，接着便去了火边。他还是没有走出屋子；他想知道他们会做些什么或说些什么。他开始装烟斗，低头看着狗，装腔作势地高声说道："跟我去？跟我去吧你？那比刚才的还要合算，听到没？"狗轻轻地摇着尾巴，男人伸着下巴，双手握着烟斗，狠劲地抽着烟，陶醉在烟雾之中，同时闭着一只棕色的眼睛心不在焉地注视着狗。狗带着令人悲伤的不信任的眼光抬头望着他。乔站着，就像真的骑马那样弯着膝。“你收到露西的信了吗？”弗雷德·亨利问妹妹。“上星期，”传来一句不痛不痒的回答。“她怎么说？”没有回答。“她有没有要你去待上一段？”弗雷德·亨利继续问道。“她说我要愿意就可以。”“好，那么，你最好还是去吧。告诉她你星期一去。”回答的是沉默。“你就这么做，对不对？”弗雷德·亨利说，有点儿恼怒。可她没有回答。

屋子里的沉默无聊而又令人烦躁。马尔科姆傻乎乎地咧着嘴笑。“你得在下个星期三之前做出决定，”乔大声地说，“要不你就露宿街头吧。”年轻女子的脸沉了下来，但她还是纹丝不动地坐着。“杰克·弗格森来了！”马尔科姆叫道，他正漫无目的地往窗外张望。“在哪？”乔大声地叫道。“刚过去。”“进来了吗？”马尔科姆伸长脖子望着门口。“进来了，”他说。一阵沉默。马蓓娜坐在餐桌的头上，像个被判了死刑的人。这时，从厨房传来一声口哨声。狗站了起来，吠叫着。乔打开门，喊道：“进来吧。”过了一会儿，进来一个年轻人。他裹着一件大衣，围着一条紫色羊毛围巾，花呢帽子没有摘下来，而是低低地扣在头上。他中等的个儿，脸是又长又苍白，两眼疲惫。“你好，杰克！好吗，杰克！”马尔科姆和乔大叫。弗雷德·亨利只说了一声“杰克”。“怎么样？”新来的人说，显然是跟弗雷德·亨利说话。“老样子。星期三以前我们得搬出去。感冒了？”“对——而且很重。”“干吗不待在家里别出来？”“我别出来？等到我站不起来了，大概就有机会了。”年轻人声音沙哑地说。他略微带点儿苏格兰口音。“真有意思，是不是？”乔嚷道，“医生感冒嘶哑着嗓子到处转。对病人可不太妙，是吧？”年轻的医生慢慢地看着他。“那跟您有什么关系吗？”他讽刺地问道。“就我所知还没有。你那该死的眼睛，我可不希望有。干吗？”“我刚才想，你那么为病人担心，就纳闷你自己是不是也可能是一个。”“去你的，不是，我从来没有做过可恶的医生的病人，希望永远也不要做，”乔回敬道。正在这时，马蓓娜从餐桌旁站了起来，他们这才好像意识到她的存在。她开始收拾碗碟。年轻的医生看着她，但没有跟她说话。他没有跟她打招呼。她端着碗碟出了屋，脸上无动于衷，纹丝不动。“那你们什么时候走，都走？”医生问道。“我坐十一点四十的车，”马尔科姆回答道。“你是坐马车走，乔？”“对，我告诉过你我要坐马车走，不是？”“我们还是做些安排吧。再见了，杰克，要是我走之前见不到你的话，”马尔科姆说，握手。他走了出来，后面跟着乔，乔好像两条腿之间有个尾巴。“唉，真难呐，”医生单独和弗雷德·亨利在一起的时候嚷着说。“星期三以前走，你也是？”“那是命令，”对方回答。“哪儿，去北安普敦？”“对。”“真他妈的！”弗格森带着轻轻的懊恼叫道。两人一阵沉默。“全安排好了，是吗？”弗格森问道。差不多。”又是一阵沉默。“唉，我会想念你的，弗雷德，兄弟，”年轻的医生说道。“我也会想念你的，杰克，”对方回答。“真他妈的想你，”医生沉思着。弗雷德·亨利别过脸去。没有什么可说的。马蓓娜又进来了，擦桌子。“那您打算怎么办，裴文小姐？”

弗格森问道。“去你姐姐那儿，是吗？”马蓓娜用她那双沉着而又危险的眼睛看着他，那双眼睛总是使他不舒服，打破他那表面上的自若神态。“不是，”她说道。“那么，以命运的名义起誓，你究竟要怎么做？你说你打算怎么办？”弗雷德·亨利喊道，带着于事无补的激动。可她只把头偏向一边，继续干她的活。她把白桌布折起来，铺上绳绒布。“从来没见过这样的闷货！”她哥哥嘀咕着。可她依然无动于衷地干她的活，年轻的医生一直在饶有兴趣地注视着她。然后，她便出去了。弗雷德盯着她的背，紧闭双唇，一双蓝眼睛充满深深的敌意瞪着，一边做了个恼怒的鬼脸。“你就是把她捣成碎片，从她那儿得到的也就是这些，”他压低声音轻轻地说道。医生微微地一笑。“那她打算怎么办？”他问道。

“我要知道，你打死我好了！”对方回答。一阵不满。接着，医生动了一下。“我今天晚上来看你，行吗？”他对自己的朋友说。“喔——在哪？我们去杰斯德尔怎么样？”“我不知道。我现在得了这样的感冒。不管怎么样，我要去‘星傍月’的。”“让丽和梅晚上想上一次，呃？”“没错——要是我像现在这样的感觉的话。”“都一样——”两个年轻的男人穿过走廊，一起走到后门。房子很大，可已经没有了仆人，且很荒凉。后面是一个不大的砖砌的院子，再后面就是一个大场子，铺着红色的细沙，两边是马厩。再往前走的斜坡两边，是潮湿的、冬天深色的田野。然而，马厩却已经空了。约瑟夫·裴文，是这一家人的父亲，没有受过教育，却成了一个不小的马贩子。那时，马厩里全是马，马、马贩子、马夫进进出出，整天闹哄哄的。接着，厨房里有了不少的用人。但后来，光景衰落了。老头子结了第二次婚，想重整雄风。现在，他死了，一切全完了，除了债务和恐吓，一无所有。几个月来，马蓓娜住在这幢大房子里，没有用人，为她那几个无能的兄弟拮据地操持着这个家。她操持这个家已有十年了。可以前手头不受限制。那时，无论事情是多么残酷严峻，可金钱的感觉总能使她高傲而又自信。男人们或许满口脏话，厨房的女人们或许名声不佳，她的兄弟们或许有私生子。可只要有钱，姑娘就觉得自己心里踏实，并且无情地高傲，不苟言笑。没有人到家里来，除了那些马贩子和粗鄙的男人。马蓓娜没有一个自己的同伴，自从她姐姐走了以后。可她并不在乎。她常去教堂，她照料父亲。而且她生活在对母亲的回忆之中，母亲死的时候，她才十四岁，她爱母亲。她也爱她的父亲，方式不一样，依赖他，在他身上有一种安全感，直到他五十四岁又结了婚。从那时起，她就处处跟他作对。现在，他已经死了，留给他们的是一屁股债。在穷困时期，她吃了不少的苦。然而，没有什么东西能够动摇他们家谁都具有的那种难以理解、邪恶、动物式的傲慢。现在，对于马蓓娜来说，末日已经来临。即便如此，她也不会为自己想方设法。她还会我行我素，依然故我。她会一直控制着自己的处境。虽然不爱动脑子，固执己见，她却一天一天地挺着。她为什么要思考？她为什么要回答别人的问话？这样的结局就已经够了，并且还没有出路。在大街上走着，她再也不必躲躲闪闪，避开所有人的目光了。她再也不必贬低自己，到商店买最便宜的食品了。这一切都结束了。她什么人也不想，也不想她自己。虽然不爱动脑子，固执己见，她却似乎处在一种狂喜之中：愈来愈接近她自己的抱负，她自己的荣光，走向她死去的母亲，母亲就很荣光。下午，她拿了个小袋子，带着大剪刀、海绵和一把小小的板刷，便出门了。那是一个灰暗的冬日，深绿色的田野显得黯淡，不远处铸造厂冒出的烟把天空弄得灰蒙蒙的。她沿着大道迈着快步，表情忧郁地走着，谁也不去注意，穿过镇里，往教堂墓地走去。在那儿，她总是觉得很安全，就好像没有人能够看见她，虽然事实上，只要从墓地墙下经过的人都能看见。尽管如此，只要一置身于高大教堂的阴影之中，到了这墓地，她就觉得自己恍如隔世一般，待在厚厚的墓地墙内，就像在另一个国度。她细心地修剪着坟上的草，把粉白色的小菊花放在锡制的十字架上。当做完这一切的时候，她从旁边的坟上拿了一个空罐子，打来水，细心、一丝不苟地用海绵擦洗大理石墓碑，还有压顶石。做着这一切给她一种真正的满足感。她觉得与她母亲的世界有了直接的接触。她忍着微不足道的痛苦，以一种纯粹幸福的心态穿过墓园，仿佛在完成这件事的时候，她已与她的母亲产生了一种微妙而又亲密的联系。因为她在这个世界上过的生活远不如她从母亲那儿得来的死亡世界真实。

医生的家就在教堂旁边。弗格森，只是一个受雇的助理，成了乡村的奴隶，整天跑。这时，正当他匆忙地去看诊所的门诊病人的时候，他很快地往墓地扫了一眼，看到姑娘正在坟前忙着。看起来她是那样的专心，显得那样的遥远，仿佛她是在注视着另一个世界。他身上某种神秘的东西被触动了。他步子慢了下来，注视着她，仿佛着了魔。她抬起眼睛，感觉到他的目光。他们的目光相遇了。接着他们又很快地看了对方一眼，各自似乎感觉到自己被对方发现了。他抬了抬帽，继续走路。在他的脑海里，像一个幻觉一般，他清楚地记得她的面孔，从墓地的墓碑前抬起，然后用那双迟钝、不祥的大眼睛看着他的样子。那是不祥的，她的面孔。它似乎要把他催眠了。她的眼里有一股深沉的力量，控制了他的整个人，就好像他喝了什么威力很大的药一样。他以前曾感到身体虚弱，精疲力竭。现在，生命的活力重又回到了他的身上，他感到自己从那种烦躁的日常生活中解脱出来了。他以尽快的速度做完了诊所的工作，匆忙地往那些正在等候的病人瓶子里塞满廉价的药品。然后，他又像往常一样匆匆忙忙地出发，要赶在下午茶之前，去看他巡诊区域的另外几个病人。平时，他能走路的时候，他喜欢走路，尤其是当他不太好的时候。他认为运动能够使他恢复健康。下午天暗下来。天空灰暗，沉闷，寒冷，慢慢地一股厚重潮湿的冷气袭来，使人所有的感觉都变得麻木了。可他为什么要思考或者观察？他匆匆地翻过山，穿过暗绿色的地，沿着黑乎乎的煤渣路走着。远处，隔着一个浅浅的水塘，小镇就像一堆还有火星的余烬，一座塔楼，一个尖塔，一堆低矮、简陋、年久失修的房子。而在镇的最边缘处，和水塘形成斜坡的便是“旧牧场”，裴文家的房子。他能够清楚地看到马厩和外屋，都是在斜坡上朝着他现在的方向。唉，他到那儿去的次数也不会太多了！他又少了一个可以慰藉的地方，他就要失去这个异乡丑陋的小镇里唯一在意的朋友。什么也没有了，除了工作，苦役，在矿工和打铁工中从一家匆匆地往另一家赶。这一切使他疲倦不堪，可同时他渴望这样。在工人们的家庭穿梭，走进他们的生活深处，对于他是一种兴奋剂，他的神经既激动又满足。他可以如此之近地走入那些粗犷、不善言辞而又感情丰富的男男女女的生活之中。他嘀咕抱怨，他说他痛恨这个地狱般的肮脏狭小的地方。可事实上，这个地方却又使他激动，与那些粗犷、感情强烈的人接触，是直接贴在他神经上的一副兴奋剂。在“旧牧场”下面，在浅浅的潮湿的绿色洼地上，有一个很深的方形水塘。环顾一路上的景色，医生敏锐的目光看见一个身着黑衣的身影穿过大门，往下朝水塘走去。他又看了一眼。那像马蓓娜·裴文。他的头脑突然活跃起来，精神集中。她为什么要往那儿去？他在上面的坡路上停了下来，驻足观察。从渐渐暗下去的天色中，他只能肯定那个小巧的黑色身影在洼地里移动。在这茫茫夜色中，他好像看清了她，好像他是一个“千里眼”，是用心灵的眼睛而不是肉眼在看着。然而，他在精神集中的时候，可以非常清楚地看到她。他感觉到，如果他把目光从她身上收回，在这厚重而又丑陋的暮色中，他就会彻底失去她。他注视着她，她朝前移动，身体笔直，目光专注，就像被发射出去的东西，而不是自发的移动，一直穿过庄稼地朝池塘走去。她在岸上站了一会儿。她一直没有抬过头。然后，她慢慢地往水里走去。他一动不动地站着，小巧的黑影缓慢而又从容地向水塘的中央走去，非常缓慢，渐渐地静静的水越来越深，她一直往前走，直到水齐了她的胸。接着，在这死沉沉的暮色中，他再也看不见她了。“啊呀！”他大叫。“简直难以置信！”他匆忙往下跑去，穿过潮湿有水的地，推开篱笆，在冷酷无情而又寒冷的暮色中冲向洼地。他花了好几分钟才到水塘边。他站在岸上，喘着粗气。他什么也看不见。他的眼睛仿佛要穿透死静的水。对，那可能是她的黑衣服在水下的影子。他慢慢地试探着进了水塘。塘底是深深的柔软的泥，他陷了进去，腿上的水冰冷。他一动，他就可以闻到泛到水里那种寒冷、腐烂的泥味。这使他反胃。虽然感到厌恶，也管不了那么多了，他还是往深水处走去。寒冷的水没了他的大腿，他的腰部，他的腹部。他的下身全浸在可怕而又寒冷的水中。而塘底又深又软，又不知底细，他不敢再向前走，怕嘴没到水里去。他不会游泳，并且害怕。他微微往下蹲，张开双手在水中搅动，希望能摸到她。冰冷的水塘在他胸前晃动。他又走了，又深了一点儿，又双手在水里朝周围搅动。他碰到了她的衣服。可衣服从他手中滑掉了。他孤注一掷地去抓衣服。正这么做的时候，他身体失去了平衡，摔倒在水中，可怕的是，还在难闻的泥水中呛住了，疯狂地挣扎了好一会儿。终于，经过好像没有尽头的一段时间之后，他立住了脚，重又伸出了头，朝四周一望。他倒抽了一口气，并且知道自己还在这个世界上活着。然后，他注视着水面。她就在他附近浮着。他抓住她的衣服，把她往身边拉近一点儿，便转过身子，重又往岸边走去。他走得非常慢，小心翼翼，在缓慢的前进中全神贯注。他露出水面的身子越来越多，接着就从水塘里爬了出来。这时，水只到他的腿；他谢天谢地，从水塘的魔爪中摆脱出来，大大地松了一口气。他抱起她，摇摇晃晃地往岸上走去，摆脱了令人恐怖的暗灰色稀泥。他把她放在岸上。她失去了知觉，浑身在流水。他让水从她口里流出，他想让她苏醒过来。没有多久，他便感觉到她又开始呼吸了；她呼吸正常。他又弄了一会儿。他可以感觉到她在自己的手下活过来了；她在苏醒。他擦了擦她的脸，用自己的大衣裹着她，朝黑茫茫的世界望了望，便抱起她，摇摇晃晃地从岸上走下，穿过庄稼地。路好像是不可思议的长，而他的负担又是如此的重，他都觉得自己永远到不了房子似的。但终于，他进了马厩院子，然后是房子的院子。他打开门，进了房子。在厨房里，他把她放在炉前的地毯上，便叫人。房子空无一人。但火还在燃着。接着，他又跪下看一看她。她在均匀地呼吸，她的眼睛睁得大大的，好像已经有了意识，可那神情里似乎缺了点什么东西。她是自己有了意识，可对她周围的环境还没有意识。他跑上楼，从床上拿了毛毯放在火前烘着。然后，他脱下她身上湿透了的带着泥土气味的衣服，用毛巾把她擦干，再把她赤裸裸地裹在毛毯里。然后，他去了餐厅，找酒。有一点威士忌。他自己先喝了一大口，然后往她嘴里灌了一点。效果是立竿见影。她睁大眼睛紧紧盯着他，那样子就像她已经看了他好一会儿，而实际上刚刚才意识到他的存在。“弗格森医生？”她说。“什么？”他回答。他正在脱他的衣服，准备到楼上找些干衣服。他受不了那股死气沉沉的泥土味，并且为自己的健康害怕得要死。“我做了什么？”她问道。“走到塘里去了，”他回答。他已经开始像个病人一样打颤，几乎没法顾及她了。她的眼睛一直停留在他身上，他仿佛脑袋里发黑，无助地回头望着她。他的打颤轻一点了，活力重又回到了他的身上，虽然面色发暗，显得恍惚，但又有力气了。“我是不是精神错乱？”她问，眼睛一直盯在他身上。“有可能，暂时的，”他回答。他感到平静了，因为他已经恢复了力气。

那奇怪而又令人烦躁的极度紧张已离他而去。“我现在是不是精神错乱？”她问。“你现在？”他想了一会儿。“不是，”他如实地回答，“我看不出来你是。”他扭过脸去。他现在害怕了，因为他感到晕眩，并且隐隐约约地觉得她的能力要比他强，在这个问题上。而她继续一直目不转睛地盯着他。“你能不能告诉我，在什么地方我可以找到一些干衣服穿？”他问道。“你因为我跳进了水塘？”她问道。“不是，”他回答。“我是走进去的。不过我也淹了头顶。”一阵沉默。他犹豫着。他非常想上楼换上干衣服。可他心里还有一个欲望。而她似乎抓住他了。他的意志似乎已经睡着了，离他而去，懒散地站在她面前。可他内心里觉得暖乎乎的。他一点也不打颤了，虽然他身上的衣服湿漉漉的。“你为什么？”她问道。“因为我不想让你做这样的傻事，”他说。“那不是傻事，”她说，依然盯着他，她躺在地上，头下面枕着一个沙发坐垫。“事情就该那么做。我所知道的最好的，那时候。”“我去把这些湿东西换下来，”他说。可他依然没有能力走出她的视线，除非她让他走。好像她已经把他身体中的活力掌握在手中，而他自己无法从中摆脱。要不就是他不想走。突然，她站了起来。紧接着她就意识到自己当时的处境。她感觉到自己身子周围的毛毯，她太熟悉自己的四肢了。一时之间，她好像失去了理智。她朝四周张望，眼睛瞪得大大的，好像在找什么东西。他因为害怕站在那儿一动没动。她看到自己的衣服散落在地上。“谁脱了我的衣服？”她问道，她的眼睛睁得滚圆，毫不躲闪地看着他的脸。“是我，”他回答，“是为了让你活过来。”有好一会儿，她坐在那儿，可怕地盯着他，双唇张开。

“那么，你爱我吗？”她问道。他只是站在那儿盯着她，已经出了神。他的灵魂好像熔化了。她跪着朝前挪动了一下，用双臂抱着他，抱着他的双腿，而他就站在那儿，她把自己的乳房紧紧地贴在他的膝上、大腿上，带着一种奇怪而又疯狂的自信紧紧地抓住他，把他的大腿紧紧地贴着她，当她抬头用那双变了样子的闪烁而又卑微的双眼望着他的时候，把他拉向她的脸，她的脖子，眼睛里充满了第一次占有的胜利。“你爱我，”她喃喃道，带着莫名的狂喜，渴望，胜利和自信。“我知道你爱我，我知道。”她充满激情地吻着他的双膝，隔着湿漉漉的裤子，充满激情而又不分青红皂白地吻着他的双膝，他的双腿，似乎忘却了一切。他低头看着乱蓬蓬而又湿漉漉的头发，她那裸露着的原始而又动物式的双肩。他惊愕，困惑，继而恐惧。他从来没有想过要爱她。他从来没有想去爱她。当他救她，使她苏醒过来的时候，他是一个医生，而她是一个病人。他对她从来没有个人方面的念头。何况，这样把个人因素扯进来使他很反感，违背了他的职业道德。让她这样抱着他的双膝，真是可怕。真可怕。他对此很反感，颇为反感。可是——可是——他却无力摆脱。她再一次看着他，同样带着对强烈的爱情的祈求，同样带着那种莫名而又可怕的胜利的光芒。在那似乎来自她脸上光芒一样的火焰面前，他已无能为力。可他从来没有打算爱她。他从来没有打算过。

并且他身上某种固执的东西无法让步。“你爱我，”她重复着，带着深深而又狂热的自信喃喃道。“你爱我。”她的双手在拉他，朝下往她身边拉。他害怕，甚至有点恐惧。因为他真的没有要爱她的打算。可她的双手在把他向她身上拉。为了站稳，他迅速抽出一只手，抓住她裸露的肩。一股火焰好像在灼烧那只抓住她那柔软肩膀的手。他没有爱她的打算：他所有的意志在反对他的屈服。真可怕。可摸着她的肩膀真美妙，她的脸放着光真美。她是不是疯了？他害怕在她面前屈服。可他内心又有某种东西在痛苦。他一直没有看她，而是盯着门看。可他的一只手却留在她的肩膀上。她突然静了下来。他低头看着她。她的双眼现在因为恐惧、疑虑而睁得大大的，脸上的光芒正在消失，可怕的灰色阴影重又回来。他受不了她眼睛射来的质疑的目光，还有那质疑背后所隐藏的死亡的神情。伴随着内心的呻吟，他让步了，任凭自己的心向她屈服。突然，一丝微笑浮上了他的脸。而她那双从未离开过他脸的眼睛，慢慢地，慢慢地充满了泪水。他注视着她眼里那奇怪的水往上涨，就像慢慢涌上来的泉水。他的心好像在胸膛里灼烧，熔化了。他再也受不了去看她。他跪了下来，抱着她的头，把她的脸贴在他的脖子上。她非常的静。他的心，好像已经碎了，在胸膛里因为痛苦在灼烧着。他感觉到她慢慢的滚烫的泪水沾湿了他的脖子。可是他不能动弹。他感觉到滚烫的泪水沾湿了他的脖子和颈窝，而他依然不动，一时之间便停留在人类的永恒之中。只是现在，把她的脸紧紧地贴在自己的身上，对他而言，已经是责无旁贷的了；他再也无法让她走开。他再也无法让她的头从自己紧紧搂着的怀抱中离开。他要永远保持这个姿势，虽然他的心在痛苦中伤痛，这种痛苦对他来说也是生命的活力。不知不觉之中，他在低头看着她潮湿而又柔软的金发。接着，突然地，他闻到了塘水那种令人讨厌的臭味。正在这时，她从他身边挣脱，看着他。她的眼睛充满着渴望，显得高深莫测。他害怕那双眼睛，便开始吻她，不知道自己在做什么。他不想那双眼睛有那种可怕的、渴望的而又高深莫测的神情。当她再一次面对着他的时候，脸上泛起一阵微微的红晕，眼睛里又闪烁着那可怕的喜悦的光芒，那确实使他惊恐不已，而他现在又想看到了，因为他更害怕那种疑虑的眼神。“你爱我吗？”她说，声音很颤抖。“对。”这个词是他费了好大的劲才说出来的。倒不是因为不真实。而是因为这话刚刚不久前才是真实的，这一说出口，似乎又使他那刚刚破碎的心再一次破碎了。而他几乎不想让那话是真实的，即便是现在。她抬起脸望着他，他弯下头来吻着她的嘴，轻柔地，这一吻是永远的誓言。当他吻着她的时候，他的心又在胸膛里紧缩起来。他从来没有打算去爱她。可现在一切都结束了。他已经跨过了他们之间的鸿沟，而他留在身后所有的一切已经干枯，烟消云散，化为乌有。吻过之后，她的眼里慢慢地又涌起了泪水。她静静地坐着，没有靠着他，脸垂在一旁，双手交叉着放在膝上。泪水非常缓慢地流着。一片寂静。他也坐在炉前的地毯上，一动不动，一言不发。破碎的心里那种莫名的痛苦，似乎在灼烧着他。他竟然爱她？这就是爱！他竟然是以这种方式敞开自己的胸怀！他，堂堂一个医生！他们要是知道了，又会怎样地嘲笑啊！一想起他们会知道，他就痛苦不已。在这种想法带来的莫名而又无法掩饰的痛苦中，他又朝她看了一眼。她坐在那儿，低头陷入了沉思之中。他看见一滴眼泪掉了下来，他的心又灼烧起来。他第一次发现，她的一个肩膀没有盖着，一只手臂裸露着，他还能看到她的一个小巧的乳房；隐隐约约地看到，因为屋子里差不多黑了。“你为什么在哭？”他问道，声音变了。她抬头望着他，泪眼中，第一次意识到自己的处境，使她眼里露出了羞涩带来的愁容。“我不是在哭，真的，”她说，注视着他，半是吓着了。他伸出一只手，轻柔地握住她那只裸露的手臂。“我爱你！我爱你！”他轻柔而又颤抖地低声说，都不像他自己了。她退缩着，低下了头。他的手轻柔而又强烈地抓着她的手臂，使她疼痛不已。她抬头看着他。“我要去，”她说，“我要去给你弄些干衣服来。”“干吗？”他说，“我没事。”“可我要去，”她说，“而且我要你把衣服换了。”他放了她的手，她便把自己裹在毛毯里，非常害怕地看着他。并且她还是没有起身。“吻我，”她充满渴望地说。他吻了她，但很短促，半是生气。然后，过了片刻，她紧张不安地站了起来，全身裹在毛毯里。他注视着，当她想脱出自己的身子把自己裹好，以便好走路时的那份慌乱神情。他目不转睛地注视着她，这个她知道。而当她走路的时候，当他瞥见她的双脚和雪白的大腿的时候，他在努力回想他当时把她裹在毛毯里时她是什么样子。可接着他又不想去回想了，因为在当时，她对他而言什么也不是，而他的本性也对回想她在她对他什么也不是的时候是什么样子极为反感。漆黑的房子里传来轻微的磕磕碰碰的声音，把他吓了一跳。接着，他听到了她的声音：“有衣服。”他起身来到楼梯口，拾起她扔下来的衣服。接着，他重又回到火边，擦干身子，穿上衣服。他穿好后，他对自己的样子咧嘴笑了。火在暗下去，因此他又加了煤。屋子现在已很黑了，只有冬青树后面的街灯射进来微弱的光线。他从炉台上拿了火柴，点亮了煤气灯。然后，他把自己衣服的口袋都掏了一遍，把所有的湿衣服卷作一堆，扔进了洗刷房里。之后，他又把她那些湿漉漉的衣服收拾起来，另作一堆，放在洗刷房的铜器盖子上。钟上是六点钟。他自己的表已经停了。他得回诊所去。他等着，可她还没有下来。因此，他走到楼梯口，叫道：“我得走了。”话音未落，他就听到了她下楼的声音。她穿着她那最好的黑色薄纱裙子，头发整齐，但还湿着。她看着他——不由自主地笑了。“我不想让你穿着这身衣服就走，”她说道。“我是不是样子很难看？”他回答道。他们都有点儿不喜欢对方的样子。

“我去给你沏杯茶，”她说。“不用了，我得走了。”“你非得走？”她再一次用那双大大的、紧张的、充满疑虑的眼睛看着他。而再一次地，从胸膛里的痛苦，他知道他是怎样地爱着她。他走了过去，弯腰吻她，轻轻地，充满激情，给她一个内心充满痛苦的吻。“我的头发太难闻了，”她心烦意乱地喃喃道。“并且我这么难看，我这么难看！噢，我太难看了。”说着，她便痛苦、心碎地抽泣着。“你不可能爱我的，我太糟了。”“别冒傻气，别冒傻气，”他说道，想安抚她，吻她，把她抱在怀里。“我要你，我要娶你，我们就结婚，马上，马上——要是你答应明天就结。”可她只是一味使劲儿地抽泣，并且哭叫：“我觉得难看。我觉得难看。我觉得我在你面前太糟了。”“没有，我要你，我要你，”他使劲儿地回答，心中茫然，那可怕的声调把她吓住了，其程度几乎超过了她担心他不要她时的恐惧。

（王伟凡　译）

第十五单元

哈利·波特与魔法石

词汇

astride [ə'straɪd] adv. 跨着

beefy ['biːfɪ] adj. 像牛肉的，健壮的，结实的

blow one's nose v. 擤鼻涕

bun [bʌn] n. 小圆面包，曲卷（或结）状的头发

doughnut ['dəʊnʌt] n. 油炸圈饼

drill [drɪl] n. 钻孔机，钻子

earmuff ['ɪəmʌf] n. 御寒耳罩

exasperate [ɪg'zɑːspəreɪt] v. 激怒

falter ['fɔːltə(r)] vt. 支吾地说，结巴地讲出

flinch [flɪntʃ] vi. 畏缩，退缩，畏首畏尾

getup ['getʌp] n. 服饰

gingerly ['dʒɪndʒəlɪ] adv. 小心翼翼地，谨慎地

glumly [glʌmli] adv. 阴郁地，愁苦地

grudgingly ['grʌdʒiŋli] adv. 勉强地

irritably ['ɪrɪtəbli] adv. 性急地，暴躁地

Muggle ['mʌgl] n. 普通人，不会魔法的人

owl [aʊl] n. [动] 猫头鹰，枭

petunia [pɪ'tjuːnɪə] n. [植] 矮牵牛花

pinch [pɪntʃ] n. vt. 掐，夹痛

pinprick ['pɪnprɪk] n. 小亮点，小孔

Privet Drive n. 女贞路

prod [prɔd] v. 刺

pursed lips 有皱褶的嘴唇，撅起的嘴唇

quiver ['kwɪvə(r)] vi. 颤抖，振动

rattled ['rætld] adj. 慌乱的，恼火的

ruffled ['rʌfld] adj. 被激怒的

rummage ['rʌmɪdʒ] v. 到处翻寻，搜出，检查

shaggy ['ʃægɪ] adj. 毛发粗浓杂乱的，蓬松的

slink [slɪŋk] v. 潜逃

snap [snæp] v. 突然厉声说

sorcerer ['sɔːsərə] n. 男巫，方士，施魔法者

swap [swɔp] v. 互传，交换

swish [swɪʃ] n. 嗖嗖声

swoop [swuːp] vi. 飞扑，突然袭击

tabby cat n. ['tæbɪ :'kæt] 虎斑猫

tantrum ['tæntrəm] n. 发脾气，发怒

tawny ['tɔːnɪ] adj. 茶色的

tuft [tʌft] n. 一丛，丛生植物，一簇

tyke [taɪk] n. 小孩子，小淘气

unDursleyish [ʌn'dəːsliiʃ] adj. 无德思礼家族风范的

weirdo ['wɪədəu] n. 古怪的人，奇怪的人

译文

第 1 章　大难不死的男孩

家住女贞路四号的德思礼夫妇总是得意地说他们是非常规矩的人家。拜托，拜托了。他们跟神秘古怪的事从来不沾边，因为他们根本不相信那些邪门歪道。

弗农·德思礼先生在一家名叫格朗宁的公司做主管，公司生产钻机。他高大魁梧，胖得几乎连脖子都没了，却蓄着一脸大胡子。德思礼太太是个瘦削的金发女人。她的脖子几乎比正常人长一倍。这样每当她花许多时间隔着篱墙引颈而望、窥探左邻右舍时，她的长脖子可就派上了大用场。德思礼夫妇有一个小儿子，名叫达力。在他们看来，人世间没有比达力更好的孩子了。

德思礼一家什么都不缺，但他们拥有一个秘密，他们最害怕的就是这秘密会被人发现。他们想，一旦有人发现波特一家的事，他们会承受不住的。波特太太是德思礼太太的妹妹，不过姐妹俩已经有好几年不见面了。实际上，德思礼太太佯装自己根本没有这么个妹妹，因为她妹妹和她那一无是处的妹夫与德思礼一家的为人处世完全不一样。一想到邻居们会说波特夫妇来到了，德思礼夫妇会吓得胆战心惊。他们知道波特也有个儿子，只是他们从来没有见过。这孩子也是他们不与波特夫妇来往的一个很好的借口，他们不愿让达力跟这种孩子厮混。

我们的故事开始于一个晦暗、阴沉的星期二，德思礼夫妇一早醒来，窗外浓云低垂的天空并没有丝毫迹象预示这地方即将发生神秘古怪的事情。德思礼先生哼着小曲，挑出一条最不喜欢的领带戴着上班，德思礼太太高高兴兴，一直絮絮叨叨，把唧哇乱叫的达力塞到了儿童椅里。

他们谁也没留意一只黄褐色的猫头鹰扑扇着翅膀从窗前飞过。

八点半，德思礼先生拿起公文包，在德思礼太太面颊上亲了一下，正要亲达力，跟这个小家伙道别，可是没有亲成，小家伙正在发脾气，把麦片往墙上摔。“臭小子。”德思礼先生嘟哝了一句，咯咯笑着走出家门，坐进汽车，倒出四号车道。

在街角上，他看到了第一个异常的信号——一只猫在看地图。一开始，德思礼先生还没明白他看到了什么，于是又回过头去。只见一只花斑猫站在女贞路街角，但是没有看见地图的踪影。他到底在想些什么？很可能是光线使他产生了错觉吧。德思礼

先生眨了眨眼，盯着猫看，猫也瞪着他。当德思礼先生拐过街角继续上路的时候，他从后视镜里看看那只猫。猫这时正在读女贞路的标牌，不，是在看标牌；猫是不会读地图或是读标牌的。德思礼先生定了定神，把猫从脑海里赶走。他开车进城，一路上想的是希望今天他能得到一大批钻机的订单。

但快进城时，另一件事又把钻机的事从他脑海里赶走了。当他的车汇入清晨拥堵的车流时，他突然看见路边有一群穿着奇装异服的人。他们都披着斗篷。德思礼先生最看不惯别人穿得怪模怪样，瞧年轻人的那身打扮！他猜想这大概又是一种无聊的新时尚吧。他用手指敲击着方向盘，目光落到了离他最近的一大群怪物身上。他们正兴致勃勃，交头接耳。德思礼先生很生气，因为他发现他们中间有一对根本不年轻了，那个男的显得比他年龄还大，竟然还披着一件翡翠绿的斗篷！真不知羞耻！接着，德思礼先生突然想到这些人大概是为什么事募捐吧，不错，就是这么回事。车流移动了，几分钟后德思礼先生来到了格朗宁公司的停车场，他的思绪又回到了钻机上。

德思礼先生在他九楼的办公室里，总是习惯背窗而坐。如果不是这样，他可能会发现这一天早上他更难把思想集中到钻机的事情上了。他没有看见成群的猫头鹰在光天化日之下从天上飞过，可街上的人群都看到了；他们目瞪口呆，指指点点，盯着猫头鹰一只接一只从头顶上掠过。他们大多甚至夜里都从未见过猫头鹰。德思礼先生这天早上很正常，没有受到猫头鹰的干扰。他先后对五个人大喊大叫了一遍，又打了几个重要的电话，喊的声音更响。他的情绪很好，到吃午饭的时候，他想舒展一下筋骨，到马路对角的面包房去买一只小甜圆面包。若不是他在面包房附近又碰到那群披斗篷的人，他早就把他们忘了。他经过他们身边时，狠狠地瞪了他们一眼。他说不清这是为什么，只是觉得这些人让他心里别扭。这些人正嘁嘁喳喳，讲得起劲，但他连一只募捐箱也没有看见。当他拎着装在袋里的一只大油饼往回走，经过他们身边时，他们的话断断续续飘入他的耳鼓：

“波特夫妇，不错，我正是听说……”

“……没错，他们的儿子，哈利……”

他突然停下脚步，恐惧万分。他回头朝窃窃私语的人群看了一眼，似乎想听他们说点什么，后来又改变了主意。

他急忙冲到马路对面，回到办公室，厉声吩咐秘书不要来打扰他，然后抓起话筒，刚要拨通家里的电话，临时又变了卦。他放下话筒，摸着胡须，琢磨起来……不，他太愚蠢了。

波特并不是一个稀有的姓，肯定有许多人姓波特，而且有儿子叫哈利。想到这里，他甚至连自己的外甥是不是哈利·波特都拿不定了。他甚至没有见过这孩子。说不定叫哈维，或者叫哈罗德。没有必要让太太烦心，只要一提起她妹妹，她总是心烦意乱。他并不责怪她，要是他自己有一个那样的妹妹呢？可不管怎么说，这群披斗篷的人……那天下午，他发现自己很难专心考虑钻机的事。五点钟他走出办公室大楼，依旧心事重重，与站在门口的一个人撞了个满怀。

这个小老头打了个趔趄，差点儿摔倒。“对不起。”德思礼先生嘟哝着说。过了几秒钟，他才发现这人披了一件紫罗兰色斗篷。他几乎被撞倒在地，可他似乎一点儿也不生气，脸上反而绽出灿烂的笑容。“您不用道歉，尊贵的先生，因为今天没有事会惹我生气！太高兴了，因为‘神秘人’总算走了！就连像你这种麻瓜，也应该好好庆贺这大喜大庆的日子！”他说话的声音尖细刺耳，令过往的人侧目。

老头说完，搂了搂德思礼先生的腰，就走开了。

德思礼先生站在原地一动不动，仿佛生了根。他刚刚被一个完全陌生的人搂过。他还想到自己被称作“麻瓜”，不知这是什么意思。他心乱如麻，连忙朝自己的汽车跑去，开车回家。他希望这一切只是幻想出来的景象，尽管他从来没有幻想过什么，因为他根本不赞同幻想。

当他驶入四号车道时，第一个映入眼帘的就是早上他见过的那只花斑猫，这并没有使他的心情好转。这时猫正坐在他家花园的院墙上。他肯定这只猫和早上的是同一只：眼睛周围的纹路一模一样。

“去……去！”德思礼先生大喝道。

猫纹丝不动，只是狠狠地瞪了他一眼。这难道是一只正常的猫的行为吗？德思礼先生感到怀疑。他先让自己镇定下来，随后就进屋去了。他仍决定对太太只字不提。

德思礼太太这一天过得很好，一切正常。晚饭桌上，德思礼太太向他讲述了邻居家的母女矛盾，还说达力又学会一个新词（“决不”），德思礼先生也尽量表现得正常。安顿达力睡下之后，他来到起居室，听到晚间新闻的最后一段报道：“最后，据各地鸟类观察者反映，今天全国猫头鹰表现反常。通常情况下，它们都是在夜间捕食，白天很少露面，可是今天，日出时猫头鹰就四处纷飞。专家们也无法解释猫头鹰为什么改变了它们的睡眠习惯。”新闻播音员说到这里，咧嘴一笑，“真是太奇妙了。现在我把话筒交给吉姆·麦古，问问他天气情况如何。吉姆，今天夜里还会下猫头鹰雨吗？”

“噢，泰德，”气象播音员说，“这我可不知道，今天不仅是猫头鹰表现反常。全国各地远至肯特郡、约克郡、丹地等地的目击者都纷纷打来电话说，我们原来预报昨天有雨，结果下的不是雨而是流星！也许人们把本该在一星期后举行的庆祝篝火之夜晚会提前举行了，朋友们！不过我向你们保证，今晚一定有雨。”

德思礼先生坐在扶手椅里惊呆了。英国普遍下流星雨……猫头鹰光天化日之下四处纷飞……到处都是披着斗篷的怪人……还有一些传闻，关于波特一家的传闻……

德思礼太太端着两杯茶来到起居室。情况不妙。他应该向她透露一些。他心神不定，清了清嗓子，“唔……佩妮，亲爱的……最近有你妹妹的消息吗？”

不出所料，德思礼太太大为吃惊，也很生气。不管怎么说，他们通常都说自己没有这么个妹妹。

“没有，”她厉声说，“怎么了？”

“今天的新闻有点奇怪，”德思礼先生咕哝说，“成群的猫头鹰……流星雨……今天城里又有那么多怪模怪样的人……”

“那又怎么样？”德思礼太太急赤白脸地说。

“哦，我是想……说不定……这跟……你知道……她那一群人有关系……”

德思礼太太嘬起嘴唇呷了一口茶。德思礼先生不知道自己是不是该大胆地把听到“哈利”名字的事告诉她。他决定还是不要太冒失。于是他尽量漫不经心地改口说：“他们的儿子，他现在该有达力这么大了吧？”

“我想是吧。”德思礼太太干巴巴地说。

“他叫什么名字来着？是叫霍华德吧？”

“叫哈利，要我说，这是一个不讨人喜欢的普通名字。”

“哦，是的。”德思礼先生说着，感到心里突然往下一沉，“不错，我也这么想。”

他们上楼睡觉时，他就再也没有提到这个话题了。德思礼太太进浴室以后，德思礼先生就轻手轻脚来到卧室窗前，看看前面的花园。那只猫还在原地，正目不转睛地盯着女贞路路口，好像在等待什么。

他是在想入非非吗？这一切会与波特一家有关吗？如果真有关系……如果最后真跟他们夫妇有关……那么，他认为他是承受不住的。

德思礼夫妇睡下了。德思礼太太很快就睡着了，德思礼先生却思绪万千，怎么也睡不着觉。不过在他入睡前，最后一个想法使他感到安慰：即使波特一家真的被卷了进去，也没有理由牵连他和他太太。波特夫妇很清楚德思礼夫妇对他们和他们那群人的看法。他打了个哈欠，翻过身去。不会影响他们的……他可是大错特错了。

德思礼先生迷迷糊糊，本来可能胡乱睡上一觉，可花园墙头上的那只猫却没有丝毫睡意。它卧在墙头上，宛如一座雕像，纹丝不动，目不转睛地盯着女贞路远处的街角。邻街的一辆汽车砰的一声关上车门，两只猫头鹰扑扇着从头顶上飞过，它也一动不动。实际上，快到午夜时，它才开始动了动。

猫一直眺望着的那个街角出现了一个男人，他来得那样突然，悄无声息，简直像是从地里冒出来的。猫尾巴抖动了一下，眼睛眯成了一条缝。

女贞路上从来没有见过这个男人。他个子瘦高，银发和银须长到都能够塞到腰带里了，凭这一点就可以断定他年纪已经很大了。他穿一件长袍，披一件拖到地的紫色斗篷，蹬一双带搭扣的高跟靴子。半月形的眼镜后边一双湛蓝湛蓝的明亮眼睛炯炯有神。他的鼻子很长，但是歪歪扭扭的，看来至少断过两次。他的名字叫阿不思·邓布利多。

阿不思·邓布利多似乎并没有意识到从他的名字到他的靴子，在他来到的这条街上都不受欢迎。他忙着在斗篷口袋里翻寻，好像在找什么东西。他也没有发现有人监视他，因为他突然抬头看见一直在街那头注视着他的那只猫，出于某种原因，他觉得这只猫的样子很好笑。他咯咯笑着，咕哝说："我早就该想到了。"

他在里边衣袋里找出了他要找的东西，看起来像一只银质打火机。他把它轻轻弹开，高举起来，咔嗒一声，离得最近的一盏路灯噗的一声熄灭了。他又打了一下，第二盏灯也熄灭了。他用熄灯器打了十二次，整条街上只剩下远处两个小小的光点，那就是监视他的那只猫的两只眼睛。如果这时有人向窗外看，即使是眼尖的德思礼太太，也不会看到马路上发生的一切。邓布利多把熄灯器放回斗篷里边的口袋里，之后就顺着街道向四号走去。他在墙头猫的身边坐下来。他没有看它，但过了一会儿便跟它说起话来。

"真没想到会在这里见到您，麦格教授。"

他回头朝花斑猫微微一笑。花斑猫不见了，换成一个神情严肃的女人，戴一副方形眼镜，看起来跟猫眼睛周围的纹路一模一样。她也披了一件翠绿色斗篷，乌黑的头发绾成一个很紧的发髻。她显得非常激动。

"您怎么认出那是我？"她问。

"我亲爱的教授，我从来没有见过一只猫像这样僵硬地待着。"

"您要是在砖墙上坐一整天，您也会变僵的。"麦格教授说。

"一整天？您本来应当参加庆祝会的呀？我一路来到这里，至少遇上了十二场欢快的聚会和庆祝活动。"

麦格教授气呼呼地哼了一声。

"哦，不错，人人都在庆贺，很好！"她恼火地说，"您以为他们会更小心谨慎，其实不然，连麻瓜们都注意到有什么事情发生了，都上了他们的电视新闻了。"她猛地把头转向德思礼家漆黑的起居室窗口，"我都听见了。成群的猫头鹰……流星雨……好了，他们也不是十足的傻瓜。有些事也会引起他们的注意。肯特郡下的那场流星雨……我敢说准是迪歌干的。他本来就没多少头脑。"

"您不能责怪他们，"邓布利多心平气和地说，"十一年来值得我们庆贺的事太少了。"

"这我知道，"麦格教授气呼呼地说，"但这些并不是冒险胡来的理由。他们也太不小心了，大白天跑到街上去，也不穿上麻瓜们的衣服，还在那里传递消息。"

说到这里，她机敏地朝邓布利多斜瞟了一眼，似乎希望他能告诉她些什么，但邓布利多没有吱声，于是她接着说："神秘人终于不见了，如果正好在他失踪的那一天，麻瓜们发现了我们的一切，那可真太奇妙了。我想他真的走了吧，邓布利多？"

"好像是这样，"邓布利多说，"我们应该感到欣慰。您来一块柠檬雪糕好吗？"

"一块什么？"

" 一块柠檬雪糕。这是麻瓜们的一种甜点。我非常喜欢。"

"不了，谢谢。"麦格教授冷冷地说，看来她认为现在不是吃柠檬雪糕的时候。"像我说的，即使'神秘人'真的走了……"

"我亲爱的教授，像您这样的明白人，总该可以直呼他的大名吧？什么神秘人不神秘人的，全都是瞎扯淡……十一年了，我一直想方设法说服大家，直呼他本人的名字：伏地魔。"麦格教授打了个寒噤，可邓布利多在掰两块粘在一起的雪糕，似乎没有留意。"要是我们还继续叫神秘人神秘人的，一切就都乱套了。我看直呼伏地魔的大名也没有任何理由害怕。"

"我知道您不害怕，"麦格教授半是恼怒，半是夸赞地说，"尽人皆知，您与众不同。神秘人……哦，好吧，伏地魔……唯一害怕的就是您。"

"您太抬举我了。"邓布利多平静地说，"伏地魔拥有我永远也不会有的功力。"

"那是因为您太……哦……太高尚了，不愿意运用它。"

"幸亏这里很黑，庞弗雷夫人说她喜欢我的新耳套以后，我还没有像现在这样脸红过呢。"

麦格教授狠狠地瞪了邓布利多一眼，说："猫头鹰和沸沸扬扬的谣言毫不相干。您知道大伙都在说什么吗？说他为什么失踪？说最终是什么制止了他？"

这一来，麦格教授似乎点到了她急于想讨论的问题核心，这也正是她在冰冷的砖墙上守候了一整天的原因。不管她是一只猫，或是一个女人，她从来都不曾用现在这样锐利的眼光看邓布利多。显然，不管大家怎么说，只有从邓布利多口中得到证实，她才会相信。邓布利多却挑了另一块柠檬雪糕，没有答话。

"他们说，"她不依不饶地说，"昨天夜里伏地魔绕到高锥克山谷。他们是去找波特夫妇的，谣传莉莉和詹姆·波特都……都他们都已经……死了。"

邓布利多低下头。麦格教授倒抽了一口气，"这……这是真的吗？莉莉和詹姆……我不相信……我也不愿相信……哦，阿不思……"

邓布利多伸手拍了拍她的肩膀。"我知道……我知道……"他心情沉重地说。

麦格教授接着往下说，她的声音颤抖了。"还不止这些。他们说，他还想杀波特夫妇的儿子哈利，可是没有成功。他杀不死那个孩子。没有人知道为什么，也没有人知道怎么会杀不死。不过他们说，当伏地魔杀不死哈利的时候，他的功法就不知怎的失灵了，所以他才走掉了。"

邓布利多愁眉不展地点了点头。

"这……这是真的吗？"麦格教授用颤巍巍的声音说，"他做了这么多坏事……杀了这么多人……可竟然杀不了一个孩子？这简直令人震惊……我们想了那么多办法去阻止他……可苍天在上，哈利究竟是怎么幸免于难的呢？"

"我们只能猜测，"邓布利多说，"我们可能永远也不会知道。"

麦格教授掏出一块花边手帕轻轻拭了拭镜片后边的眼睛。邓布利多深深吸了一口气，从衣袋里掏出一块金表，认真看起来。那只表样子很奇怪，有十二根指针，却没有数字，还有一些小星沿着表盘边缘转动。邓布利多显然看明白了，他把表放回衣袋，说："海格肯定迟到了。顺便问一句，我想，大概是他告诉您我要到这里来的吧？"

"是的，"麦格教授说，"可去的地方多了，您为什么偏偏要到这里来呢？我想，您大概不会告诉我吧？"

"我是来接哈利，把他送到他姨妈姨父家的。现在他们是他唯一的亲人。"

"您不会是指……您不可能是指住在这里的那家人吧？"

她噌地跳起来，指着四号那一家，"邓布利多……您可不能这么做。我观察他们一整天了。您找不到比他们更不像你我这样的人了。他们还有一个儿子……我看见他在大街上一路用脚踢他母亲，吵着要糖吃。要哈利·波特住在这里？！"

"这对他是最合适的地方了。"邓布利多坚定地说，"等他长大一些，他的姨妈姨父会向他说明一切。我给他们写了一封信。"

"一封信？"麦格教授有气无力地重复说，又坐回到墙头上。"邓布利多，您当真认为用一封信您就能把一切都解释清楚吗？这些人永远也不会理解他的！他会成名……一个传奇人物……如果将来有一天把今天定为哈利·波特日，我一点儿也不会觉得奇怪……会有许多写哈利的书……我们世界里的每一个孩子都会知道他的名字！"

"说得对极了，"邓布利多说，他那半月形眼镜上方的目光显得非常严肃，"这足以使任何一个孩子冲昏头脑。不会走路、不会说话的时候就一举成名！甚至为他根本不记得的事情而成名！让他在远离过去的地方成长，直到他能接受这一切，再让他知道，不是更好吗？"

麦格教授张开嘴，改变了看法。她咽了口唾沫，接着说："是啊……是啊，当然您是对的。可怎么把孩子弄到这里来呢，邓布利多？"她突然朝他的斗篷看了一眼，好像他会把哈利藏在斗篷里。

"海格会把他带到这里来。""把这么重要的事情托付给海格去办……您觉得……明智吗？""我可以把我的身家性命托付给他。"邓布利多说。

"我不是说他心术不正，"麦格教授不以为然地说，"可是您不能不看到他很粗心。他总是……那是什么声音？"

一阵低沉的隆隆声划破了周围的寂静。当他们来回搜索街道上是否有汽车前灯的灯光时，响声越来越大，最后变成一阵吼叫。他们抬眼望着天空，只见一辆巨型摩托自天而降，停在他们面前的街道上。

如果说摩托是一辆巨型摩托，那么骑车人就更不在话下了。那人比普通人高一倍，宽度至少有五倍，似乎显得出奇地高大，而且粗野地纠结在一起的乱蓬蓬的黑色长发和胡须几乎遮住了大部分脸庞，那双手有垃圾桶盖那么大，一双穿着皮靴的脚像两只小海豚。他那肌肉发达的粗壮双臂抱着一卷毛毯。

“海格，”邓布利多说，听起来像松了一口气，“你总算来了。这辆摩托车你是从哪里弄来的？”

“是借来的，邓布利多教授，”巨人一边小心翼翼地跨下摩托车，一边说，“是小天狼星布莱克借给我的。我把他带来了，先生。”

“没有遇到麻烦吧？”

“没有，先生。房子几乎全毁了。我们赶在麻瓜们从四面八方汇拢来之前把他抱了出来。当我们飞越布里斯托尔上空的时候，他睡着了……”

邓布利多和麦格教授朝那卷毛毯俯下身去。他们看见毛毯里裹着一个男婴，睡得正香。孩子前额上一绺乌黑的头发下边有一处刀伤，伤口形状很奇怪，像一道闪电。

“这地方就是……”麦格教授低声说。

“是的，”邓布利多说，“他一辈子都要带着这道伤疤了。”

“你不能想想办法吗？邓布利多？”

“即使有办法，我也不会去做。伤疤今后可能会有用处。我左边膝盖上就有一个疤，是一幅完整的伦敦地铁图。好了，把他给我吧。海格，咱们最好还是把事情办妥。”

邓布利多把哈利托在怀里，朝德思礼家走去。

“我能……我能跟他告别一下吗？先生？”海格问。

他把毛发蓬乱的大头凑到哈利脸上，给了他一个胡子拉碴、痒乎乎的吻。接着海格突然像一只受伤的狗号叫了一声。

“嘘！”麦格教授嘘了他一声，“你会把麻瓜们吵醒的！”

“对……对……对不起，”海格抽抽搭搭地说，掏出一块污渍斑斑的大手帕来，把脸埋在手帕里，“我……我实在受……受不了……莉莉和詹姆死了……可怜的小哈利又要住在麻瓜们家里……”

“是啊，是啊，是令人难过，可你得把握住自己，不然我们会被发现的。”麦格教授小声说，轻轻拍了一下海格的臂膀。

这时邓布利多正跨过花园低矮的院墙，朝大门走去。他轻轻把哈利放到大门口的台阶上，从斗篷里掏出一封信，塞到哈利的毛毯里，然后回到另外两个人身边。他们三人站在那里对小小的毯子注视了足有一分钟。海格的肩膀在抖动，麦格教授拼命眨眼，邓布利多一向闪光的眼睛也暗淡无光了。

“好了，”邓布利多终于说，“到此结束了。我们没有必要继续待在这里。咱们还是去参加庆祝会吧。”

“是啊，”海格咕哝说，“我得去把车还给小天狼星。晚安，麦格教授。晚安，邓布利多教授。”

海格用外衣衣袖揩了揩流泪的眼睛，跨上摩托，踩着了发动机，随着一声吼叫，摩托车腾空而起，消失在夜色里。

“希望很快和您见面，麦格教授。”邓布利多朝麦格教授点头说。她擤了擤鼻子作为回答。

邓布利多转身来到街上。他在街角上掏出银质熄灯器，咔嗒弹了一下，只见十二个火球又回到各自的路灯上，女贞路顿时映照出一片橙黄，他看见一只花斑猫正悄悄从街那头的拐角溜掉了。他恰好可以看见四号台阶上放着的那个用毯子裹着的小包。

“祝你好运，哈利。”他喃喃地说道，接着踩脚跟一转身，只听斗篷嗖的一声，他已经消失得无影无踪了。

微风拂动着女贞路两旁整洁的树篱，街道在漆黑的天空下寂静无声，一尘不染，谁也不会想到这里会发生骇人听闻的事情。哈利·波特在毯子包里翻了个身，但他并没有醒。他的一只小手正好放在那封信旁边。他还继续沉睡，一点不知道他很特殊，不知道他名气很大，不知道再过几小时，等德思礼太太开大门放奶瓶时，他会被她的尖叫声吵醒；更不会知道，在未来的几个星期，他表哥达力会对他连捅带戳，连掐带拧…… 他也不可能知道，就在此刻，全国人都在秘密聚会。人们高举酒杯悄声说：“祝福大难不死的孩子—— 哈利·波特！”

（苏农 译）

Bibliography

In English:

ANNE VARTY. 王尔德导读［M］. 北京：北京大学出版社，2005.

MERRYN WILLIAMS. 哈代导读［M］. 北京：北京大学出版社，2005.

JOHN PURKIS. 华兹华斯导读［M］. 北京：北京大学出版社，2005.

SYDNEY BOLT. 乔伊斯导读［M］. 北京：北京大学出版社，2005.

M. H. ABRAMS, The Norton anthology of English literature[M]. Fifth Edition. New York: W. W. Norton & Company, Inc, 1986.

In Chinese:

乔叟. 坎特伯雷故事［M］. 黄杲炘，译. 南京：译林出版社，1999.

王佐良，李赋宁，周珏良，等. 英国文学名篇选注［M］. 北京：商务印书馆，1983.

狄更斯. 大卫·科波菲尔（上册）［M］. 董秋斯，译. 北京：人民文学出版社，1980.

狄更斯. 大卫·科波菲尔（下册）［M］. 董秋斯，译. 北京：人民文学出版社，1980.

菲尔丁. 弃儿汤姆·琼斯史（上册）［M］. 张谷若，译. 上海：上海译文出版社，1993.

菲尔丁. 弃儿汤姆·琼斯史（下册）［M］. 张谷若，译. 上海：上海译文出版社，1993.

奥斯丁. 傲慢与偏见［M］. 张玲，张扬，译. 北京：人民文学出版社，1993.

勃朗特. 呼啸山庄［M］. 方平，译. 上海：上海译文出版社，1993.

哈代. 苔丝［M］. 吴笛，译. 杭州：浙江文艺出版社，1991.

雪莱. 雪莱诗选［M］. 江枫，译. 长沙：湖南人民出版社，1980.

李乃坤. 伍尔夫作品精粹［M］. 石家庄：河北教育出版社，1991.

王佐良．并非舞文弄墨［M］．北京：生活·读书·新知三联书店，1994.

莎士比亚．莎士比亚十四行诗集（第二版）［M］．屠岸，译．上海：上海译文出版社，1988.

莎士比亚．哈姆雷特——莎士比亚戏剧集［M］．卞之琳，曹禺，方平，译．杭州：浙江文艺出版社，1991.

笛福．鲁滨孙漂流记［M］．徐霞村，译．北京：人民文学出版社，1959.

黄杲炘．英国抒情诗100首［M］．上海：上海译文出版社，1986.

田乃钊．英美名诗一百首赏析［M］．天津：天津人民出版社，1993.

奥斯丁．傲慢与偏见［M］．王科一，译．上海：上海译文出版社，2010.

勃朗特．呼啸山庄［M］．杨苡，译．南京：译林出版社，2010.

哈代．德伯家的苔丝［M］．王忠祥，聂珍钊，译．武汉：长江文艺出版社，2011.

图书在版编目(CIP)数据

英国文学经典名篇选读 / 顾铁军编. -- 北京 : 中国传媒大学出版社, 2022.12
ISBN 978-7-5657-3280-5

Ⅰ. ①英… Ⅱ. ①顾… Ⅲ. ①英语－语言读物②英国文学－作品综合集 Ⅳ.
①H319.4: I

中国版本图书馆CIP数据核字(2022)第167526号

声明：本书选文若涉及版权问题，请联系13261849235

英国文学经典名篇选读

YINGGUO WENXUE JINGDIAN MINGPIAN XUANDU

编　　者 顾铁军
策划编辑 王雁来
责任编辑 王雁来
责任印制 李志鹏
封面设计 拓美设计

出版发行 中国传媒大学出版社
社　　址 北京市朝阳区定福庄东街 1 号　　**邮　　编** 100024
电　　话 86-10-65450528　65450532　　**传　　真** 65779405
网　　址 http://cucp.cuc.edu.cn
经　　销 全国新华书店

印　　刷 唐山玺诚印务有限公司
开　　本 787mm × 1092mm　1 / 16
印　　张 17.25
字　　数 403 千字
版　　次 2022 年 12 月第 1 版
印　　次 2022 年 12 月第 1 次印刷

书　　号 ISBN 978-7-5657-3280-5/H · 3280　　**定　　价** 68.00 元

本社法律顾问：北京嘉润律师事务所　郭建平